The Ultimate Ninja Air Fryer Cookbook for Beginners 2022-2023

800 Effortless and Delicious Air Fryer Recipes for Family and Busy People on a Budget Healthy and Hot Air Fryer Cookbook

Dillan Marvin

Copyright© 2022 By Dillan Marvin

All rights reserved worldwide.

No part of this book may be reproduced or transmitted in any form or by any means, electronic or mechanical, including photo-copying, recording or by any information storage and retrieval system, without written permission from the publisher, except for the inclusion of brief quotations in a review.

Warning-Disclaimer

The purpose of this book is to educate and entertain. The author or publisher does not guarantee that anyone following the techniques, suggestions, tips, ideas, or strategies will become successful. The author and publisher shall have neither liability or responsibility to anyone with respect to any loss or damage caused, or alleged to be caused, directly or indirectly by the information contained in this book.

Table of Contents

Introduction 1

Chapter 1 You Must Have the Ninja Air Fryer 2
What Is a Ninja Air Fryer? 3
Getting To Know Your Ninja Air Fryer 3
Must-Have Air Fryer Accessories 5
Cleaning Tips 6
Troubleshooting Tips 6

Chapter 2 Breakfasts 7
Johnny Cakes 8
Breakfast Cobbler 8
Whole Wheat Blueberry Muffins 8
Savory Sweet Potato Hash 8
Peppered Maple Bacon Knots 9
Baked Egg and Mushroom Cups 9
Egg in a Hole 9
Parmesan Sausage Egg Muffins 9
Red Pepper and Feta Frittata 9
Cajun Breakfast Sausage 9
Keto Quiche 10
Creamy Cinnamon Rolls 10
Cheesy Bell Pepper Eggs 10
Cinnamon Rolls 10
Sausage and Cheese Balls 11
Scotch Eggs 11
Honey-Apricot Granola with Greek Yogurt 11
Whole Wheat Banana-Walnut Bread 11
Mozzarella Bacon Calzones 11
Lemon-Blueberry Muffins 12
Golden Avocado Tempura 12
Fried Chicken Wings with Waffles 12
Pumpkin Spice Muffins 12
Breakfast Pizza 12
Butternut Squash and Ricotta Frittata 13
Poached Eggs on Whole Grain Avocado Toast 13
Italian Egg Cups 13
BLT Breakfast Wrap 13
Apple Rolls 13

Jalapeño Popper Egg Cups 14
Portobello Eggs Benedict 14
Homemade Cherry Breakfast Tarts 14
Easy Sausage Pizza 14

Chapter 3 Fish and Seafood 15
Baked Monkfish 16
Roasted Cod with Lemon-Garlic Potatoes 16
Garlic Lemon Scallops 16
Oyster Po'Boy 16
Lemony Shrimp 17
Tuna Casserole 17
Scallops and Spinach with Cream Sauce 17
Blackened Salmon 17
Chili Tilapia 17
Roasted Salmon Fillets 17
Shrimp Kebabs 18
Asian Swordfish 18
Crab Cake Sandwich 18
Fish Cakes 18
Garlicky Cod Fillets 18
Country Shrimp 19
Butter-Wine Baked Salmon 19
Tilapia with Pecans 19
Garlic Shrimp 19
Crustless Shrimp Quiche 19
South Indian Fried Fish 20
Foil-Packet Lobster Tail 20
Roasted Halibut Steaks with Parsley 20
Thai Shrimp Skewers with Peanut Dipping Sauce 20
Panko Catfish Nuggets 20
Easy Scallops 21
Asian Marinated Salmon 21
Mouthwatering Cod over Creamy Leek Noodles 21
Roasted Fish with Almond-Lemon Crumbs 21
Tortilla Shrimp Tacos 22
Ahi Tuna Steaks 22
Shrimp Caesar Salad 22

Salmon on Bed of Fennel and Carrot	22
Greek Fish Pitas	22
Snapper Scampi	23
Chinese Ginger-Scallion Fish	23
Almond Pesto Salmon	23
Smoky Shrimp and Chorizo Tapas	23
Golden Shrimp	24
Lemony Salmon	24

Chapter 4 Poultry — 25

Porchetta-Style Chicken Breasts	26
Korean Honey Wings	26
Easy Chicken Nachos	26
Cheesy Pepperoni and Chicken Pizza	26
Spice-Rubbed Chicken Thighs	27
Chicken Kiev	27
Sriracha-Honey Chicken Nuggets	27
Chicken Paillard	27
Gold Livers	28
Chicken Shawarma	28
Jerk Chicken Kebabs	28
Stuffed Chicken Florentine	28
Peachy Chicken Chunks with Cherries	28
Ethiopian Chicken with Cauliflower	29
Buffalo Chicken Cheese Sticks	29
Peruvian Chicken with Green Herb Sauce	29
Barbecue Chicken	29
Chicken Cordon Bleu	29
Chicken Croquettes with Creole Sauce	30
Chicken Legs with Leeks	30
Nacho Chicken Fries	30
Pecan Turkey Cutlets	30
Crisp Paprika Chicken Drumsticks	30
Garlic Soy Chicken Thighs	31
Turkey and Cranberry Quesadillas	31
Chicken Hand Pies	31
Israeli Chicken Schnitzel	31
Chipotle Drumsticks	31
Hoisin Turkey Burgers	32
Potato-Crusted Chicken	32
Chicken Schnitzel	32
South Indian Pepper Chicken	32
Pork Rind Fried Chicken	32
Juicy Paprika Chicken Breast	33
Honey-Glazed Chicken Thighs	33

Chapter 5 Beef, Pork, and Lamb — 34

Beef Flank Steak with Sage	35
Southern Chili	35
Herb-Roasted Beef Tips with Onions	35
Carne Asada	35
Cantonese BBQ Pork	35
Smoky Pork Tenderloin	36
Beef Empanadas	36
Honey-Baked Pork Loin	36
Swedish Meatloaf	36
Spice-Rubbed Pork Loin	37
Meat and Rice Stuffed Bell Peppers	37
Stuffed Beef Tenderloin with Feta Cheese	37
Spicy Lamb Sirloin Chops	37
Macadamia Nuts Crusted Pork Rack	37
German Rouladen-Style Steak	38
Fajita Meatball Lettuce Wraps	38
Hoisin BBQ Pork Chops	38
Bulgogi Burgers	38
Pork Loin Roast	39
Garlic Butter Steak Bites	39
Sausage and Pork Meatballs	39
Greek Pork with Tzatziki Sauce	39
Greek Lamb Pita Pockets	39
Greek-Style Meatloaf	40
Chinese-Style Baby Back Ribs	40
Roast Beef with Horseradish Cream	40
Sausage and Peppers	40
Lebanese Malfouf (Stuffed Cabbage Rolls)	40
Beef and Goat Cheese Stuffed Peppers	41
Beef and Broccoli Stir-Fry	41
Air Fried Beef Satay with Peanut Dipping Sauce	41
Beefy Poppers	41
Rosemary Ribeye Steaks	41
Kheema Burgers	42
Asian Glazed Meatballs	42
London Broil with Herb Butter	42
Lamb Chops with Horseradish Sauce	42
Tomato and Bacon Zoodles	43
Sichuan Cumin Lamb	43

Chapter 6 Snacks and Appetizers — 44

Garlicky and Cheesy French Fries	45
Golden Onion Rings	45
Zucchini Fries with Roasted Garlic Aïoli	45

Taco-Spiced Chickpeas	46
Peppery Chicken Meatballs	46
Classic Spring Rolls	46
Crispy Cajun Dill Pickle Chips	46
Spicy Tortilla Chips	46
Egg Roll Pizza Sticks	47
Roasted Grape Dip	47
Greek Potato Skins with Olives and Feta	47
Skinny Fries	47
Mozzarella Arancini	47
Garlic-Roasted Tomatoes and Olives	48
Stuffed Figs with Goat Cheese and Honey	48
Caramelized Onion Dip	48
Kale Chips with Tex-Mex Dip	48
Jalapeño Poppers	48
Asian Five-Spice Wings	48
Onion Pakoras	49
Lemon-Pepper Chicken Drumsticks	49
Grilled Ham and Cheese on Raisin Bread	49
Lemon Shrimp with Garlic Olive Oil	49
Cheesy Hash Brown Bruschetta	49
Pickle Chips	50

Chapter 7 Vegetables and Sides — 51

Spiced Butternut Squash	52
Baked Jalapeño and Cheese Cauliflower Mash	52
Garlic and Thyme Tomatoes	52
Green Bean Casserole	52
Sausage-Stuffed Mushroom Caps	52
Garlic Herb Radishes	53
Butternut Squash Croquettes	53
Air-Fried Okra	53
Glazed Sweet Potato Bites	53
Cheesy Cauliflower Tots	53
Sweet and Crispy Roasted Pearl Onions	53
Garlic-Parmesan Jícama Fries	54
Roasted Potatoes and Asparagus	54
Breaded Green Tomatoes	54
Chermoula-Roasted Beets	54
Asparagus Fries	54
Sesame-Ginger Broccoli	55
Broccoli Tots	55
Mashed Sweet Potato Tots	55
Gorgonzola Mushrooms with Horseradish Mayo	55
Dill-and-Garlic Beets	55

Marinara Pepperoni Mushroom Pizza	55
Spinach and Sweet Pepper Poppers	56
Hasselback Potatoes with Chive Pesto	56
Easy Rosemary Green Beans	56
Buttery Green Beans	56
Spinach and Cheese Stuffed Tomatoes	56
Hawaiian Brown Rice	56
Mexican Corn in a Cup	57
Tahini-Lemon Kale	57

Chapter 8 Vegetarian Mains — 58

Garlic White Zucchini Rolls	59
Three-Cheese Zucchini Boats	59
Cauliflower, Chickpea, and Avocado Mash	59
Baked Zucchini	59
Crustless Spinach Cheese Pie	59
Lush Vegetables Roast	60
Italian Baked Egg and Veggies	60
Super Vegetable Burger	60
Lush Summer Rolls	60
Sweet Pepper Nachos	60
Pesto Vegetable Skewers	60
Quiche-Stuffed Peppers	61
Tangy Asparagus and Broccoli	61
Cheesy Cauliflower Pizza Crust	61
Black Bean and Tomato Chili	61
Spinach-Artichoke Stuffed Mushrooms	61
Baked Turnip and Zucchini	61
Whole Roasted Lemon Cauliflower	62
Mediterranean Pan Pizza	62
Cheese Stuffed Zucchini	62

Chapter 9 Holiday Specials — 63

Golden Nuggets	64
Classic Churros	64
Cinnamon Rolls with Cream Glaze	64
Teriyaki Shrimp Skewers	64
Simple Butter Cake	65
Lush Snack Mix	65
Jewish Blintzes	65
Fried Dill Pickles with Buttermilk Dressing	65
Hasselback Potatoes	65
Shrimp with Sriracha and Worcestershire Sauce	66
Kale Salad Sushi Rolls with Sriracha Mayonnaise	66
Hearty Honey Yeast Rolls	66
Air Fried Spicy Olives	66

Mushroom and Green Bean Casserole ... 67
Air Fried Blistered Tomatoes ... 67
Custard Donut Holes with Chocolate Glaze ... 67
Whole Chicken Roast ... 67
Garlicky Olive Stromboli ... 68
Arancini ... 68

Chapter 10 Family Favorites 69

Pecan Rolls ... 70
Phyllo Vegetable Triangles ... 70
Beignets ... 70
Elephant Ears ... 70
Beef Jerky ... 71
Veggie Tuna Melts ... 71
Fish and Vegetable Tacos ... 71
Mixed Berry Crumble ... 71
Buffalo Cauliflower ... 71
Chinese-Inspired Spareribs ... 71
Steak Tips and Potatoes ... 72
Pork Stuffing Meatballs ... 72
Apple Pie Egg Rolls ... 72
Cajun Shrimp ... 72
Meringue Cookies ... 72
Churro Bites ... 73
Puffed Egg Tarts ... 73
Fried Green Tomatoes ... 73
Meatball Subs ... 73
Old Bay Tilapia ... 73

Chapter 11 Desserts 74

Peaches and Apple Crumble ... 75
Vanilla Scones ... 75
Pumpkin-Spice Bread Pudding ... 75
Double Chocolate Brownies ... 75
Crispy Pineapple Rings ... 75
Dark Chocolate Lava Cake ... 76
Fried Golden Bananas ... 76
Caramelized Fruit Skewers ... 76
Shortcut Spiced Apple Butter ... 76
Baked Brazilian Pineapple ... 76
Funnel Cake ... 76
Chocolate Cake ... 77
Apple Hand Pies ... 77
Coconut Mixed Berry Crisp ... 77

Bourbon Bread Pudding ... 77
Berry Crumble ... 77
Ricotta Lemon Poppy Seed Cake ... 78
Strawberry Shortcake ... 78
Peanut Butter-Honey-Banana Toast ... 78
Zucchini Nut Muffins ... 78
Pears with Honey-Lemon Ricotta ... 78
Chickpea Brownies ... 79
Breaded Bananas with Chocolate Topping ... 79
Brown Sugar Banana Bread ... 79
Blackberry Cobbler ... 79
Eggless Farina Cake ... 79
Cream Cheese Shortbread Cookies ... 80
Gluten-Free Spice Cookies ... 80
Cream-Filled Sandwich Cookies ... 80
Pumpkin Cookie with Cream Cheese Frosting ... 80
Easy Chocolate Donuts ... 80
Cinnamon-Sugar Almonds ... 81

Chapter 12 Staples, Sauces, Dips, and Dressings 82

Traditional Caesar Dressing ... 83
Blue Cheese Dressing ... 83
Sweet Ginger Teriyaki Sauce ... 83
Vegan Lentil Dip ... 83
Cauliflower Alfredo Sauce ... 83
Cashew Mayo ... 84
Gochujang Dip ... 84
Lemon Cashew Dip ... 84
Tahini Dressing ... 84
Red Buffalo Sauce ... 84
Pepper Sauce ... 84
Artichoke Dip ... 84
Peachy Barbecue Sauce ... 85
Apple Cider Dressing ... 85
Lemony Tahini ... 85

Appendix 1 Measurement Conversion Chart 87

Appendix 2 Air Fryer Cooking Chart 88

INTRODUCTION

If you enjoy fried meals beyond everything else and you're concerned about the health consequences of eating fried foods all the time, just like me, I highly recommend my new Ninja Air Fryer for you.

It employs a mix of hot air and quick air circulation to crisp up any dish without the usage of gallons of oil.

This flexible air fryer, which has four modes – air fry, roast, reheat, and dehydrate – is a great equipment for household kitchens and doesn't occupy as much room as some of the other versions we looked at.

The Ninja Foodi can achieve temperatures of up to 400°F, which allows it to cook the crispiest fries, chicken wings, and more.

It has a huge capacity basket that can fit up to 2 pounds of fries or six chicken tenders, making it easy to feed a family, unlike many other air fryers we've tested.

It also contains two crisping covers, one for the 5-quart main cooking pot and one for the 3-quart inner pot, allowing you to effectively cook little quantities of food.

By dividing the basket into distinct areas, the Ninja Foodi's dual-zone technology allows you to cook two different meals at the same time. This is quite beneficial if you want to cook many items at the same time without having to worry about them mixing.

Not only has Ninja created an air fryer that cooks food more healthily, but they've also created a product that is super easy to use. With just a press of a button, you can cook delicious meals in no time. You can also cook different foods at once! How amazing!

This Ninja Air Fryer Guide will handle all aspects of learning how to cook using your air fryer. This guide will help you through all of your culinary adventures, whether you are a novice or an expert. It also offers delectable and mouth-watering recipes that will have you coming back for more.

The book also includes instructions for utilising the air fryer, which will make your meals taste better and be healthier than before. Because the recipes are quick and simple to follow, you will be able to save time, money, and effort when cooking.

Chapter 1 You Must Have the Ninja Air Fryer

Chapter 1 You Must Have the Ninja Air Fryer

What Is a Ninja Air Fryer?

The popular ninja air fryer is a simple frying device that uses very hot, fast-circulating air to flash-roast meals inside an enclosed frying basket. Though little or no oil is usually used, the outcomes can be close to typical frying in that the food comes out crunchy on the exterior and moist on the inside.

The ninja air fryer uses convection to circulate hot air around your food at high speed. The result is evenly cooked food that's crispy on the outside and tender on the inside, with little to no oil required.

Ninja air fryers are designed to quickly and evenly heat any type of food. Their fans can circulate hot air at a very high speed, which cooks foods quickly and makes them crispy.

Getting To Know Your Ninja Air Fryer

Getting to know your Ninja Air Fryer may seem intimidating at first, but don't worry. We are here to help.

The Ninja Air Fryer is a revolutionary product that has been crafted with care and precision to ensure you get the best performance. Let's take a look at how you can get the most out of your Air Fryer.

The first thing we want to do is familiarize ourselves with the buttons on our Ninja Foodi Air Fryer.

Air fry

This function uses Rapid Air Technology to cook food. You can also adjust the time and temperature by pressing the Time/Temp button. This function is best used for frozen foods.

Roast

This function, like the others, uses Rapid Air Technology to elevate the temperature within the pot to 450 degrees Fahrenheit. As a result, the Ninja Air Fryer is ideal for roasting vegetables and meats. By tapping the Time/Temp button, you may easily change the time and temperature.

Reheat

The reheat function quickly raises the interior temperature to 380 degrees Fahrenheit, making it perfect for leftovers or frozen foods that you don't have time to cook in an oven or microwave.

Dehydrate

The dehydrate function allows you to create your homemade snacks like dried fruit and jerky at home without added sugars or preservatives that are found in store-bought options.

Power Button

This button turns your air fryer on and off, obvious enough. The light next to it will show red when it's on, and white when it's off.

Start/Pause

This pauses and resumes cooking. If you want to check on how it is coming along without stopping the cooking process, just press this button if it has started, and then press it again to resume cooking.

Time

Sets the duration of your cooking process. This can be anywhere from 15 seconds for a smaller item like an onion slice, to 240 minutes for crisping up frozen fries.

Temp

Set the temperature with the convenient up to and down button. The temperature display shows both the set temperature and the actual temperature in the inner cooking chamber. The selectable temperature range is from 200 to 400 degrees (Fahrenheit), so you can adjust it to your needs.

Must-Have Air Fryer Accessories

Take your air fryer to the next level with this trio of useful accessories.

Air Fryer Liners

Air fryer accessories make your Air Fryer experience even better. While air frying, food can splatter and stick to the basket. An air fryer liner is one way to tackle this issue. Air fryers come with a basket but it's also possible to use liners. Make air frying easier by purchasing some air fryer accessories today!

Air fryer liners are made of heavy-duty polypropylene, a high-quality heat resistant material. They are perfect for protecting your Air Fryer from splatter and also make clean up a breeze. And the fact that you can, roast and fry in them are just amazing.

Skewers and Rack

Skewers and racks are must-have accessories for your air fryer. Rack makes it easy to add or remove food while still keeping other foods in place. Skewers rest comfortably across the upper edges, ensuring that they won't fall out or become obstructed with food.

Heat-Resistant Tongs

Using tongs is one of the easiest ways to safely remove food from your fryer. The heat-resistant, non-slip silicone material makes it possible for you to do this without burning yourself. The tongs and spatula are easy to clean and dishwasher safe.

Oil Sprayer

The oil sprayer is the perfect companion for your Air Fryer. It has a 60ml capacity and allows you to precisely coat your food with oil, chocolate, butter or marinades. The ideal addition to your Air Fryer for healthier and tastier cooking.

Thermapen

The Thermapen is a fast, accurate, and reliable thermometer. It is designed to help in verifying the results of your temperature measurements and making sure food reaches safe cooking temperatures.

Ramekins

Ramekins are the perfect accessory for our Air Fryer. Perfect for frying quesadillas, fish and more, the clear glass lets you see your food as it cooks to give you added confidence. Also great for sauces, condiments or side dishes.

By following these tips, you can keep your Ninja Foodi Air Fryer clean and working well for a long time.

Cleaning Tips

- Always clean the air fryer after completing each use.
- To help prevent food odours from spreading, turn off the unit before cleaning it and allow it to cool down completely.
- Wash the inside of the bowl with water and soap, but do not wet the base; do not use harsh cleaners or scouring pads on any part of your equipment.
- Fill the bowl with warm water and a few drops of dishwashing liquid if food becomes stuck or hardens within the air fryer's shell.
- Slowly turn the power back on and run the appliance through its cycle to loosen food particles.
- If the food remains in hard-to-reach places, take a few Q-tips, dip them in water and alcohol, then gently scrub at pieces of stuck food until they can be dislodged from their hiding spot.

Troubleshooting Tips

How do I avoid the air frying from my blowing food around?

Lightweight items may be blown around by the air fryer's blower on occasion. To avoid this, use toothpicks to fasten goods (such as the top slice of bread on a sandwich).

Is it possible to air-fry wet battered ingredients?

Absolutely, but make sure you're using the right breading process. It's critical to cover dishes with flour first, then egg, and last bread crumbs. Use your hands to squeeze the bread pieces onto the meal. Because the air fryer's system includes a strong fan, breading can occasionally be blasted off. The bread crumbs will stick better if you press them down hard.

How do I make sure my food never gets burned?

Check progress during cooking for optimal results, and remove food when a desirable amount of brownness is reached. To avoid overcooking, take the food as soon as the cooking time is up.

Is it safe to set the basket on my counter?

While cooking, the basket will overheat. Handle with care and only set on heat-safe areas.

Chapter 2 Breakfasts

Chapter 2 Breakfasts

Johnny Cakes

Prep time: 10 minutes | Cook time: 10 to 12 minutes | Serves 4

½ cup all-purpose flour
1½ cups yellow cornmeal
2 tablespoons sugar
1 teaspoon baking powder
1 teaspoon salt
1 cup milk, whole or 2%
1 tablespoon butter, melted
1 large egg, lightly beaten
1 to 2 tablespoons oil

1. In a large bowl, whisk the flour, cornmeal, sugar, baking powder, and salt until blended. Whisk in the milk, melted butter, and egg until the mixture is sticky but still lumpy. 2. Preheat the air fryer to 350°F (177°C). Line the air fryer basket with parchment paper. 3. For each cake, drop 1 heaping tablespoon of batter onto the parchment paper. The fryer should hold 4 cakes. 4. Spritz the cakes with oil and cook for 3 minutes. Turn the cakes, spritz with oil again, and cook for 2 to 3 minutes more. Repeat with a second batch of cakes.

Breakfast Cobbler

Prep time: 20 minutes | Cook time: 30 minutes | Serves 4

Filling:
10 ounces (283 g) bulk pork sausage, crumbled
¼ cup minced onions
2 cloves garlic, minced
½ teaspoon fine sea salt
½ teaspoon ground black pepper
1 (8-ounce / 227-g) package cream cheese (or Kite Hill brand cream cheese style spread for dairy-free), softened
¾ cup beef or chicken broth
Biscuits:
3 large egg whites
¾ cup blanched almond flour
1 teaspoon baking powder
¼ teaspoon fine sea salt
2½ tablespoons very cold unsalted butter, cut into ¼-inch pieces
Fresh thyme leaves, for garnish

1. Preheat the air fryer to 400°F (204°C). 2. Place the sausage, onions, and garlic in a pie pan. Using your hands, break up the sausage into small pieces and spread it evenly throughout the pie pan. Season with the salt and pepper. Place the pan in the air fryer and cook for 5 minutes. 3. While the sausage cooks, place the cream cheese and broth in a food processor or blender and purée until smooth. 4. Remove the pork from the air fryer and use a fork or metal spatula to crumble it more. Pour the cream cheese mixture into the sausage and stir to combine. Set aside. 5. Make the biscuits: Place the egg whites in a medium-sized mixing bowl or the bowl of a stand mixer and whip with a hand mixer or stand mixer until stiff peaks form. 6. In a separate medium-sized bowl, whisk together the almond flour, baking powder, and salt, then cut in the butter. When you are done, the mixture should still have chunks of butter. Gently fold the flour mixture into the egg whites with a rubber spatula. 7. Use a large spoon or ice cream scoop to scoop the dough into 4 equal-sized biscuits, making sure the butter is evenly distributed. Place the biscuits on top of the sausage and cook in the air fryer for 5 minutes, then turn the heat down to 325°F (163°C) and cook for another 17 to 20 minutes, until the biscuits are golden brown. Serve garnished with fresh thyme leaves. 8. Store leftovers in an airtight container in the refrigerator for up to 3 days. Reheat in a preheated 350°F (177°C) air fryer for 5 minutes, or until warmed through.

Whole Wheat Blueberry Muffins

Prep time: 10 minutes | Cook time: 15 minutes | Serves 6

Olive oil cooking spray
½ cup unsweetened applesauce
¼ cup raw honey
½ cup nonfat plain Greek yogurt
1 teaspoon vanilla extract
1 large egg
1½ cups plus 1 tablespoon
whole wheat flour, divided
½ teaspoon baking soda
½ teaspoon baking powder
½ teaspoon salt
½ cup blueberries, fresh or frozen

1. Preheat the air fryer to 360°F (182°C). Lightly coat the inside of six silicone muffin cups or a six-cup muffin tin with olive oil cooking spray. 2. In a large bowl, combine the applesauce, honey, yogurt, vanilla, and egg and mix until smooth. 3. Sift in 1½ cups of the flour, the baking soda, baking powder, and salt into the wet mixture, then stir until just combined. 4. In a small bowl, toss the blueberries with the remaining 1 tablespoon flour, then fold the mixture into the muffin batter. 5. Divide the mixture evenly among the prepared muffin cups and place into the basket of the air fryer. Cook for 12 to 15 minutes, or until golden brown on top and a toothpick inserted into the middle of one of the muffins comes out clean. 6. Allow to cool for 5 minutes before serving.

Savory Sweet Potato Hash

Prep time: 15 minutes | Cook time: 18 minutes | Serves 6

2 medium sweet potatoes, peeled and cut into 1-inch cubes
½ green bell pepper, diced
½ red onion, diced
4 ounces (113 g) baby bella mushrooms, diced
2 tablespoons olive oil
1 garlic clove, minced
½ teaspoon salt
½ teaspoon black pepper
½ tablespoon chopped fresh rosemary

1. Preheat the air fryer to 380°F (193°C). 2. In a large bowl, toss all ingredients together until the vegetables are well coated and seasonings distributed. 3. Pour the vegetables into the air fryer basket, making sure they are in a single even layer. (If using a smaller air fryer, you may need to do this in two batches.) 4. Roast for 9 minutes, then toss or flip the vegetables. Roast for 9 minutes more. 5. Transfer to a serving bowl or individual plates and enjoy.

Peppered Maple Bacon Knots

Prep time: 5 minutes | Cook time: 7 to 8 minutes | Serves 6

1 pound (454 g) maple smoked center-cut bacon
¼ cup maple syrup
¼ cup brown sugar
Coarsely cracked black peppercorns, to taste

1. Preheat the air fryer to 390°F (199°C). 2. On a clean work surface, tie each bacon strip in a loose knot. 3. Stir together the maple syrup and brown sugar in a bowl. Generously brush this mixture over the bacon knots. 4. Working in batches, arrange the bacon knots in the air fryer basket. Sprinkle with the coarsely cracked black peppercorns. 5. Air fry for 5 minutes. Flip the bacon knots and continue cooking for 2 to 3 minutes more, or until the bacon is crisp. 6. Remove from the basket to a paper towel-lined plate. Repeat with the remaining bacon knots. 7. Let the bacon knots cool for a few minutes and serve warm.

Baked Egg and Mushroom Cups

Prep time: 5 minutes | Cook time: 15 minutes | Serves 6

Olive oil cooking spray
6 large eggs
1 garlic clove, minced
½ teaspoon salt
½ teaspoon black pepper
Pinch red pepper flakes
8 ounces (227 g) baby bella mushrooms, sliced
1 cup fresh baby spinach
2 scallions, white parts and green parts, diced

1. Preheat the air fryer to 320°F (160°C). Lightly coat the inside of six silicone muffin cups or a six-cup muffin tin with olive oil cooking spray. 2. In a large bowl, beat the eggs, garlic, salt, pepper, and red pepper flakes for 1 to 2 minutes, or until well combined. 3. Fold in the mushrooms, spinach, and scallions. 4. Divide the mixture evenly among the muffin cups. 5. Place into the air fryer and cook for 12 to 15 minutes, or until the eggs are set. 6. Remove and allow to cool for 5 minutes before serving.

Egg in a Hole

Prep time: 5 minutes | Cook time: 5 minutes | Serves 1

1 slice bread
1 teaspoon butter, softened
1 egg
Salt and pepper, to taste
1 tablespoon shredded Cheddar cheese
2 teaspoons diced ham

1. Preheat the air fryer to 330°F (166°C). Place a baking dish in the air fryer basket. 2. On a flat work surface, cut a hole in the center of the bread slice with a 2½-inch-diameter biscuit cutter. 3. Spread the butter evenly on each side of the bread slice and transfer to the baking dish. 4. Crack the egg into the hole and season as desired with salt and pepper. Scatter the shredded cheese and diced ham on top. 5. Cook in the preheated air fryer for 5 minutes until the bread is lightly browned and the egg is cooked to your preference. 6. Remove from the basket and serve hot.

Parmesan Sausage Egg Muffins

Prep time: 5 minutes | Cook time: 20 minutes | Serves 4

6 ounces (170 g) Italian sausage, sliced
6 eggs
⅛ cup heavy cream
Salt and ground black pepper, to taste
3 ounces (85 g) Parmesan cheese, grated

1. Preheat the air fryer to 350°F (177°C). Grease a muffin pan. 2. Put the sliced sausage in the muffin pan. 3. Beat the eggs with the cream in a bowl and season with salt and pepper. 4. Pour half of the mixture over the sausages in the pan. 5. Sprinkle with cheese and the remaining egg mixture. 6. Cook in the preheated air fryer for 20 minutes or until set. 7. Serve immediately.

Red Pepper and Feta Frittata

Prep time: 10 minutes | Cook time: 20 minutes | Serves 4

Olive oil cooking spray
8 large eggs
1 medium red bell pepper, diced
½ teaspoon salt
½ teaspoon black pepper
1 garlic clove, minced
½ cup feta, divided

1. Preheat the air fryer to 360°F (182°C). Lightly coat the inside of a 6-inch round cake pan with olive oil cooking spray. 2. In a large bowl, beat the eggs for 1 to 2 minutes, or until well combined. 3. Add the bell pepper, salt, black pepper, and garlic to the eggs, and mix together until the bell pepper is distributed throughout. 4. Fold in ¼ cup of the feta cheese. 5. Pour the egg mixture into the prepared cake pan, and sprinkle the remaining ¼ cup of feta over the top. 6. Place into the air fryer and cook for 18 to 20 minutes, or until the eggs are set in the center. 7. Remove from the air fryer and allow to cool for 5 minutes before serving.

Cajun Breakfast Sausage

Prep time: 10 minutes | Cook time: 15 to 20 minutes | Serves 8

1½ pounds (680 g) 85% lean ground turkey
3 cloves garlic, finely chopped
¼ onion, grated
1 teaspoon Tabasco sauce
1 teaspoon Creole seasoning
1 teaspoon dried thyme
½ teaspoon paprika
½ teaspoon cayenne

1. Preheat the air fryer to 370°F (188°C). 2. In a large bowl, combine the turkey, garlic, onion, Tabasco, Creole seasoning, thyme, paprika, and cayenne. Mix with clean hands until thoroughly combined. Shape into 16 patties, about ½ inch thick. (Wet your hands slightly if you find the sausage too sticky to handle.) 3. Working in batches if necessary, arrange the patties in a single layer in the air fryer basket. Pausing halfway through the cooking time to flip the patties, air fry for 15 to 20 minutes until a thermometer inserted into the thickest portion registers 165°F (74°C).

Keto Quiche

Prep time: 10 minutes | Cook time: 1 hour | Makes 1 (6-inch) quiche

Crust:
1¼ cups blanched almond flour
1¼ cups grated Parmesan or Gouda cheese
¼ teaspoon fine sea salt
1 large egg, beaten
Filling:
½ cup chicken or beef broth (or vegetable broth for vegetarian)
1 cup shredded Swiss cheese (about 4 ounces / 113 g)
4 ounces (113 g) cream cheese (½ cup)
1 tablespoon unsalted butter, melted
4 large eggs, beaten
⅓ cup minced leeks or sliced green onions
¾ teaspoon fine sea salt
⅛ teaspoon cayenne pepper
Chopped green onions, for garnish

1. Preheat the air fryer to 325ºF (163ºC). Grease a pie pan. Spray two large pieces of parchment paper with avocado oil and set them on the countertop. 2. Make the crust: In a medium-sized bowl, combine the flour, cheese, and salt and mix well. Add the egg and mix until the dough is well combined and stiff. 3. Place the dough in the center of one of the greased pieces of parchment. Top with the other piece of parchment. Using a rolling pin, roll out the dough into a circle about 1/16 inch thick. 4. Press the pie crust into the prepared pie pan. Place it in the air fryer and cook for 12 minutes, or until it starts to lightly brown. 5. While the crust cooks, make the filling: In a large bowl, combine the broth, Swiss cheese, cream cheese, and butter. Stir in the eggs, leeks, salt, and cayenne pepper. When the crust is ready, pour the mixture into the crust. 6. Place the quiche in the air fryer and cook for 15 minutes. Turn the heat down to 300ºF (149ºC) and cook for an additional 30 minutes, or until a knife inserted 1 inch from the edge comes out clean. You may have to cover the edges of the crust with foil to prevent burning. 7. Allow the quiche to cool for 10 minutes before garnishing it with chopped green onions and cutting it into wedges. 8. Store leftovers in an airtight container in the refrigerator for up to 4 days or in the freezer for up to a month. Reheat in a preheated 350ºF (177ºC) air fryer for a few minutes, until warmed through.

Creamy Cinnamon Rolls

Prep time: 10 minutes | Cook time: 9 minutes | Serves 8

1 pound (454 g) frozen bread dough, thawed
¼ cup butter, melted
¾ cup brown sugar
1½ tablespoons ground cinnamon
Cream Cheese Glaze:
4 ounces (113 g) cream cheese, softened
2 tablespoons butter, softened
1¼ cups powdered sugar
½ teaspoon vanilla extract

1. Let the bread dough come to room temperature on the counter. On a lightly floured surface, roll the dough into a 13-inch by 11-inch rectangle. Position the rectangle so the 13-inch side is facing you. Brush the melted butter all over the dough, leaving a 1-inch border uncovered along the edge farthest away from you. 2. Combine the brown sugar and cinnamon in a small bowl. Sprinkle the mixture evenly over the buttered dough, keeping the 1-inch border uncovered. Roll the dough into a log, starting with the edge closest to you. Roll the dough tightly, rolling evenly, and push out any air pockets. When you get to the uncovered edge of the dough, press the dough onto the roll to seal it together. 3. Cut the log into 8 pieces, slicing slowly with a sawing motion so you don't flatten the dough. Turn the slices on their sides and cover with a clean kitchen towel. Let the rolls sit in the warmest part of the kitchen for 1½ to 2 hours to rise. 4. To make the glaze, place the cream cheese and butter in a microwave-safe bowl. Soften the mixture in the microwave for 30 seconds at a time until it is easy to stir. Gradually add the powdered sugar and stir to combine. Add the vanilla extract and whisk until smooth. Set aside. 5. When the rolls have risen, preheat the air fryer to 350ºF (177ºC). 6. Transfer 4 of the rolls to the air fryer basket. Air fry for 5 minutes. Turn the rolls over and air fry for another 4 minutes. Repeat with the remaining 4 rolls. 7. Let the rolls cool for two minutes before glazing. Spread large dollops of cream cheese glaze on top of the warm cinnamon rolls, allowing some glaze to drip down the side of the rolls. Serve warm.

Cheesy Bell Pepper Eggs

Prep time: 10 minutes | Cook time: 15 minutes | Serves 4

4 medium green bell peppers
3 ounces (85 g) cooked ham, chopped
¼ medium onion, peeled and chopped
8 large eggs
1 cup mild Cheddar cheese

1. Cut the tops off each bell pepper. Remove the seeds and the white membranes with a small knife. Place ham and onion into each pepper. 2. Crack 2 eggs into each pepper. Top with ¼ cup cheese per pepper. Place into the air fryer basket. 3. Adjust the temperature to 390ºF (199ºC) and air fry for 15 minutes. 4. When fully cooked, peppers will be tender and eggs will be firm. Serve immediately.

Cinnamon Rolls

Prep time: 10 minutes | Cook time: 20 minutes | Makes 12 rolls

2½ cups shredded Mozzarella cheese
2 ounces (57 g) cream cheese, softened
1 cup blanched finely ground almond flour
½ teaspoon vanilla extract
½ cup confectioners' erythritol
1 tablespoon ground cinnamon

1. In a large microwave-safe bowl, combine Mozzarella cheese, cream cheese, and flour. Microwave the mixture on high 90 seconds until cheese is melted. 2. Add vanilla extract and erythritol, and mix 2 minutes until a dough forms. 3. Once the dough is cool enough to work with your hands, about 2 minutes, spread it out into a 12 × 4-inch rectangle on ungreased parchment paper. Evenly sprinkle dough with cinnamon. 4. Starting at the long side of the dough, roll lengthwise to form a log. Slice the log into twelve even pieces. 5. Divide rolls between two ungreased round nonstick baking dishes. Place one dish into air fryer basket. Adjust the temperature to 375ºF (191ºC) and cook for 10 minutes. 6. Cinnamon rolls will be done when golden around the edges and mostly firm. Repeat with second dish. Allow rolls to cool in dishes 10 minutes before serving.

Sausage and Cheese Balls

Prep time: 10 minutes | Cook time: 12 minutes | Makes 16 balls

1 pound (454 g) pork breakfast sausage
½ cup shredded Cheddar cheese
1 ounce (28 g) full-fat cream cheese, softened
1 large egg

1. Mix all ingredients in a large bowl. Form into sixteen (1-inch) balls. Place the balls into the air fryer basket. 2. Adjust the temperature to 400°F (204°C) and air fry for 12 minutes. 3. Shake the basket two or three times during cooking. Sausage balls will be browned on the outside and have an internal temperature of at least 145°F (63°C) when completely cooked. 4. Serve warm.

Scotch Eggs

Prep time: 10 minutes | Cook time: 20 to 25 minutes | Serves 4

2 tablespoons flour, plus extra for coating
1 pound (454 g) ground breakfast sausage
4 hard-boiled eggs, peeled
1 raw egg
1 tablespoon water
Oil for misting or cooking spray
Crumb Coating:
¾ cup panko bread crumbs
¾ cup flour

1. Combine flour with ground sausage and mix thoroughly. 2. Divide into 4 equal portions and mold each around a hard-boiled egg so the sausage completely covers the egg. 3. In a small bowl, beat together the raw egg and water. 4. Dip sausage-covered eggs in the remaining flour, then the egg mixture, then roll in the crumb coating. 5. Air fry at 360°F (182°C) for 10 minutes. Spray eggs, turn, and spray other side. 6. Continue cooking for another 10 to 15 minutes or until sausage is well done.

Honey-Apricot Granola with Greek Yogurt

Prep time: 10 minutes | Cook time: 30 minutes | Serves 6

1 cup rolled oats
¼ cup dried apricots, diced
¼ cup almond slivers
¼ cup walnuts, chopped
¼ cup pumpkin seeds
¼ cup hemp hearts
¼ to ⅓ cup raw honey, plus more for drizzling
1 tablespoon olive oil
1 teaspoon ground cinnamon
¼ teaspoon ground nutmeg
¼ teaspoon salt
2 tablespoons sugar-free dark chocolate chips (optional)
3 cups nonfat plain Greek yogurt

1. Preheat the air fryer to 260°F (127°C). Line the air fryer basket with parchment paper. 2. In a large bowl, combine the oats, apricots, almonds, walnuts, pumpkin seeds, hemp hearts, honey, olive oil, cinnamon, nutmeg, and salt, mixing so that the honey, oil, and spices are well distributed. 3. Pour the mixture onto the parchment paper and spread it into an even layer. 4. Cook for 10 minutes, then shake or stir and spread back out into an even layer. Continue baking for 10 minutes more, then repeat the process of shaking or stirring the mixture. Cook for an additional 10 minutes before removing from the air fryer. 5. Allow the granola to cool completely before stirring in the chocolate chips (if using) and pouring into an airtight container for storage. 6. For each serving, top ½ cup Greek yogurt with ⅓ cup granola and a drizzle of honey, if needed.

Whole Wheat Banana-Walnut Bread

Prep time: 10 minutes | Cook time: 23 minutes | Serves 6

Olive oil cooking spray
2 ripe medium bananas
1 large egg
¼ cup nonfat plain Greek yogurt
¼ cup olive oil
½ teaspoon vanilla extract
2 tablespoons raw honey
1 cup whole wheat flour
¼ teaspoon salt
¼ teaspoon baking soda
½ teaspoon ground cinnamon
¼ cup chopped walnuts

1. Preheat the air fryer to 360°F (182°C). Lightly coat the inside of a 8-by-4-inch loaf pan with olive oil cooking spray. (Or use two 5 ½-by-3-inch loaf pans.) 2. In a large bowl, mash the bananas with a fork. Add the egg, yogurt, olive oil, vanilla, and honey. Mix until well combined and mostly smooth. 3. Sift the whole wheat flour, salt, baking soda, and cinnamon into the wet mixture, then stir until just combined. Do not overmix. 4. Gently fold in the walnuts. 5. Pour into the prepared loaf pan and spread to distribute evenly. 6. Place the loaf pan in the air fryer basket and cook for 20 to 23 minutes, or until golden brown on top and a toothpick inserted into the center comes out clean. 7. Allow to cool for 5 minutes before serving.

Mozzarella Bacon Calzones

Prep time: 15 minutes | Cook time: 12 minutes | Serves 4

2 large eggs
1 cup blanched finely ground almond flour
2 cups shredded Mozzarella cheese
2 ounces (57 g) cream cheese, softened and broken into small pieces
4 slices cooked sugar-free bacon, crumbled

1. Beat eggs in a small bowl. Pour into a medium nonstick skillet over medium heat and scramble. Set aside. 2. In a large microwave-safe bowl, mix flour and Mozzarella. Add cream cheese to the bowl. 3. Place bowl in microwave and cook 45 seconds on high to melt cheese, then stir with a fork until a soft dough ball forms. 4. Cut a piece of parchment to fit air fryer basket. Separate dough into two sections and press each out into an 8-inch round. 5. On half of each dough round, place half of the scrambled eggs and crumbled bacon. Fold the other side of the dough over and press to seal the edges. 6. Place calzones on ungreased parchment and into air fryer basket. Adjust the temperature to 350°F (177°C) and set the timer for 12 minutes, turning calzones halfway through cooking. Crust will be golden and firm when done. 7. Let calzones cool on a cooking rack 5 minutes before serving.

Lemon-Blueberry Muffins

Prep time: 5 minutes | Cook time: 20 to 25 minutes | Makes 6 muffins

1¼ cups almond flour
3 tablespoons Swerve
1 teaspoon baking powder
2 large eggs
3 tablespoons melted butter
1 tablespoon almond milk
1 tablespoon fresh lemon juice
½ cup fresh blueberries

1. Preheat the air fryer to 350ºF (177ºC). Lightly coat 6 silicone muffin cups with vegetable oil. Set aside. 2. In a large mixing bowl, combine the almond flour, Swerve, and baking soda. Set aside. 3. In a separate small bowl, whisk together the eggs, butter, milk, and lemon juice. Add the egg mixture to the flour mixture and stir until just combined. Fold in the blueberries and let the batter sit for 5 minutes. 4. Spoon the muffin batter into the muffin cups, about two-thirds full. Air fry for 20 to 25 minutes, or until a toothpick inserted into the center of a muffin comes out clean. 5. Remove the basket from the air fryer and let the muffins cool for about 5 minutes before transferring them to a wire rack to cool completely.

Golden Avocado Tempura

Prep time: 5 minutes | Cook time: 10 minutes | Serves 4

½ cup bread crumbs
½ teaspoons salt
1 Haas avocado, pitted, peeled and sliced
Liquid from 1 can white beans

1. Preheat the air fryer to 350ºF (177ºC). 2. Mix the bread crumbs and salt in a shallow bowl until well-incorporated. 3. Dip the avocado slices in the bean liquid, then into the bread crumbs. 4. Put the avocados in the air fryer, taking care not to overlap any slices, and air fry for 10 minutes, giving the basket a good shake at the halfway point. 5. Serve immediately.

Fried Chicken Wings with Waffles

Prep time: 10 minutes | Cook time: 30 minutes | Serves 4

8 whole chicken wings
1 teaspoon garlic powder
Chicken seasoning, for preparing the chicken
Freshly ground black pepper, to taste
½ cup all-purpose flour
Cooking oil spray
8 frozen waffles
Pure maple syrup, for serving (optional)

1. In a medium bowl, combine the chicken and garlic powder and season with chicken seasoning and pepper. Toss to coat. 2. Transfer the chicken to a resealable plastic bag and add the flour. Seal the bag and shake it to coat the chicken thoroughly. 3. Insert the crisper plate into the basket and the basket into the unit. Preheat the unit by selecting AIR FRY, setting the temperature to 400ºF (204ºC), and setting the time to 3 minutes. Select START/PAUSE to begin. 4. Once the unit is preheated, spray the crisper plate with cooking oil. Using tongs, transfer the chicken from the bag to the basket. It is okay to stack the chicken wings on top of each other. Spray them with cooking oil. 5. Select AIR FRY, set the temperature to 400ºF (204ºC), and set the time to 20 minutes. Select START/PAUSE to begin. 6. After 5 minutes, remove the basket and shake the wings. Reinsert the basket to resume cooking. Remove and shake the basket every 5 minutes until the chicken is fully cooked. 7. When the cooking is complete, remove the cooked chicken from the basket; cover to keep warm. 8. Rinse the basket and crisper plate with warm water. Insert them back into the unit. 9. Select AIR FRY, set the temperature to 360ºF (182ºC), and set the time to 3 minutes. Select START/PAUSE to begin. 10. Once the unit is preheated, spray the crisper plate with cooking spray. Working in batches, place the frozen waffles into the basket. Do not stack them. Spray the waffles with cooking oil. 11. Select AIR FRY, set the temperature to 360ºF (182ºC), and set the time to 6 minutes. Select START/PAUSE to begin. 12. When the cooking is complete, repeat steps 10 and 11 with the remaining waffles. 13. Serve the waffles with the chicken and a touch of maple syrup, if desired.

Pumpkin Spice Muffins

Prep time: 10 minutes | Cook time: 15 minutes | Serves 6

1 cup blanched finely ground almond flour
½ cup granular erythritol
½ teaspoon baking powder
¼ cup unsalted butter, softened
¼ cup pure pumpkin purée
½ teaspoon ground cinnamon
¼ teaspoon ground nutmeg
1 teaspoon vanilla extract
2 large eggs

1. In a large bowl, mix almond flour, erythritol, baking powder, butter, pumpkin purée, cinnamon, nutmeg, and vanilla. 2. Gently stir in eggs. 3. Evenly pour the batter into six silicone muffin cups. Place muffin cups into the air fryer basket, working in batches if necessary. 4. Adjust the temperature to 300ºF (149ºC) and cook for 15 minutes. 5. When completely cooked, a toothpick inserted in center will come out mostly clean. Serve warm.

Breakfast Pizza

Prep time: 5 minutes | Cook time: 8 minutes | Serves 1

2 large eggs
¼ cup unsweetened, unflavored almond milk (or unflavored hemp milk for nut-free)
¼ teaspoon fine sea salt
⅛ teaspoon ground black pepper
¼ cup diced onions
¼ cup shredded Parmesan cheese (omit for dairy-free)
6 pepperoni slices (omit for vegetarian)
¼ teaspoon dried oregano leaves
¼ cup pizza sauce, warmed, for serving

1. Preheat the air fryer to 350ºF (177ºC). Grease a cake pan. 2. In a small bowl, use a fork to whisk together the eggs, almond milk, salt, and pepper. Add the onions and stir to mix. Pour the mixture into the greased pan. Top with the cheese (if using), pepperoni slices (if using), and oregano. 3. Place the pan in the air fryer and cook for 8 minutes, or until the eggs are cooked to your liking. 4. Loosen the eggs from the sides of the pan with a spatula and place them on a serving plate. Drizzle the pizza sauce on top. Best served fresh.

Butternut Squash and Ricotta Frittata

Prep time: 10 minutes | Cook time: 33 minutes | Serves 2 to 3

1 cup cubed (½-inch) butternut squash (5½ ounces / 156 g)
2 tablespoons olive oil
Kosher salt and freshly ground black pepper, to taste
4 fresh sage leaves, thinly sliced
6 large eggs, lightly beaten
½ cup ricotta cheese
Cayenne pepper

1. In a bowl, toss the squash with the olive oil and season with salt and black pepper until evenly coated. Sprinkle the sage on the bottom of a cake pan and place the squash on top. Place the pan in the air fryer and cook at 400°F (204°C) for 10 minutes. Stir to incorporate the sage, then cook until the squash is tender and lightly caramelized at the edges, about 3 minutes more. 2. Pour the eggs over the squash, dollop the ricotta all over, and sprinkle with cayenne. Cook at 300°F (149°C) until the eggs are set and the frittata is golden brown on top, about 20 minutes. Remove the pan from the air fryer and cut the frittata into wedges to serve.

Poached Eggs on Whole Grain Avocado Toast

Prep time: 5 minutes | Cook time: 7 minutes | Serves 4

Olive oil cooking spray
4 large eggs
Salt
Black pepper
4 pieces whole grain bread
1 avocado
Red pepper flakes (optional)

1. Preheat the air fryer to 320°F (160°C). Lightly coat the inside of four small oven-safe ramekins with olive oil cooking spray. 2. Crack one egg into each ramekin, and season with salt and black pepper. 3. Place the ramekins into the air fryer basket. Close and set the timer to 7 minutes. 4. While the eggs are cooking, toast the bread in a toaster. 5. Slice the avocado in half lengthwise, remove the pit, and scoop the flesh into a small bowl. Season with salt, black pepper, and red pepper flakes, if desired. Using a fork, smash the avocado lightly. 6. Spread a quarter of the smashed avocado evenly over each slice of toast. 7. Remove the eggs from the air fryer, and gently spoon one onto each slice of avocado toast before serving.

Italian Egg Cups

Prep time: 5 minutes | Cook time: 10 minutes | Serves 4

Olive oil
1 cup marinara sauce
4 eggs
4 tablespoons shredded Mozzarella cheese
4 teaspoons grated Parmesan cheese
Salt and freshly ground black pepper, to taste
Chopped fresh basil, for garnish

1. Lightly spray 4 individual ramekins with olive oil. 2. Pour ¼ cup of marinara sauce into each ramekin. 3. Crack one egg into each ramekin on top of the marinara sauce. 4. Sprinkle 1 tablespoon of Mozzarella and 1 tablespoon of Parmesan on top of each egg. Season with salt and pepper. 5. Cover each ramekin with aluminum foil. Place two of the ramekins in the air fryer basket. 6. Air fry at 350°F (177°C) for 5 minutes and remove the aluminum foil. Air fry until the top is lightly browned and the egg white is cooked, another 2 to 4 minutes. If you prefer the yolk to be firmer, cook for 3 to 5 more minutes. 7. Repeat with the remaining two ramekins. Garnish with basil and serve.

BLT Breakfast Wrap

Prep time: 5 minutes | Cook time: 10 minutes | Serves 4

8 ounces (227 g) reduced-sodium bacon
8 tablespoons mayonnaise
8 large romaine lettuce leaves
4 Roma tomatoes, sliced
Salt and freshly ground black pepper, to taste

1. Arrange the bacon in a single layer in the air fryer basket. (It's OK if the bacon sits a bit on the sides.) Set the air fryer to 350°F (177°C) and air fry for 10 minutes. Check for crispiness and air fry for 2 to 3 minutes longer if needed. Cook in batches, if necessary, and drain the grease in between batches. 2. Spread 1 tablespoon of mayonnaise on each of the lettuce leaves and top with the tomatoes and cooked bacon. Season to taste with salt and freshly ground black pepper. Roll the lettuce leaves as you would a burrito, securing with a toothpick if desired.

Apple Rolls

Prep time: 20 minutes | Cook time: 20 to 24 minutes | Makes 12 rolls

Apple Rolls:
2 cups all-purpose flour, plus more for dusting
2 tablespoons granulated sugar
1 teaspoon salt
3 tablespoons butter, at room temperature
¾ cup milk, whole or 2%
½ cup packed light brown sugar
1 teaspoon ground cinnamon
1 large Granny Smith apple, peeled and diced
1 to 2 tablespoons oil
Icing:
½ cup confectioners' sugar
½ teaspoon vanilla extract
2 to 3 tablespoons milk, whole or 2%

Make the Apple Rolls 1. In a large bowl, whisk the flour, granulated sugar, and salt until blended. Stir in the butter and milk briefly until a sticky dough forms. 2. In a small bowl, stir together the brown sugar, cinnamon, and apple. 3. Place a piece of parchment paper on a work surface and dust it with flour. Roll the dough on the prepared surface to ¼ inch thickness. 4. Spread the apple mixture over the dough. Roll up the dough jelly roll-style, pinching the ends to seal. Cut the dough into 12 rolls. 5. Preheat the air fryer to 320°F (160°C). 6. Line the air fryer basket with parchment paper and spritz it with oil. Place 6 rolls on the prepared parchment. 7. Cook for 5 minutes. Flip the rolls and cook for 5 to 7 minutes more until lightly browned. Repeat with the remaining rolls. Make the Icing 8. In a medium bowl, whisk the confectioners' sugar, vanilla, and milk until blended. 9. Drizzle over the warm rolls.

Jalapeño Popper Egg Cups

Prep time: 10 minutes | Cook time: 10 minutes | Serves 2

4 large eggs
¼ cup chopped pickled jalapeños
2 ounces (57 g) full-fat cream cheese
½ cup shredded sharp Cheddar cheese

1. In a medium bowl, beat the eggs, then pour into four silicone muffin cups. 2. In a large microwave-safe bowl, place jalapeños, cream cheese, and Cheddar. Microwave for 30 seconds and stir. Take a spoonful, approximately ¼ of the mixture, and place it in the center of one of the egg cups. Repeat with remaining mixture. 3. Place egg cups into the air fryer basket. 4. Adjust the temperature to 320°F (160°C) and cook for 10 minutes. 5. Serve warm.

Portobello Eggs Benedict

Prep time: 10 minutes | Cook time: 10 to 14 minutes | Serves 2

1 tablespoon olive oil
2 cloves garlic, minced
¼ teaspoon dried thyme
2 portobello mushrooms, stems removed and gills scraped out
2 Roma tomatoes, halved lengthwise
Salt and freshly ground black pepper, to taste
2 large eggs
2 tablespoons grated Pecorino Romano cheese
1 tablespoon chopped fresh parsley, for garnish
1 teaspoon truffle oil (optional)

1. Preheat the air fryer to 400°F (204°C). 2. In a small bowl, combine the olive oil, garlic, and thyme. Brush the mixture over the mushrooms and tomatoes until thoroughly coated. Season to taste with salt and freshly ground black pepper. 3. Arrange the vegetables, cut side up, in the air fryer basket. Crack an egg into the center of each mushroom and sprinkle with cheese. Air fry for 10 to 14 minutes until the vegetables are tender and the whites are firm. When cool enough to handle, coarsely chop the tomatoes and place on top of the eggs. Scatter parsley on top and drizzle with truffle oil, if desired, just before serving.

Homemade Cherry Breakfast Tarts

Prep time: 15 minutes | Cook time: 20 minutes | Serves 6

Tarts:
2 refrigerated piecrusts
⅓ cup cherry preserves
1 teaspoon cornstarch
Cooking oil

Frosting:
½ cup vanilla yogurt
1 ounce (28 g) cream cheese
1 teaspoon stevia
Rainbow sprinkles

Make the Tarts 1. Place the piecrusts on a flat surface. Using a knife or pizza cutter, cut each piecrust into 3 rectangles, for 6 total. (I discard the unused dough left from slicing the edges.) 2. In a small bowl, combine the preserves and cornstarch. Mix well. 3. Scoop 1 tablespoon of the preserves mixture onto the top half of each piece of piecrust. 4. Fold the bottom of each piece up to close the tart. Using the back of a fork, press along the edges of each tart to seal. 5. Spray the breakfast tarts with cooking oil and place them in the air fryer. I do not recommend stacking the breakfast tarts. They will stick together if stacked. You may need to prepare them in two batches. Cook at 375°F for 10 minutes. 6. Allow the breakfast tarts to cool fully before removing from the air fryer. 7. If necessary, repeat steps 5 and 6 for the remaining breakfast tarts. Make the Frosting 8. In a small bowl, combine the yogurt, cream cheese, and stevia. Mix well. 9. Spread the breakfast tarts with frosting and top with sprinkles, and serve.

Easy Sausage Pizza

Prep time: 10 minutes | Cook time: 6 minutes | Serves 4

2 tablespoons ketchup
1 pita bread
⅓ cup sausage
½ pound (227 g) Mozzarella cheese
1 teaspoon garlic powder
1 tablespoon olive oil

1. Preheat the air fryer to 340°F (171°C). 2. Spread the ketchup over the pita bread. 3. Top with the sausage and cheese. Sprinkle with the garlic powder and olive oil. 4. Put the pizza in the air fryer basket and cook for 6 minutes. 5. Serve warm.

Chapter 3 Fish and Seafood

Chapter 3 Fish and Seafood

Baked Monkfish

Prep time: 20 minutes | Cook time: 12 minutes | Serves 2

2 teaspoons olive oil
1 cup celery, sliced
2 bell peppers, sliced
1 teaspoon dried thyme
½ teaspoon dried marjoram
½ teaspoon dried rosemary
2 monkfish fillets
1 tablespoon coconut aminos
2 tablespoons lime juice
Coarse salt and ground black pepper, to taste
1 teaspoon cayenne pepper
½ cup Kalamata olives, pitted and sliced

1. In a nonstick skillet, heat the olive oil for 1 minute. Once hot, sauté the celery and peppers until tender, about 4 minutes. Sprinkle with thyme, marjoram, and rosemary and set aside. 2. Toss the fish fillets with the coconut aminos, lime juice, salt, black pepper, and cayenne pepper. Place the fish fillets in the lightly greased air fryer basket and cook at 390ºF (199ºC) for 8 minutes. 3. Turn them over, add the olives, and cook an additional 4 minutes. Serve with the sautéed vegetables on the side. Bon appétit!

Roasted Cod with Lemon-Garlic Potatoes

Prep time: 10 minutes | Cook time: 28 minutes | Serves 2

3 tablespoons unsalted butter, softened, divided
2 garlic cloves, minced
1 lemon, grated to yield 2 teaspoons zest and sliced ¼ inch thick
Salt and pepper, to taste
1 large russet potato (12 ounce / 340-g), unpeeled, sliced ¼ inch thick
1 tablespoon minced fresh parsley, chives, or tarragon
2 (8-ounce / 227-g) skinless cod fillets, 1¼ inches thick
Vegetable oil spray

1. Preheat the air fryer to 400ºF (204ºC). 2. Make foil sling for air fryer basket by folding 1 long sheet of aluminum foil so it is 4 inches wide. Lay sheet of foil widthwise across basket, pressing foil into and up sides of basket. Fold excess foil as needed so that edges of foil are flush with top of basket. Lightly spray the foil and basket with vegetable oil spray. 3. Microwave 1 tablespoon butter, garlic, 1 teaspoon lemon zest, ¼ teaspoon salt, and ⅛ teaspoon pepper in a medium bowl, stirring once, until the butter is melted and the mixture is fragrant, about 30 seconds. Add the potato slices and toss to coat. Shingle the potato slices on sling in prepared basket to create 2 even layers. Air fry until potato slices are spotty brown and just tender, 16 to 18 minutes, using a sling to rotate potatoes halfway through cooking. 4. Combine the remaining 2 tablespoons butter, remaining 1 teaspoon lemon zest, and parsley in a small bowl. Pat the cod dry with paper towels and season with salt and pepper. Place the fillets, skinned-side down, on top of potato slices, spaced evenly apart. (Tuck thinner tail ends of fillets under themselves as needed to create uniform pieces.) Dot the fillets with the butter mixture and top with the lemon slices. Return the basket to the air fryer and air fry until the cod flakes apart when gently prodded with a paring knife and registers 140ºF (60ºC), 12 to 15 minutes, using a sling to rotate the potato slices and cod halfway through cooking. 5. Using a sling, carefully remove potatoes and cod from air fryer. Cut the potato slices into 2 portions between fillets using fish spatula. Slide spatula along underside of potato slices and transfer with cod to individual plates. Serve.

Garlic Lemon Scallops

Prep time: 5 minutes | Cook time: 10 minutes | Serves 4

4 tablespoons salted butter, melted
4 teaspoons peeled and finely minced garlic
½ small lemon, zested and juiced
8 (1-ounce / 28-g) sea scallops, cleaned and patted dry
¼ teaspoon salt
¼ teaspoon ground black pepper

1. In a small bowl, mix butter, garlic, lemon zest, and lemon juice. Place scallops in an ungreased round nonstick baking dish. Pour butter mixture over scallops, then sprinkle with salt and pepper. 2. Place dish into air fryer basket. Adjust the temperature to 360ºF (182ºC) and cook for 10 minutes. Scallops will be opaque and firm, and have an internal temperature of 135ºF (57ºC) when done. Serve warm.

Oyster Po'Boy

Prep time: 20 minutes | Cook time: 5 minutes | Serves 4

¾ cup all-purpose flour
¼ cup yellow cornmeal
1 tablespoon Cajun seasoning
1 teaspoon salt
2 large eggs, beaten
1 teaspoon hot sauce
1 pound (454 g) pre-shucked oysters
1 (12-inch) French baguette, quartered and sliced horizontally
Tartar Sauce, as needed
2 cups shredded lettuce, divided
2 tomatoes, cut into slices
Cooking spray

1. In a shallow bowl, whisk the flour, cornmeal, Cajun seasoning, and salt until blended. In a second shallow bowl, whisk together the eggs and hot sauce. 2. One at a time, dip the oysters in the cornmeal mixture, the eggs, and again in the cornmeal, coating thoroughly. 3. Preheat the air fryer to 400ºF (204ºC). Line the air fryer basket with parchment paper. 4. Place the oysters on the parchment and spritz with oil. 5. Air fry for 2 minutes. Shake the basket, spritz the oysters with oil, and air fry for 3 minutes more until lightly browned and crispy. 6. Spread each sandwich half with Tartar Sauce. Assemble the po'boys by layering each sandwich with fried oysters, ½ cup shredded lettuce, and 2 tomato slices. 7. Serve immediately.

Lemony Shrimp

Prep time: 10 minutes | Cook time: 7 to 8 minutes | Serves 4

1 pound (454 g) shrimp, deveined
4 tablespoons olive oil
1½ tablespoons lemon juice
1½ tablespoons fresh parsley, roughly chopped
2 cloves garlic, finely minced
1 teaspoon crushed red pepper flakes, or more to taste
Garlic pepper, to taste
Sea salt flakes, to taste

1. Preheat the air fryer to 385ºF (196ºC). 2. Toss all the ingredients in a large bowl until the shrimp are coated on all sides. 3. Arrange the shrimp in the air fryer basket and air fry for 7 to 8 minutes, or until the shrimp are pink and cooked through. 4. Serve warm.

Tuna Casserole

Prep time: 15 minutes | Cook time: 15 minutes | Serves 4

2 tablespoons salted butter
¼ cup diced white onion
¼ cup chopped white mushrooms
2 stalks celery, finely chopped
½ cup heavy cream
½ cup vegetable broth
2 tablespoons full-fat mayonnaise
¼ teaspoon xanthan gum
½ teaspoon red pepper flakes
2 medium zucchini, spiralized
2 (5-ounce / 142-g) cans albacore tuna
1 ounce (28 g) pork rinds, finely ground

1. In a large saucepan over medium heat, melt butter. Add onion, mushrooms, and celery and sauté until fragrant, about 3 to 5 minutes. 2. Pour in heavy cream, vegetable broth, mayonnaise, and xanthan gum. Reduce heat and continue cooking an additional 3 minutes, until the mixture begins to thicken. 3. Add red pepper flakes, zucchini, and tuna. Turn off heat and stir until zucchini noodles are coated. 4. Pour into a round baking dish. Top with ground pork rinds and cover the top of the dish with foil. Place into the air fryer basket. 5. Adjust the temperature to 370ºF (188ºC) and set the timer for 15 minutes. 6. When 3 minutes remain, remove the foil to brown the top of the casserole. Serve warm.

Scallops and Spinach with Cream Sauce

Prep time: 5 minutes | Cook time: 10 minutes | Serves 2

Vegetable oil spray
1 (10-ounce / 283-g) package frozen spinach, thawed and drained
8 jumbo sea scallops
Kosher salt and black pepper, to taste
¾ cup heavy cream
1 tablespoon tomato paste
1 tablespoon chopped fresh basil
1 teaspoon minced garlic

1. Spray a baking pan with vegetable oil spray. Spread the thawed spinach in an even layer in the bottom of the pan. 2. Spray both sides of the scallops with vegetable oil spray. Season lightly with salt and pepper. Arrange the scallops on top of the spinach. 3. In a small bowl, whisk together the cream, tomato paste, basil, garlic, ½ teaspoon salt, and ½ teaspoon pepper. Pour the sauce over the scallops and spinach. 4. Place the pan in the air fryer basket. Set the air fryer to 350ºF (177ºC) for 10 minutes. Use a meat thermometer to ensure the scallops have an internal temperature of 135ºF (57ºC).

Blackened Salmon

Prep time: 10 minutes | Cook time: 8 minutes | Serves 2

10 ounces (283 g) salmon fillet
½ teaspoon ground coriander
1 teaspoon ground cumin
1 teaspoon dried basil
1 tablespoon avocado oil

1. In the shallow bowl, mix ground coriander, ground cumin, and dried basil. 2. Then coat the salmon fillet in the spices and sprinkle with avocado oil. 3. Put the fish in the air fryer basket and cook at 395ºF (202ºC) for 4 minutes per side.

Chili Tilapia

Prep time: 5 minutes | Cook time: 20 minutes | Serves 4

4 tilapia fillets, boneless
1 teaspoon chili flakes
1 teaspoon dried oregano
1 tablespoon avocado oil
1 teaspoon mustard

1. Rub the tilapia fillets with chili flakes, dried oregano, avocado oil, and mustard and put in the air fryer. 2. Cook it for 10 minutes per side at 360ºF (182ºC).

Roasted Salmon Fillets

Prep time: 5 minutes | Cook time: 10 minutes | Serves 2

2 (8-ounce / 227-g) skin-on salmon fillets, 1½ inches thick
1 teaspoon vegetable oil
Salt and pepper, to taste
Vegetable oil spray

1. Preheat the air fryer to 400ºF (204ºC). 2. Make foil sling for air fryer basket by folding 1 long sheet of aluminum foil so it is 4 inches wide. Lay sheet of foil widthwise across basket, pressing foil into and up sides of basket. Fold excess foil as needed so that edges of foil are flush with top of basket. Lightly spray foil and basket with vegetable oil spray. 3. Pat salmon dry with paper towels, rub with oil, and season with salt and pepper. Arrange fillets skin side down on sling in prepared basket, spaced evenly apart. Air fry salmon until center is still translucent when checked with the tip of a paring knife and registers 125ºF (52ºC) (for medium-rare), 10 to 14 minutes, using sling to rotate fillets halfway through cooking. 4. Using the sling, carefully remove salmon from air fryer. Slide fish spatula along underside of fillets and transfer to individual serving plates, leaving skin behind. Serve.

Shrimp Kebabs

Prep time: 15 minutes | Cook time: 6 minutes | Serves 4

Oil, for spraying
1 pound (454 g) medium raw shrimp, peeled and deveined
4 tablespoons unsalted butter, melted
1 tablespoon Old Bay seasoning
1 tablespoon packed light brown sugar
1 teaspoon granulated garlic
1 teaspoon onion powder
½ teaspoon freshly ground black pepper

1. Line the air fryer basket with parchment and spray lightly with oil. 2. Thread the shrimp onto the skewers and place them in the prepared basket. 3. In a small bowl, mix together the butter, Old Bay, brown sugar, garlic, onion powder, and black pepper. Brush the sauce on the shrimp. 4. Air fry at 400ºF (204ºC) for 5 to 6 minutes, or until pink and firm. Serve immediately.

Asian Swordfish

Prep time: 10 minutes | Cook time: 6 to 11 minutes | Serves 4

4 (4-ounce / 113-g) swordfish steaks
½ teaspoon toasted sesame oil
1 jalapeño pepper, finely minced
2 garlic cloves, grated
1 tablespoon grated fresh ginger
½ teaspoon Chinese five-spice powder
⅛ teaspoon freshly ground black pepper
2 tablespoons freshly squeezed lemon juice

1. Place the swordfish steaks on a work surface and drizzle with the sesame oil. 2. In a small bowl, mix the jalapeño, garlic, ginger, five-spice powder, pepper, and lemon juice. Rub this mixture into the fish and let it stand for 10 minutes. 3. Roast the swordfish in the air fryer at 380ºF (193ºC) for 6 to 11 minutes, or until the swordfish reaches an internal temperature of at least 140ºF (60ºC) on a meat thermometer. Serve immediately.

Crab Cake Sandwich

Prep time: 15 minutes | Cook time: 10 minutes | Serves 4

Crab Cakes:
½ cup panko bread crumbs
1 large egg, beaten
1 large egg white
1 tablespoon mayonnaise
1 teaspoon Dijon mustard
¼ cup minced fresh parsley
1 tablespoon fresh lemon juice
½ teaspoon Old Bay seasoning
⅛ teaspoon sweet paprika
⅛ teaspoon kosher salt
Freshly ground black pepper, to taste
10 ounces (283 g) lump crab meat
Cooking spray
Cajun Mayo:
¼ cup mayonnaise
1 tablespoon minced dill pickle
1 teaspoon fresh lemon juice
¾ teaspoon Cajun seasoning
For Serving:
4 Boston lettuce leaves
4 whole wheat potato buns or gluten-free buns

1. For the crab cakes: In a large bowl, combine the panko, whole egg, egg white, mayonnaise, mustard, parsley, lemon juice, Old Bay, paprika, salt, and pepper to taste and mix well. Fold in the crab meat, being careful not to over mix. Gently shape into 4 round patties, about ½ cup each, ¾ inch thick. Spray both sides with oil. 2. Preheat the air fryer to 370ºF (188ºC). 3. Working in batches, place the crab cakes in the air fryer basket. Air fry for about 10 minutes, flipping halfway, until the edges are golden. 4. Meanwhile, for the Cajun mayo: In a small bowl, combine the mayonnaise, pickle, lemon juice, and Cajun seasoning. 5. To serve: Place a lettuce leaf on each bun bottom and top with a crab cake and a generous tablespoon of Cajun mayonnaise. Add the bun top and serve.

Fish Cakes

Prep time: 30 minutes | Cook time: 10 to 12 minutes | Serves 4

¾ cup mashed potatoes (about 1 large russet potato)
12 ounces (340 g) cod or other white fish
Salt and pepper, to taste
Oil for misting or cooking spray
1 large egg
¼ cup potato starch
½ cup panko bread crumbs
1 tablespoon fresh chopped chives
2 tablespoons minced onion

1. Peel potatoes, cut into cubes, and cook on stovetop till soft. 2. Salt and pepper raw fish to taste. Mist with oil or cooking spray, and air fry at 360ºF (182ºC) for 6 to 8 minutes, until fish flakes easily. If fish is crowded, rearrange halfway through cooking to ensure all pieces cook evenly. 3. Transfer fish to a plate and break apart to cool. 4. Beat egg in a shallow dish. 5. Place potato starch in another shallow dish, and panko crumbs in a third dish. 6. When potatoes are done, drain in colander and rinse with cold water. 7. In a large bowl, mash the potatoes and stir in the chives and onion. Add salt and pepper to taste, then stir in the fish. 8. If needed, stir in a tablespoon of the beaten egg to help bind the mixture. 9. Shape into 8 small, fat patties. Dust lightly with potato starch, dip in egg, and roll in panko crumbs. Spray both sides with oil or cooking spray. 10. Air fry at 360ºF (182ºC) for 10 to 12 minutes, until golden brown and crispy.

Garlicky Cod Fillets

Prep time: 10 minutes | Cook time: 10 to 12 minutes | Serves 4

1 teaspoon olive oil
4 cod fillets
¼ teaspoon fine sea salt
¼ teaspoon ground black pepper, or more to taste
1 teaspoon cayenne pepper
½ cup fresh Italian parsley, coarsely chopped
½ cup nondairy milk
1 Italian pepper, chopped
4 garlic cloves, minced
1 teaspoon dried basil
½ teaspoon dried oregano

1. Lightly coat the sides and bottom of a baking dish with the olive oil. Set aside. 2. In a large bowl, sprinkle the fillets with salt, black pepper, and cayenne pepper. 3. In a food processor, pulse the remaining ingredients until smoothly puréed. 4. Add the purée to the bowl of fillets and toss to coat, then transfer to the prepared baking dish. 5. Preheat the air fryer to 380ºF (193ºC). 6. Put the baking dish in the air fryer basket and cook for 10 to 12 minutes, or until the fish flakes when pressed lightly with a fork. 7. Remove from the basket and serve warm.

Country Shrimp

Prep time: 10 minutes | Cook time: 15 to 20 minutes | Serves 4

1 pound (454 g) large shrimp, deveined, with tails on
1 pound (454 g) smoked turkey sausage, cut into thick slices
2 corn cobs, quartered
1 zucchini, cut into bite-sized pieces
1 red bell pepper, cut into chunks
1 tablespoon Old Bay seasoning
2 tablespoons olive oil
Cooking spray

1. Preheat the air fryer to 400°F (204°C). Spray the air fryer basket lightly with cooking spray. 2. In a large bowl, mix the shrimp, turkey sausage, corn, zucchini, bell pepper, and Old Bay seasoning, and toss to coat with the spices. Add the olive oil and toss again until evenly coated. 3. Spread the mixture in the air fryer basket in a single layer. You will need to cook in batches. 4. Air fry for 15 to 20 minutes, or until cooked through, shaking the basket every 5 minutes for even cooking. 5. Serve immediately.

Butter-Wine Baked Salmon

Prep time: 5 minutes | Cook time: 10 minutes | Serves 4

4 tablespoons butter, melted
2 cloves garlic, minced
Sea salt and ground black pepper, to taste
¼ cup dry white wine
1 tablespoon lime juice
1 teaspoon smoked paprika
½ teaspoon onion powder
4 salmon steaks
Cooking spray

1. Place all the ingredients except the salmon and oil in a shallow dish and stir to mix well. 2. Add the salmon steaks, turning to coat well on both sides. Transfer the salmon to the refrigerator to marinate for 30 minutes. 3. Preheat the air fryer to 360°F (182°C). 4. Place the salmon steaks in the air fryer basket, discarding any excess marinade. Spray the salmon steaks with cooking spray. 5. Air fry for about 10 minutes, flipping the salmon steaks halfway through, or until cooked to your preferred doneness. 6. Divide the salmon steaks among four plates and serve.

Tilapia with Pecans

Prep time: 20 minutes | Cook time: 16 minutes | Serves 5

2 tablespoons ground flaxseeds
1 teaspoon paprika
Sea salt and white pepper, to taste
1 teaspoon garlic paste
2 tablespoons extra-virgin olive oil
½ cup pecans, ground
5 tilapia fillets, sliced into halves

1. Combine the ground flaxseeds, paprika, salt, white pepper, garlic paste, olive oil, and ground pecans in a Ziploc bag. Add the fish fillets and shake to coat well. 2. Spritz the air fryer basket with cooking spray. Cook in the preheated air fryer at 400°F (204°C) for 10 minutes; turn them over and cook for 6 minutes more. Work in batches. 3. Serve with lemon wedges, if desired. Enjoy!

Garlic Shrimp

Prep time: 15 minutes | Cook time: 10 minutes | Serves 3

Shrimp:
Oil, for spraying
1 pound (454 g) medium raw shrimp, peeled and deveined
6 tablespoons unsalted butter, melted
1 cup panko bread crumbs
2 tablespoons granulated garlic
1 teaspoon salt
½ teaspoon freshly ground black pepper
Garlic Butter Sauce:
½ cup unsalted butter
2 teaspoons granulated garlic
¾ teaspoon salt (omit if using salted butter)

Make the Shrimp 1. Preheat the air fryer to 400°F (204°C). Line the air fryer basket with parchment and spray lightly with oil. 2. Place the shrimp and melted butter in a zip-top plastic bag, seal, and shake well, until evenly coated. 3. In a medium bowl, mix together the bread crumbs, garlic, salt, and black pepper. 4. Add the shrimp to the panko mixture and toss until evenly coated. Shake off any excess coating. 5. Place the shrimp in the prepared basket and spray lightly with oil. 6. Cook for 8 to 10 minutes, flipping and spraying with oil after 4 to 5 minutes, until golden brown and crispy. Make the Garlic Butter Sauce 7. In a microwave-safe bowl, combine the butter, garlic, and salt and microwave on 50% power for 30 to 60 seconds, stirring every 15 seconds, until completely melted. 8. Serve the shrimp immediately with the garlic butter sauce on the side for dipping.

Crustless Shrimp Quiche

Prep time: 15 minutes | Cook time: 20 minutes | Serves 2

Vegetable oil
4 large eggs
½ cup half-and-half
4 ounces (113 g) raw shrimp, chopped (about 1 cup)
1 cup shredded Parmesan or Swiss cheese
¼ cup chopped scallions
1 teaspoon sweet smoked paprika
1 teaspoon herbes de Provence
1 teaspoon black pepper
½ to 1 teaspoon kosher salt

1. Generously grease a baking pan with vegetable oil. (Be sure to grease the pan well, the proteins in eggs stick something fierce. Alternatively, line the bottom of the pan with parchment paper cut to fit and spray the parchment and sides of the pan generously with vegetable oil spray.) 2. In a large bowl, beat together the eggs and half-and-half. Add the shrimp, ¾ cup of the cheese, the scallions, paprika, herbes de Provence, pepper, and salt. Stir with a fork to thoroughly combine. Pour the egg mixture into the prepared pan. 3. Place the pan in the air fryer basket. Set the air fryer to 300°F (149°C) for 20 minutes. After 17 minutes, sprinkle the remaining ¼ cup cheese on top and cook for the remaining 3 minutes, or until the cheese has melted, the eggs are set, and a toothpick inserted into the center comes out clean. 4. Serve the quiche warm or at room temperature.

South Indian Fried Fish

Prep time: 20 minutes | Cook time: 8 minutes | Serves 4

2 tablespoons olive oil
2 tablespoons fresh lime or lemon juice
1 teaspoon minced fresh ginger
1 clove garlic, minced
1 teaspoon ground turmeric
½ teaspoon kosher salt
¼ to ½ teaspoon cayenne pepper
1 pound (454 g) tilapia fillets (2 to 3 fillets)
Olive oil spray
Lime or lemon wedges (optional)

1. In a large bowl, combine the oil, lime juice, ginger, garlic, turmeric, salt, and cayenne. Stir until well combined; set aside. 2. Cut each tilapia fillet into three or four equal-size pieces. Add the fish to the bowl and gently mix until all of the fish is coated in the marinade. Marinate for 10 to 15 minutes at room temperature. (Don't marinate any longer or the acid in the lime juice will "cook" the fish.) 3. Spray the air fryer basket with olive oil spray. Place the fish in the basket and spray the fish. Set the air fryer to 325°F (163°C) for 3 minutes to partially cook the fish. Set the air fryer to 400°F (204°C) for 5 minutes to finish cooking and crisp up the fish. (Thinner pieces of fish will cook faster so you may want to check at the 3-minute mark of the second cooking time and remove those that are cooked through, and then add them back toward the end of the second cooking time to crisp.) 4. Carefully remove the fish from the basket. Serve hot, with lemon wedges if desired.

Foil-Packet Lobster Tail

Prep time: 15 minutes | Cook time: 12 minutes | Serves 2

2 (6-ounce / 170-g) lobster tails, halved
2 tablespoons salted butter, melted
½ teaspoon Old Bay seasoning
Juice of ½ medium lemon
1 teaspoon dried parsley

1. Place the two halved tails on a sheet of aluminum foil. Drizzle with butter, Old Bay seasoning, and lemon juice. 2. Seal the foil packets, completely covering tails. Place into the air fryer basket. 3. Adjust the temperature to 375°F (191°C) and air fry for 12 minutes. 4. Once done, sprinkle with dried parsley and serve immediately.

Roasted Halibut Steaks with Parsley

Prep time: 5 minutes | Cook time: 10 minutes | Serves 4

1 pound (454 g) halibut steaks
¼ cup vegetable oil
2½ tablespoons Worcester sauce
2 tablespoons honey
2 tablespoons vermouth
1 tablespoon freshly squeezed lemon juice
1 tablespoon fresh parsley leaves, coarsely chopped
Salt and pepper, to taste
1 teaspoon dried basil

1. Preheat the air fryer to 390°F (199°C). 2. Put all the ingredients in a large mixing dish and gently stir until the fish is coated evenly. 3. Transfer the fish to the air fryer basket and roast for 10 minutes, flipping the fish halfway through, or until the fish reaches an internal temperature of at least 145°F (63°C) on a meat thermometer. 4. Let the fish cool for 5 minutes and serve.

Thai Shrimp Skewers with Peanut Dipping Sauce

Prep time: 15 minutes | Cook time: 6 minutes | Serves 2

Salt and pepper, to taste
12 ounces (340 g) extra-large shrimp, peeled and deveined
1 tablespoon vegetable oil
1 teaspoon honey
½ teaspoon grated lime zest plus 1 tablespoon juice, plus lime wedges for serving
6 (6-inch) wooden skewers
3 tablespoons creamy peanut butter
3 tablespoons hot tap water
1 tablespoon chopped fresh cilantro
1 teaspoon fish sauce

1. Preheat the air fryer to 400°F (204°C). 2. Dissolve 2 tablespoons salt in 1 quart cold water in a large container. Add shrimp, cover, and refrigerate for 15 minutes. 3. Remove shrimp from brine and pat dry with paper towels. Whisk oil, honey, lime zest, and ¼ teaspoon pepper together in a large bowl. Add shrimp and toss to coat. Thread shrimp onto skewers, leaving about ¼ inch between each shrimp (3 or 4 shrimp per skewer). 4. Arrange 3 skewers in air fryer basket, parallel to each other and spaced evenly apart. Arrange remaining 3 skewers on top, perpendicular to the bottom layer. Air fry until shrimp are opaque throughout, 6 to 8 minutes, flipping and rotating skewers halfway through cooking. 5. Whisk peanut butter, hot tap water, lime juice, cilantro, and fish sauce together in a bowl until smooth. Serve skewers with peanut dipping sauce and lime wedges.

Panko Catfish Nuggets

Prep time: 10 minutes | Cook time: 7 to 8 minutes | Serves 4

2 medium catfish fillets, cut into chunks (approximately 1 × 2 inch)
Salt and pepper, to taste
2 eggs
2 tablespoons skim milk
½ cup cornstarch
1 cup panko bread crumbs
Cooking spray

1. Preheat the air fryer to 390°F (199°C). 2. In a medium bowl, season the fish chunks with salt and pepper to taste. 3. In a small bowl, beat together the eggs with milk until well combined. 4. Place the cornstarch and bread crumbs into separate shallow dishes. 5. Dredge the fish chunks one at a time in the cornstarch, coating well on both sides, then dip in the egg mixture, shaking off any excess, finally press well into the bread crumbs. Spritz the fish chunks with cooking spray. 6. Arrange the fish chunks in the air fryer basket in a single layer. You may need to cook in batches depending on the size of your air fryer basket. 7. Fry the fish chunks for 7 to 8 minutes until they are no longer translucent in the center and golden brown. Shake the basket once during cooking. 8. Remove the fish chunks from the basket to a plate. Repeat with the remaining fish chunks. 9. Serve warm.

Easy Scallops

Prep time: 5 minutes | Cook time: 4 minutes | Serves 2

12 medium sea scallops, rinsed and patted dry
1 teaspoon fine sea salt
¾ teaspoon ground black pepper, plus more for garnish
Fresh thyme leaves, for garnish (optional)
Avocado oil spray

1. Preheat the air fryer to 390ºF (199ºC). Coat the air fryer basket with avocado oil spray. 2. Place the scallops in a medium bowl and spritz with avocado oil spray. Sprinkle the salt and pepper to season. 3. Transfer the seasoned scallops to the air fryer basket, spacing them apart. You may need to work in batches to avoid overcrowding. 4. Air fry for 4 minutes, flipping the scallops halfway through, or until the scallops are firm and reach an internal temperature of just 145ºF (63ºC) on a meat thermometer. 5. Remove from the basket and repeat with the remaining scallops. 6. Sprinkle the pepper and thyme leaves on top for garnish, if desired. Serve immediately.

Asian Marinated Salmon

Prep time: 30 minutes | Cook time: 6 minutes | Serves 2

Marinade:
¼ cup wheat-free tamari or coconut aminos
2 tablespoons lime or lemon juice
2 tablespoons sesame oil
2 tablespoons Swerve confectioners'-style sweetener, or a few drops liquid stevia
2 teaspoons grated fresh ginger
2 cloves garlic, minced
½ teaspoon ground black pepper
2 (4-ounce / 113-g) salmon fillets (about 1¼ inches thick)
Sliced green onions, for garnish
Sauce (Optional):
¼ cup beef broth
¼ cup wheat-free tamari
3 tablespoons Swerve confectioners'-style sweetener or equivalent amount of liquid or powdered sweetener
1 tablespoon tomato sauce
1 teaspoon stevia glycerite (optional)
⅛ teaspoon guar gum or xanthan gum (optional, for thickening)

1. Make the marinade: In a medium-sized shallow dish, stir together all the ingredients for the marinade until well combined. Place the salmon in the marinade. Cover and refrigerate for at least 2 hours or overnight. 2. Preheat the air fryer to 400ºF (204ºC). 3. Remove the salmon fillets from the marinade and place them in the air fryer, leaving space between them. Air fry for 6 minutes, or until the salmon is cooked through and flakes easily with a fork. 4. While the salmon cooks, make the sauce, if using: Place all the sauce ingredients except the guar gum in a medium-sized bowl and stir until well combined. Taste and adjust the sweetness to your liking. While whisking slowly, add the guar gum. Allow the sauce to thicken for 3 to 5 minutes. (The sauce can be made up to 3 days ahead and stored in an airtight container in the fridge.) Drizzle the sauce over the salmon before serving. 5. Garnish the salmon with sliced green onions before serving. Store leftovers in an airtight container in the fridge for up to 3 days. Reheat in a preheated 350ºF (177ºC) air fryer for 3 minutes, or until heated through.

Mouthwatering Cod over Creamy Leek Noodles

Prep time: 10 minutes | Cook time: 24 minutes | Serves 4

1 small leek, sliced into long thin noodles (about 2 cups)
½ cup heavy cream
2 cloves garlic, minced
1 teaspoon fine sea salt, divided
4 (4-ounce / 113-g) cod fillets (about 1 inch thick)
½ teaspoon ground black pepper
Coating:
¼ cup grated Parmesan cheese
2 tablespoons mayonnaise
2 tablespoons unsalted butter, softened
1 tablespoon chopped fresh thyme, or ½ teaspoon dried thyme leaves, plus more for garnish

1. Preheat the air fryer to 350ºF (177ºC). 2. Place the leek noodles in a casserole dish or a pan that will fit in your air fryer. 3. In a small bowl, stir together the cream, garlic, and ½ teaspoon of the salt. Pour the mixture over the leeks and cook in the air fryer for 10 minutes, or until the leeks are very tender. 4. Pat the fish dry and season with the remaining ½ teaspoon of salt and the pepper. When the leeks are ready, open the air fryer and place the fish fillets on top of the leeks. Air fry for 8 to 10 minutes, until the fish flakes easily with a fork (the thicker the fillets, the longer this will take). 5. While the fish cooks, make the coating: In a small bowl, combine the Parmesan, mayo, butter, and thyme. 6. When the fish is ready, remove it from the air fryer and increase the heat to 425ºF (218ºC) (or as high as your air fryer can go). Spread the fillets with a ½-inch-thick to ¾-inch-thick layer of the coating. 7. Place the fish back in the air fryer and air fry for 3 to 4 minutes, until the coating browns. 8. Garnish with fresh or dried thyme, if desired. Store leftovers in an airtight container in the refrigerator for up to 3 days. Reheat in a casserole dish in a preheated 350ºF (177ºC) air fryer for 6 minutes, or until heated through.

Roasted Fish with Almond-Lemon Crumbs

Prep time: 10 minutes | Cook time: 7 to 8 minutes | Serves 4

½ cup raw whole almonds
1 scallion, finely chopped
Grated zest and juice of 1 lemon
½ tablespoon extra-virgin olive oil
¾ teaspoon kosher salt, divided
Freshly ground black pepper, to taste
4 (6 ounces / 170 g each) skinless fish fillets
Cooking spray
1 teaspoon Dijon mustard

1. In a food processor, pulse the almonds to coarsely chop. Transfer to a small bowl and add the scallion, lemon zest, and olive oil. Season with ¼ teaspoon of the salt and pepper to taste and mix to combine. 2. Spray the top of the fish with oil and squeeze the lemon juice over the fish. Season with the remaining ½ teaspoon salt and pepper to taste. Spread the mustard on top of the fish. Dividing evenly, press the almond mixture onto the top of the fillets to adhere. 3. Preheat the air fryer to 375ºF (191ºC). 4. Working in batches, place the fillets in the air fryer basket in a single layer. Air fry for 7 to 8 minutes, until the crumbs start to brown and the fish is cooked through. 5. Serve immediately.

Tortilla Shrimp Tacos

Prep time: 10 minutes | Cook time: 6 minutes | Serves 4

Spicy Mayo:
3 tablespoons mayonnaise
1 tablespoon Louisiana-style hot pepper sauce
Cilantro-Lime Slaw:
2 cups shredded green cabbage
½ small red onion, thinly sliced
1 small jalapeño, thinly sliced
2 tablespoons chopped fresh cilantro
Juice of 1 lime
¼ teaspoon kosher salt
Shrimp:
1 large egg, beaten
1 cup crushed tortilla chips
24 jumbo shrimp (about 1 pound / 454 g), peeled and deveined
⅛ teaspoon kosher salt
Cooking spray
8 corn tortillas, for serving

1. For the spicy mayo: In a small bowl, mix the mayonnaise and hot pepper sauce. 2. For the cilantro-lime slaw: In a large bowl, toss together the cabbage, onion, jalapeño, cilantro, lime juice, and salt to combine. Cover and refrigerate to chill. 3. For the shrimp: Place the egg in a shallow bowl and the crushed tortilla chips in another. Season the shrimp with the salt. Dip the shrimp in the egg, then in the crumbs, pressing gently to adhere. Place on a work surface and spray both sides with oil. 4. Preheat the air fryer to 360°F (182°C). 5. Working in batches, arrange a single layer of the shrimp in the air fryer basket. Air fry for 6 minutes, flipping halfway, until golden and cooked through in the center. 6. To serve, place 2 tortillas on each plate and top each with 3 shrimp. Top each taco with ¼ cup slaw, then drizzle with spicy mayo.

Ahi Tuna Steaks

Prep time: 5 minutes | Cook time: 14 minutes | Serves 2

2 (6-ounce / 170-g) ahi tuna steaks
2 tablespoons olive oil
3 tablespoons everything bagel seasoning

1. Drizzle both sides of each steak with olive oil. Place seasoning on a medium plate and press each side of tuna steaks into seasoning to form a thick layer. 2. Place steaks into ungreased air fryer basket. Adjust the temperature to 400°F (204°C) and air fry for 14 minutes, turning steaks halfway through cooking. Steaks will be done when internal temperature is at least 145°F (63°C) for well-done. Serve warm.

Shrimp Caesar Salad

Prep time: 30 minutes | Cook time: 4 to 6 minutes | Serves 4

12 ounces (340 g) fresh large shrimp, peeled and deveined
1 tablespoon plus 1 teaspoon freshly squeezed lemon juice, divided
4 tablespoons olive oil or avocado oil, divided
2 garlic cloves, minced, divided
¼ teaspoon sea salt, plus additional to season the marinade
¼ teaspoon freshly ground black pepper, plus additional to season the marinade
⅓ cup sugar-free mayonnaise
2 tablespoons freshly grated Parmesan cheese
1 teaspoon Dijon mustard
1 tinned anchovy, mashed
12 ounces (340 g) romaine hearts, torn

1. Place the shrimp in a large bowl. Add 1 tablespoon of lemon juice, 1 tablespoon of olive oil, and 1 minced garlic clove. Season with salt and pepper. Toss well and refrigerate for 15 minutes. 2. While the shrimp marinates, make the dressing: In a blender, combine the mayonnaise, Parmesan cheese, Dijon mustard, the remaining 1 teaspoon of lemon juice, the anchovy, the remaining minced garlic clove, ¼ teaspoon of salt, and ¼ teaspoon of pepper. Process until smooth. With the blender running, slowly stream in the remaining 3 tablespoons of oil. Transfer the mixture to a jar; seal and refrigerate until ready to serve. 3. Remove the shrimp from its marinade and place it in the air fryer basket in a single layer. Set the air fryer to 400°F (204°C) and air fry for 2 minutes. Flip the shrimp and cook for 2 to 4 minutes more, until the flesh turns opaque. 4. Place the romaine in a large bowl and toss with the desired amount of dressing. Top with the shrimp and serve immediately.

Salmon on Bed of Fennel and Carrot

Prep time: 15 minutes | Cook time: 13 to 14 minutes | Serves 2

1 fennel bulb, thinly sliced
1 large carrot, peeled and sliced
1 small onion, thinly sliced
¼ cup low-fat sour cream
¼ teaspoon coarsely ground pepper
2 (5-ounce / 142-g) salmon fillets

1. Combine the fennel, carrot, and onion in a bowl and toss. 2. Put the vegetable mixture into a baking pan. Roast in the air fryer at 400°F (204°C) for 4 minutes or until the vegetables are crisp-tender. 3. Remove the pan from the air fryer. Stir in the sour cream and sprinkle the vegetables with the pepper. 4. Top with the salmon fillets. 5. Return the pan to the air fryer. Roast for another 9 to 10 minutes or until the salmon just barely flakes when tested with a fork.

Greek Fish Pitas

Prep time: 10 minutes | Cook time: 15 minutes | Serves 4

1 pound (454 g) pollock, cut into 1-inch pieces
¼ cup olive oil
1 teaspoon salt
½ teaspoon dried oregano
½ teaspoon dried thyme
½ teaspoon garlic powder
¼ teaspoon cayenne
4 whole wheat pitas
1 cup shredded lettuce
2 Roma tomatoes, diced
Nonfat plain Greek yogurt
Lemon, quartered

1. Preheat the air fryer to 380°F (193°C). 2. In a medium bowl, combine the pollock with olive oil, salt, oregano, thyme, garlic powder, and cayenne. 3. Put the pollock into the air fryer basket and roast for 15 minutes. 4. Serve inside pitas with lettuce, tomato, and Greek yogurt with a lemon wedge on the side.

Snapper Scampi

Prep time: 5 minutes | Cook time: 8 to 10 minutes | Serves 4

4 (6-ounce / 170-g) skinless snapper or arctic char fillets
1 tablespoon olive oil
3 tablespoons lemon juice, divided
½ teaspoon dried basil
Pinch salt
Freshly ground black pepper, to taste
2 tablespoons butter
2 cloves garlic, minced

1. Rub the fish fillets with olive oil and 1 tablespoon of the lemon juice. Sprinkle with the basil, salt, and pepper, and place in the air fryer basket. 2. Air fry the fish at 380ºF (193ºC) for 7 to 8 minutes or until the fish just flakes when tested with a fork. Remove the fish from the basket and put on a serving plate. Cover to keep warm. 3. In a baking pan, combine the butter, remaining 2 tablespoons lemon juice, and garlic. Cook in the air fryer for 1 to 2 minutes or until the garlic is sizzling. Pour this mixture over the fish and serve

Chinese Ginger-Scallion Fish

Prep time: 15 minutes | Cook time: 15 minutes | Serves 2

Bean Sauce:
2 tablespoons soy sauce
1 tablespoon rice wine
1 tablespoon doubanjiang (Chinese black bean paste)
1 teaspoon minced fresh ginger
1 clove garlic, minced
Vegetables and Fish:
1 tablespoon peanut oil
¼ cup julienned green onions (white and green parts)
¼ cup chopped fresh cilantro
2 tablespoons julienned fresh ginger
2 (6-ounce / 170-g) white fish fillets, such as tilapia

Bean Sauce:
2 tablespoons soy sauce
1 tablespoon rice wine
1 tablespoon doubanjiang (Chinese black bean paste)
1 teaspoon minced fresh ginger
1 clove garlic, minced
Vegetables and Fish:
1 tablespoon peanut oil
¼ cup julienned green onions (white and green parts)
¼ cup chopped fresh cilantro
2 tablespoons julienned fresh ginger
2 (6-ounce / 170-g) white fish fillets, such as tilapia

1. For the sauce: In a small bowl, combine all the ingredients and stir until well combined; set aside. 2. For the vegetables and fish: In a medium bowl, combine the peanut oil, green onions, cilantro, and ginger. Toss to combine. 3. Cut two squares of parchment large enough to hold one fillet and half of the vegetables. Place one fillet on each parchment square, top with the vegetables, and pour over the sauce. Fold over the parchment paper and crimp the sides in small, tight folds to hold the fish, vegetables, and sauce securely inside the packet. 4. Place the packets in a single layer in the air fryer basket. Set fryer to 350ºF (177ºC) for 15 minutes. 5. Transfer each packet to a dinner plate. Cut open with scissors just before serving. 1. For the sauce: In a small bowl, combine all the ingredients and stir until well combined; set aside. 2. For the vegetables and fish: In a medium bowl, combine the peanut oil, green onions, cilantro, and ginger. Toss to combine. 3. Cut two squares of parchment large enough to hold one fillet and half of the vegetables. Place one fillet on each parchment square, top with the vegetables, and pour over the sauce. Fold over the parchment paper and crimp the sides in small, tight folds to hold the fish, vegetables, and sauce securely inside the packet. 4. Place the packets in a single layer in the air fryer basket. Set fryer to 350ºF (177ºC) for 15 minutes. 5. Transfer each packet to a dinner plate. Cut open with scissors just before serving. 1. For the sauce: In a small bowl, combine all the ingredients and stir until well combined; set aside. 2. For the vegetables and fish: In a medium bowl, combine the peanut oil, green onions, cilantro, and ginger. Toss to combine. 3. Cut two squares of parchment large enough to hold one fillet and half of the vegetables. Place one fillet on each parchment square, top with the vegetables, and pour over the sauce. Fold over the parchment paper and crimp the sides in small, tight folds to hold the fish, vegetables, and sauce securely inside the packet. 4. Place the packets in a single layer in the air fryer basket. Set fryer to 350ºF (177ºC) for 15 minutes. 5. Transfer each packet to a dinner plate. Cut open with scissors just before serving.

Almond Pesto Salmon

Prep time: 5 minutes | Cook time: 12 minutes | Serves 2

¼ cup pesto
¼ cup sliced almonds, roughly chopped
2 (1½-inch-thick) salmon fillets
(about 4 ounces / 113 g each)
2 tablespoons unsalted butter, melted

1. In a small bowl, mix pesto and almonds. Set aside. 2. Place fillets into a round baking dish. 3. Brush each fillet with butter and place half of the pesto mixture on the top of each fillet. Place dish into the air fryer basket. 4. Adjust the temperature to 390ºF (199ºC) and set the timer for 12 minutes. 5. Salmon will easily flake when fully cooked and reach an internal temperature of at least 145ºF (63ºC). Serve warm.

Smoky Shrimp and Chorizo Tapas

Prep time: 15 minutes | Cook time: 10 minutes | Serves 2 to 4

4 ounces (113 g) Spanish (cured) chorizo, halved horizontally and sliced crosswise
½ pound (227 g) raw medium shrimp, peeled and deveined
1 tablespoon extra-virgin olive oil
1 small shallot, halved and thinly sliced
1 garlic clove, minced
1 tablespoon finely chopped fresh oregano
½ teaspoon smoked Spanish paprika
¼ teaspoon kosher salt
¼ teaspoon black pepper
3 tablespoons fresh orange juice
1 tablespoon minced fresh parsley

1. Place the chorizo in a baking pan. Set the pan in the air fryer basket. Set the air fryer to 375ºF (191ºC) for 5 minutes, or until the chorizo has started to brown and render its fat. 2. Meanwhile, in a large bowl, combine the shrimp, olive oil, shallot, garlic, oregano, paprika, salt, and pepper. Toss until the shrimp is well coated. 3. Transfer the shrimp to the pan with the chorizo. Stir to combine. Place the pan in the air fryer basket. Cook for 10 minutes, stirring halfway through the cooking time. 4. Transfer the shrimp and chorizo to a serving dish. Drizzle with the orange juice and toss to combine. Sprinkle with the parsley.

Golden Shrimp

Prep time: 20 minutes | Cook time: 7 minutes | Serves 4

2 egg whites
½ cup coconut flour
1 cup Parmigiano-Reggiano, grated
½ teaspoon celery seeds
½ teaspoon porcini powder
½ teaspoon onion powder
1 teaspoon garlic powder
½ teaspoon dried rosemary
½ teaspoon sea salt
½ teaspoon ground black pepper
1½ pounds (680 g) shrimp, deveined

1. Whisk the egg with coconut flour and Parmigiano-Reggiano. Add in seasonings and mix to combine well. 2. Dip your shrimp in the batter. Roll until they are covered on all sides. 3. Cook in the preheated air fryer at 390°F (199°C) for 5 to 7 minutes or until golden brown. Work in batches. Serve with lemon wedges if desired.

Lemony Salmon

Prep time: 30 minutes | Cook time: 10 minutes | Serves 4

1½ pounds (680 g) salmon steak
½ teaspoon grated lemon zest
Freshly cracked mixed peppercorns, to taste
⅓ cup lemon juice
Fresh chopped chives, for garnish
½ cup dry white wine
½ teaspoon fresh cilantro, chopped
Fine sea salt, to taste

1. To prepare the marinade, place all ingredients, except for salmon steak and chives, in a deep pan. Bring to a boil over medium-high flame until it has reduced by half. Allow it to cool down. 2. After that, allow salmon steak to marinate in the refrigerator approximately 40 minutes. Discard the marinade and transfer the fish steak to the preheated air fryer. 3. Air fry at 400°F (204°C) for 9 to 10 minutes. To finish, brush hot fish steaks with the reserved marinade, garnish with fresh chopped chives, and serve right away!

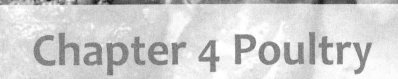

Chapter 4 Poultry

Chapter 4 Poultry

Porchetta-Style Chicken Breasts

Prep time: 10 minutes | Cook time: 15 minutes | Serves 4

½ cup fresh parsley leaves
¼ cup roughly chopped fresh chives
4 cloves garlic, peeled
2 tablespoons lemon juice
3 teaspoons fine sea salt
1 teaspoon dried rubbed sage
1 teaspoon fresh rosemary leaves
1 teaspoon ground fennel
½ teaspoon red pepper flakes
4 (4-ounce / 113-g) boneless, skinless chicken breasts, pounded to ¼ inch thick
8 slices bacon
Sprigs of fresh rosemary, for garnish (optional)

1. Spray the air fryer basket with avocado oil. Preheat the air fryer to 340ºF (171ºC). 2. Place the parsley, chives, garlic, lemon juice, salt, sage, rosemary, fennel, and red pepper flakes in a food processor and purée until a smooth paste forms. 3. Place the chicken breasts on a cutting board and rub the paste all over the tops. With a short end facing you, roll each breast up like a jelly roll to make a log and secure it with toothpicks. 4. Wrap 2 slices of bacon around each chicken breast log to cover the entire breast. Secure the bacon with toothpicks. 5. Place the chicken breast logs in the air fryer basket and air fry for 5 minutes, flip the logs over, and cook for another 5 minutes. Increase the heat to 390ºF (199ºC) and cook until the bacon is crisp, about 5 minutes more. 6. Remove the toothpicks and garnish with fresh rosemary sprigs, if desired, before serving. Store leftovers in an airtight container in the refrigerator for up to 4 days or in the freezer for up to a month. Reheat in a preheated 350ºF (177ºC) air fryer for 5 minutes, then increase the heat to 390ºF (199ºC) and cook for 2 minutes to crisp the bacon.

Korean Honey Wings

Prep time: 10 minutes | Cook time: 25 minutes per batch | Serves 4

¼ cup gochujang, or red pepper paste
¼ cup mayonnaise
2 tablespoons honey
1 tablespoon sesame oil
2 teaspoons minced garlic
1 tablespoon sugar
2 teaspoons ground ginger
3 pounds (1.4 kg) whole chicken wings
Olive oil spray
1 teaspoon salt
½ teaspoon freshly ground black pepper

1. In a large bowl, whisk the gochujang, mayonnaise, honey, sesame oil, garlic, sugar, and ginger. Set aside. 2. Insert the crisper plate into the basket and the basket into the unit. Preheat the unit by selecting AIR FRY, setting the temperature to 400ºF (204ºC), and setting the time to 3 minutes. Select START/PAUSE to begin. 3. To prepare the chicken wings, cut the wings in half. The meatier part is the drumette. Cut off and discard the wing tip from the flat part (or save the wing tips in the freezer to make chicken stock). 4. Once the unit is preheated, spray the crisper plate with olive oil. Working in batches, place half the chicken wings into the basket, spray them with olive oil, and sprinkle with the salt and pepper. 5. Select AIR FRY, set the temperature to 400ºF (204ºC), and set the time to 20 minutes. Select START/PAUSE to begin. 6. After 10 minutes, remove the basket, flip the wings, and spray them with more olive oil. Reinsert the basket to resume cooking. 7. Cook the wings to an internal temperature of 165ºF (74ºC), then transfer them to the bowl with the prepared sauce and toss to coat. 8. Repeat steps 4, 5, 6, and 7 for the remaining chicken wings. 9. Return the coated wings to the basket and air fry for 4 to 6 minutes more until the sauce has glazed the wings and the chicken is crisp. After 3 minutes, check the wings to make sure they aren't burning. Serve hot.

Easy Chicken Nachos

Prep time: 5 minutes | Cook time: 5 minutes | Serves 8

Oil, for spraying
3 cups shredded cooked chicken
1 (1-ounce / 28-g) package ranch seasoning
¼ cup sour cream
2 cups corn tortilla chips
⅓ cup bacon bits
1 cup shredded Cheddar cheese
1 tablespoon chopped scallions

1. Line the air fryer basket with parchment and spray lightly with oil. 2. In a small bowl, mix together the chicken, ranch seasoning, and sour cream. 3. Place the tortilla chips in the prepared basket and top with the chicken mixture. Add the bacon bits, Cheddar cheese, and scallions. 4. Air fry at 425ºF (218ºC) for 3 to 5 minutes, or until heated through and the cheese is melted.

Cheesy Pepperoni and Chicken Pizza

Prep time: 15 minutes | Cook time: 15 minutes | Serves 6

2 cups cooked chicken, cubed
1 cup pizza sauce
20 slices pepperoni
¼ cup grated Parmesan cheese
1 cup shredded Mozzarella cheese
Cooking spray

1. Preheat the air fryer to 375ºF (191ºC). Spritz a baking pan with cooking spray. 2. Arrange the chicken cubes in the prepared baking pan, then top the cubes with pizza sauce and pepperoni. Stir to coat the cubes and pepperoni with sauce. 3. Scatter the cheeses on top, then place the baking pan in the preheated air fryer. Air fryer for 15 minutes or until frothy and the cheeses melt. 4. Serve immediately.

Spice-Rubbed Chicken Thighs

Prep time: 10 minutes | Cook time: 25 minutes | Serves 4

4 (4-ounce / 113-g) bone-in, skin-on chicken thighs
½ teaspoon salt
½ teaspoon garlic powder
2 teaspoons chili powder
1 teaspoon paprika
1 teaspoon ground cumin
1 small lime, halved

1. Pat chicken thighs dry and sprinkle with salt, garlic powder, chili powder, paprika, and cumin. 2. Squeeze juice from ½ lime over thighs. Place thighs into ungreased air fryer basket. Adjust the temperature to 380ºF (193ºC) and roast for 25 minutes, turning thighs halfway through cooking. Thighs will be crispy and browned with an internal temperature of at least 165ºF (74ºC) when done. 3. Transfer thighs to a large serving plate and drizzle with remaining lime juice. Serve warm.

Chicken Kiev

Prep time: 15 minutes | Cook time: 25 minutes | Serves 4

1 cup (2 sticks) unsalted butter, softened (or butter-flavored coconut oil for dairy-free)
2 tablespoons lemon juice
2 tablespoons plus 1 teaspoon chopped fresh parsley leaves, divided, plus more for garnish
2 tablespoons chopped fresh tarragon leaves
3 cloves garlic, minced
1 teaspoon fine sea salt, divided
4 (4-ounce / 113-g) boneless, skinless chicken breasts
2 large eggs
2 cups pork dust
1 teaspoon ground black pepper
Sprig of fresh parsley, for garnish
Lemon slices, for serving

1. Spray the air fryer basket with avocado oil. Preheat the air fryer to 350ºF (177ºC). 2. In a medium-sized bowl, combine the butter, lemon juice, 2 tablespoons of the parsley, the tarragon, garlic, and ¼ teaspoon of the salt. Cover and place in the fridge to harden for 7 minutes. 3. While the butter mixture chills, place one of the chicken breasts on a cutting board. With a sharp knife held parallel to the cutting board, make a 1-inch-wide incision at the top of the breast. Carefully cut into the breast to form a large pocket, leaving a ½-inch border along the sides and bottom. Repeat with the other 3 breasts. 4. Stuff one-quarter of the butter mixture into each chicken breast and secure the openings with toothpicks. 5. Beat the eggs in a small shallow dish. In another shallow dish, combine the pork dust, the remaining 1 teaspoon of parsley, the remaining ¾ teaspoon of salt, and the pepper. 6. One at a time, dip the chicken breasts in the egg, shake off the excess egg, and dredge the breasts in the pork dust mixture. Use your hands to press the pork dust onto each breast to form a nice crust. If you desire a thicker coating, dip it again in the egg and pork dust. As you finish, spray each coated chicken breast with avocado oil and place it in the air fryer basket. 7. Roast the chicken in the air fryer for 15 minutes, flip the breasts, and cook for another 10 minutes, or until the internal temperature of the chicken is 165ºF (74ºC) and the crust is golden brown. 8. Serve garnished with chopped fresh parsley and a parsley sprig, with lemon slices on the side. 9. Store leftovers in an airtight container in the refrigerator for up to 4 days or in the freezer for up to a month. Reheat in a preheated 350ºF (177ºC) air fryer for 5 minutes, or until heated through.

Sriracha-Honey Chicken Nuggets

Prep time: 15 minutes | Cook time: 19 minutes | Serves 6

Oil, for spraying
1 large egg
¾ cup milk
1 cup all-purpose flour
2 tablespoons confectioners' sugar
½ teaspoon paprika
½ teaspoon salt
½ teaspoon freshly ground black pepper
2 boneless, skinless chicken breasts, cut into bite-size pieces
½ cup barbecue sauce
2 tablespoons honey
1 tablespoon Sriracha

1. Line the air fryer basket with parchment and spray lightly with oil. 2. In a small bowl, whisk together the egg and milk. 3. In a medium bowl, combine the flour, confectioners' sugar, paprika, salt, and black pepper and stir. 4. Coat the chicken in the egg mixture, then dredge in the flour mixture until evenly coated. 5. Place the chicken in the prepared basket and spray liberally with oil. 6. Air fry at 390ºF (199ºC) for 8 minutes, flip, spray with more oil, and cook for another 6 to 8 minutes, or until the internal temperature reaches 165ºF (74ºC) and the juices run clear. 7. In a large bowl, mix together the barbecue sauce, honey, and Sriracha. 8. Transfer the chicken to the bowl and toss until well coated with the barbecue sauce mixture. 9. Line the air fryer basket with fresh parchment, return the chicken to the basket, and cook for another 2 to 3 minutes, until browned and crispy.

Chicken Paillard

Prep time: 10 minutes | Cook time: 10 minutes | Serves 2

2 large eggs, room temperature
1 tablespoon water
½ cup powdered Parmesan cheese (about 1½ ounces / 43 g) or pork dust
2 teaspoons dried thyme leaves
1 teaspoon ground black pepper
2 (5-ounce / 142-g) boneless, skinless chicken breasts, pounded to ½ inch thick

Lemon Butter Sauce:
2 tablespoons unsalted butter, melted
2 teaspoons lemon juice
¼ teaspoon finely chopped fresh thyme leaves, plus more for garnish
⅛ teaspoon fine sea salt
Lemon slices, for serving

1. Spray the air fryer basket with avocado oil. Preheat the air fryer to 390ºF (199ºC). 2. Beat the eggs in a shallow dish, then add the water and stir well. 3. In a separate shallow dish, mix together the Parmesan, thyme, and pepper until well combined. 4. One at a time, dip the chicken breasts in the eggs and let any excess drip off, then dredge both sides of the chicken in the Parmesan mixture. As you finish, set the coated chicken in the air fryer basket. 5. Roast the chicken in the air fryer for 5 minutes, then flip the chicken and cook for another 5 minutes, or until cooked through and the internal temperature reaches 165ºF (74ºC). 6. While the chicken cooks, make the lemon butter sauce: In a small bowl, mix together all the sauce ingredients until well combined. 7. Plate the chicken and pour the sauce over it. Garnish with chopped fresh thyme and serve with lemon slices. 8. Store leftovers in an airtight container in the refrigerator for up to 4 days. Reheat in a preheated 390ºF (199ºC) air fryer for 5 minutes, or until heated through.

Gold Livers

Prep time: 10 minutes | Cook time: 20 minutes | Serves 4

2 eggs
2 tablespoons water
¾ cup flour
2 cups panko breadcrumbs
1 teaspoon salt
½ teaspoon ground black pepper
20 ounces (567 g) chicken livers
Cooking spray

1. Preheat the air fryer to 390ºF (199ºC). Spritz the air fryer basket with cooking spray. 2. Whisk the eggs with water in a large bowl. Pour the flour in a separate bowl. Pour the panko on a shallow dish and sprinkle with salt and pepper. 3. Dredge the chicken livers in the flour. Shake the excess off, then dunk the livers in the whisked eggs, and then roll the livers over the panko to coat well. 4. Arrange the livers in the preheated air fryer and spritz with cooking spray. Work in batches to avoid overcrowding. 5. Air fry for 10 minutes or until the livers are golden and crispy. Flip the livers halfway through. Repeat with remaining livers. 6. Serve immediately.

Chicken Shawarma

Prep time: 30 minutes | Cook time: 15 minutes | Serves 4

Shawarma Spice:
2 teaspoons dried oregano
1 teaspoon ground cinnamon
1 teaspoon ground cumin
1 teaspoon ground coriander
1 teaspoon kosher salt
½ teaspoon ground allspice
½ teaspoon cayenne pepper
Chicken:
1 pound (454 g) boneless, skinless chicken thighs, cut into large bite-size chunks
2 tablespoons vegetable oil
For Serving:
Tzatziki
Pita bread

1. For the shawarma spice: In a small bowl, combine the oregano, cayenne, cumin, coriander, salt, cinnamon, and allspice. 2. For the chicken: In a large bowl, toss together the chicken, vegetable oil, and shawarma spice to coat. Marinate at room temperature for 30 minutes or cover and refrigerate for up to 24 hours. 3. Place the chicken in the air fryer basket. Set the air fryer to 350ºF (177ºC) for 15 minutes, or until the chicken reaches an internal temperature of 165ºF (74ºC). 4. Transfer the chicken to a serving platter. Serve with tzatziki and pita bread.

Jerk Chicken Kebabs

Prep time: 10 minutes | Cook time: 14 minutes | Serves 4

8 ounces (227 g) boneless, skinless chicken thighs, cut into 1-inch cubes
2 tablespoons jerk seasoning
2 tablespoons coconut oil
½ medium red bell pepper, seeded and cut into 1-inch pieces
¼ medium red onion, peeled and cut into 1-inch pieces
½ teaspoon salt

1. Place chicken in a medium bowl and sprinkle with jerk seasoning and coconut oil. Toss to coat on all sides. 2. Using eight (6-inch) skewers, build skewers by alternating chicken, pepper, and onion pieces, about three repetitions per skewer. 3. Sprinkle salt over skewers and place into ungreased air fryer basket. Adjust the temperature to 370ºF (188ºC) and air fry for 14 minutes, turning skewers halfway through cooking. Chicken will be golden and have an internal temperature of at least 165ºF (74ºC) when done. Serve warm.

Stuffed Chicken Florentine

Prep time: 10 minutes | Cook time: 20 minutes | Serves 4

3 tablespoons pine nuts
¾ cup frozen spinach, thawed and squeezed dry
⅓ cup ricotta cheese
2 tablespoons grated Parmesan cheese
3 cloves garlic, minced
Salt and freshly ground black pepper, to taste
4 small boneless, skinless chicken breast halves (about 1½ pounds / 680 g)
8 slices bacon

1. Place the pine nuts in a small pan and set in the air fryer basket. Set the air fryer to 400ºF (204ºC) and air fry for 2 to 3 minutes until toasted. Remove the pine nuts to a mixing bowl and continue preheating the air fryer. 2. In a large bowl, combine the spinach, ricotta, Parmesan, and garlic. Season to taste with salt and pepper and stir well until thoroughly combined. 3. Using a sharp knife, cut into the chicken breasts, slicing them across and opening them up like a book, but be careful not to cut them all the way through. Sprinkle the chicken with salt and pepper. 4. Spoon equal amounts of the spinach mixture into the chicken, then fold the top of the chicken breast back over the top of the stuffing. Wrap each chicken breast with 2 slices of bacon. 5. Working in batches if necessary, air fry the chicken for 18 to 20 minutes until the bacon is crisp and a thermometer inserted into the thickest part of the chicken registers 165ºF (74ºC).

Peachy Chicken Chunks with Cherries

Prep time: 8 minutes | Cook time: 14 to 16 minutes | Serves 4

⅓ cup peach preserves
1 teaspoon ground rosemary
½ teaspoon black pepper
½ teaspoon salt
½ teaspoon marjoram
1 teaspoon light olive oil
1 pound (454 g) boneless
chicken breasts, cut in 1½-inch chunks
Oil for misting or cooking spray
1 (10-ounce / 283-g) package frozen unsweetened dark cherries, thawed and drained

1. In a medium bowl, mix together peach preserves, rosemary, pepper, salt, marjoram, and olive oil. 2. Stir in chicken chunks and toss to coat well with the preserve mixture. 3. Spray the air fryer basket with oil or cooking spray and lay chicken chunks in basket. 4. Air fry at 390ºF (199ºC) for 7 minutes. Stir. Cook for 6 to 8 more minutes or until chicken juices run clear. 5. When chicken has cooked through, scatter the cherries over and cook for additional minute to heat cherries.

Ethiopian Chicken with Cauliflower

Prep time: 15 minutes | Cook time: 28 minutes | Serves 6

2 handful fresh Italian parsley, roughly chopped
½ cup fresh chopped chives
2 sprigs thyme
6 chicken drumsticks
1½ small-sized head cauliflower, broken into large-sized florets
2 teaspoons mustard powder
⅓ teaspoon porcini powder
1½ teaspoons berbere spice
⅓ teaspoon sweet paprika
½ teaspoon shallot powder
1 teaspoon granulated garlic
1 teaspoon freshly cracked pink peppercorns
½ teaspoon sea salt

1. Simply combine all items for the berbere spice rub mix. After that, coat the chicken drumsticks with this rub mix on all sides. Transfer them to the baking dish. 2. Now, lower the cauliflower onto the chicken drumsticks. Add thyme, chives and Italian parsley and spritz everything with a pan spray. Transfer the baking dish to the preheated air fryer. 3. Next step, set the timer for 28 minutes; roast at 355ºF (179ºC), turning occasionally. Bon appétit!

Buffalo Chicken Cheese Sticks

Prep time: 5 minutes | Cook time: 8 minutes | Serves 2

1 cup shredded cooked chicken
¼ cup buffalo sauce
1 cup shredded Mozzarella cheese
1 large egg
¼ cup crumbled feta

1. In a large bowl, mix all ingredients except the feta. Cut a piece of parchment to fit your air fryer basket and press the mixture into a ½-inch-thick circle. 2. Sprinkle the mixture with feta and place into the air fryer basket. 3. Adjust the temperature to 400ºF (204ºC) and air fry for 8 minutes. 4. After 5 minutes, flip over the cheese mixture. 5. Allow to cool 5 minutes before cutting into sticks. Serve warm.

Peruvian Chicken with Green Herb Sauce

Prep time: 30 minutes | Cook time: 15 minutes | Serves 4

Chicken:
4 boneless, skinless chicken thighs (about 1½ pounds / 680 g)
2 teaspoons grated lemon zest
2 tablespoons fresh lemon juice
1 tablespoon extra-virgin olive oil
1 serrano chile, seeded and minced
1 teaspoon ground cumin
½ teaspoon dried oregano, crushed
½ teaspoon kosher salt
Sauce:
1 cup fresh cilantro leaves
1 jalapeño, seeded and coarsely chopped
1 garlic clove, minced
1 tablespoon extra-virgin olive oil
2½ teaspoons fresh lime juice
¼ teaspoon kosher salt
⅓ cup mayonnaise

1. For the chicken: Use a fork to pierce the chicken all over to allow the marinade to penetrate better. In a small bowl, combine the lemon zest, lemon juice, olive oil, serrano, cumin, oregano, and salt. Place the chicken in a large bowl or large resealable plastic bag. Pour the marinade over the chicken. Toss to coat. Marinate at room temperature for 30 minutes, or cover and refrigerate for up to 24 hours. 2. Place the chicken in the air fryer basket. (Discard remaining marinade.) Set the air fryer to 350ºF (177ºC) for 15 minutes, turning halfway through the cooking time. 3. Meanwhile, for the sauce: Combine the cilantro, jalapeño, garlic, olive oil, lime juice, and salt in a blender. Blend until combined. Add the mayonnaise and blend until puréed. Transfer to a small bowl. Cover and chill until ready to serve. 4. At the end of the cooking time, use a meat thermometer to ensure the chicken has reached an internal temperature of 165ºF (74ºC). Serve the chicken with the sauce.

Barbecue Chicken

Prep time: 10 minutes | Cook time: 18 to 20 minutes | Serves 4

⅓ cup no-salt-added tomato sauce
2 tablespoons low-sodium grainy mustard
2 tablespoons apple cider vinegar
1 tablespoon honey
2 garlic cloves, minced
1 jalapeño pepper, minced
3 tablespoons minced onion
4 (5-ounce / 142-g) low-sodium boneless, skinless chicken breasts

1. Preheat the air fryer to 370ºF (188ºC). 2. In a small bowl, stir together the tomato sauce, mustard, cider vinegar, honey, garlic, jalapeño, and onion. 3. Brush the chicken breasts with some sauce and air fry for 10 minutes. 4. Remove the air fryer basket and turn the chicken; brush with more sauce. Air fry for 5 minutes more. 5. Remove the air fryer basket and turn the chicken again; brush with more sauce. Air fry for 3 to 5 minutes more, or until the chicken reaches an internal temperature of 165ºF (74ºC) on a meat thermometer. Discard any remaining sauce. Serve immediately.

Chicken Cordon Bleu

Prep time: 20 minutes | Cook time: 15 to 20 minutes | Serves 4

4 small boneless, skinless chicken breasts
Salt and pepper, to taste
4 slices deli ham
4 slices deli Swiss cheese (about 3 to 4 inches square)
2 tablespoons olive oil
2 teaspoons marjoram
¼ teaspoon paprika

1. Split each chicken breast horizontally almost in two, leaving one edge intact. 2. Lay breasts open flat and sprinkle with salt and pepper to taste. 3. Place a ham slice on top of each chicken breast. 4. Cut cheese slices in half and place one half atop each breast. Set aside remaining halves of cheese slices. 5. Roll up chicken breasts to enclose cheese and ham and secure with toothpicks. 6. Mix together the olive oil, marjoram, and paprika. Rub all over outsides of chicken breasts. 7. Place chicken in air fryer basket and air fry at 360ºF (182ºC) for 15 to 20 minutes, until well done and juices run clear. 8. Remove all toothpicks. To avoid burns, place chicken breasts on a plate to remove toothpicks, then immediately return them to the air fryer basket. 9. Place a half cheese slice on top of each chicken breast and cook for a minute or so just to melt cheese.

Chicken Croquettes with Creole Sauce

Prep time: 30 minutes | Cook time: 10 minutes | Serves 4

2 cups shredded cooked chicken	Creole Sauce:
½ cup shredded Cheddar cheese	¼ cup mayonnaise
2 eggs	¼ cup sour cream
¼ cup finely chopped onion	1½ teaspoons Dijon mustard
¼ cup almond meal	1½ teaspoons fresh lemon juice
1 tablespoon poultry seasoning	½ teaspoon garlic powder
Olive oil	½ teaspoon Creole seasoning

1. In a large bowl, combine the chicken, Cheddar, eggs, onion, almond meal, and poultry seasoning. Stir gently until thoroughly combined. Cover and refrigerate for 30 minutes. 2. Meanwhile, to make the Creole sauce: In a small bowl, whisk together the mayonnaise, sour cream, Dijon mustard, lemon juice, garlic powder, and Creole seasoning until thoroughly combined. Cover and refrigerate until ready to serve. 3. Preheat the air fryer to 400°F (204°C). Divide the chicken mixture into 8 portions and shape into patties. 4. Working in batches if necessary, arrange the patties in a single layer in the air fryer basket and coat both sides lightly with olive oil. Pausing halfway through the cooking time to flip the patties, air fry for 10 minutes, or until lightly browned and the cheese is melted. Serve with the Creole sauce.

Chicken Legs with Leeks

Prep time: 30 minutes | Cook time: 18 minutes | Serves 6

2 leeks, sliced	skinless
2 large-sized tomatoes, chopped	½ teaspoon smoked cayenne pepper
3 cloves garlic, minced	2 tablespoons olive oil
½ teaspoon dried oregano	A freshly ground nutmeg
6 chicken legs, boneless and	

1. In a mixing dish, thoroughly combine all ingredients, minus the leeks. Place in the refrigerator and let it marinate overnight. 2. Lay the leeks onto the bottom of the air fryer basket. Top with the chicken legs. 3. Roast chicken legs at 375°F (191°C) for 18 minutes, turning halfway through. Serve with hoisin sauce.

Nacho Chicken Fries

Prep time: 20 minutes | Cook time: 6 to 7 minutes per batch | Serves 4 to 6

1 pound (454 g) chicken tenders	Oil for misting or cooking spray
Salt, to taste	Seasoning Mix:
¼ cup flour	1 tablespoon chili powder
2 eggs	1 teaspoon ground cumin
¾ cup panko bread crumbs	½ teaspoon garlic powder
¾ cup crushed organic nacho cheese tortilla chips	½ teaspoon onion powder

1. Stir together all seasonings in a small cup and set aside. 2. Cut chicken tenders in half crosswise, then cut into strips no wider than about ½ inch. 3. Preheat the air fryer to 390°F (199°C). 4. Salt chicken to taste. Place strips in large bowl and sprinkle with 1 tablespoon of the seasoning mix. Stir well to distribute seasonings. 5. Add flour to chicken and stir well to coat all sides. 6. Beat eggs together in a shallow dish. 7. In a second shallow dish, combine the panko, crushed chips, and the remaining 2 teaspoons of seasoning mix. 8. Dip chicken strips in eggs, then roll in crumbs. Mist with oil or cooking spray. 9. Chicken strips will cook best if done in two batches. They can be crowded and overlapping a little but not stacked in double or triple layers. 10. Cook for 4 minutes. Shake basket, mist with oil, and cook 2 to 3 more minutes, until chicken juices run clear and outside is crispy. 11. Repeat step 10 to cook remaining chicken fries.

Pecan Turkey Cutlets

Prep time: 10 minutes | Cook time: 10 to 12 minutes per batch | Serves 4

¾ cup panko bread crumbs	¼ cup cornstarch
¼ teaspoon salt	1 egg, beaten
¼ teaspoon pepper	1 pound (454 g) turkey cutlets, ½-inch thick
¼ teaspoon dry mustard	
¼ teaspoon poultry seasoning	Salt and pepper, to taste
½ cup pecans	Oil for misting or cooking spray

1. Place the panko crumbs, ¼ teaspoon salt, ¼ teaspoon pepper, mustard, and poultry seasoning in food processor. Process until crumbs are finely crushed. Add pecans and process in short pulses just until nuts are finely chopped. Go easy so you don't overdo it! 2. Preheat the air fryer to 360°F (182°C). 3. Place cornstarch in one shallow dish and beaten egg in another. Transfer coating mixture from food processor into a third shallow dish. 4. Sprinkle turkey cutlets with salt and pepper to taste. 5. Dip cutlets in cornstarch and shake off excess. Then dip in beaten egg and roll in crumbs, pressing to coat well. Spray both sides with oil or cooking spray. 6. Place 2 cutlets in air fryer basket in a single layer and cook for 10 to 12 minutes or until juices run clear. 7. Repeat step 6 to cook remaining cutlets.

Crisp Paprika Chicken Drumsticks

Prep time: 5 minutes | Cook time: 22 minutes | Serves 2

2 teaspoons paprika	4 (5-ounce / 142-g) chicken drumsticks, trimmed
1 teaspoon packed brown sugar	
1 teaspoon garlic powder	1 teaspoon vegetable oil
½ teaspoon dry mustard	1 scallion, green part only, sliced thin on bias
½ teaspoon salt	
Pinch pepper	

1. Preheat the air fryer to 400°F (204°C). 2. Combine paprika, sugar, garlic powder, mustard, salt, and pepper in a bowl. Pat drumsticks dry with paper towels. Using metal skewer, poke 10 to 15 holes in skin of each drumstick. Rub with oil and sprinkle evenly with spice mixture. 3. Arrange drumsticks in air fryer basket, spaced evenly apart, alternating ends. Air fry until chicken is crisp and registers 195°F (91°C), 22 to 25 minutes, flipping chicken halfway through cooking. 4. Transfer chicken to serving platter, tent loosely with aluminum foil, and let rest for 5 minutes. Sprinkle with scallion and serve.

Garlic Soy Chicken Thighs

Prep time: 10 minutes | Cook time: 30 minutes | Serves 1 to 2

2 tablespoons chicken stock
2 tablespoons reduced-sodium soy sauce
1½ tablespoons sugar
4 garlic cloves, smashed and peeled
2 large scallions, cut into 2- to 3-inch batons, plus more, thinly sliced, for garnish
2 bone-in, skin-on chicken thighs (7 to 8 ounces / 198 to 227 g each)

1. Preheat the air fryer to 375ºF (191ºC). 2. In a metal cake pan, combine the chicken stock, soy sauce, and sugar and stir until the sugar dissolves. Add the garlic cloves, scallions, and chicken thighs, turning the thighs to coat them in the marinade, then resting them skin-side up. Place the pan in the air fryer and cook, flipping the thighs every 5 minutes after the first 10 minutes, until the chicken is cooked through and the marinade is reduced to a sticky glaze over the chicken, about 30 minutes. 3. Remove the pan from the air fryer and serve the chicken thighs warm, with any remaining glaze spooned over top and sprinkled with more sliced scallions.

Turkey and Cranberry Quesadillas

Prep time: 7 minutes | Cook time: 4 to 8 minutes | Serves 4

6 low-sodium whole-wheat tortillas
⅓ cup shredded low-sodium low-fat Swiss cheese
¾ cup shredded cooked low-sodium turkey breast
2 tablespoons cranberry sauce
2 tablespoons dried cranberries
½ teaspoon dried basil
Olive oil spray, for spraying the tortillas

1. Preheat the air fryer to 400ºF (204ºC). 2. Put 3 tortillas on a work surface. 3. Evenly divide the Swiss cheese, turkey, cranberry sauce, and dried cranberries among the tortillas. Sprinkle with the basil and top with the remaining tortillas. 4. Spray the outsides of the tortillas with olive oil spray. 5. One at a time, air fry the quesadillas in the air fryer for 4 to 8 minutes, or until crisp and the cheese is melted. Cut into quarters and serve.

Chicken Hand Pies

Prep time: 30 minutes | Cook time: 10 minutes per batch | Makes 8 pies

¾ cup chicken broth
¾ cup frozen mixed peas and carrots
1 cup cooked chicken, chopped
1 tablespoon cornstarch
1 tablespoon milk
Salt and pepper, to taste
1 (8-count) can organic flaky biscuits
Oil for misting or cooking spray

1. In a medium saucepan, bring chicken broth to a boil. Stir in the frozen peas and carrots and cook for 5 minutes over medium heat. Stir in chicken. 2. Mix the cornstarch into the milk until it dissolves. Stir it into the simmering chicken broth mixture and cook just until thickened. 3. Remove from heat, add salt and pepper to taste, and let cool slightly. 4. Lay biscuits out on wax paper. Peel each biscuit apart in the middle to make 2 rounds so you have 16 rounds total. Using your hands or a rolling pin, flatten each biscuit round slightly to make it larger and thinner. 5. Divide chicken filling among 8 of the biscuit rounds. Place remaining biscuit rounds on top and press edges all around. Use the tines of a fork to crimp biscuit edges and make sure they are sealed well. 6. Spray both sides lightly with oil or cooking spray. 7. Cook in a single layer, 4 at a time, at 330ºF (166ºC) for 10 minutes or until biscuit dough is cooked through and golden brown.

Israeli Chicken Schnitzel

Prep time: 5 minutes | Cook time: 10 minutes | Serves 4

2 large boneless, skinless chicken breasts, each weighing about 1 pound (454 g)
1 cup all-purpose flour
2 teaspoons garlic powder
2 teaspoons kosher salt
1 teaspoon black pepper
1 teaspoon paprika
2 eggs beaten with 2 tablespoons water
2 cups panko bread crumbs
Vegetable oil spray
Lemon juice, for serving

1. Preheat the air fryer to 375ºF (191ºC). 2. Place 1 chicken breast between 2 pieces of plastic wrap. Use a mallet or a rolling pin to pound the chicken until it is ¼ inch thick. Set aside. Repeat with the second breast. Whisk together the flour, garlic powder, salt, pepper, and paprika on a large plate. Place the panko in a separate shallow bowl or pie plate. 3. Dredge 1 chicken breast in the flour, shaking off any excess, then dip it in the egg mixture. Dredge the chicken breast in the panko, making sure to coat it completely. Shake off any excess panko. Place the battered chicken breast on a plate. Repeat with the second chicken breast. 4. Spray the air fryer basket with oil spray. Place 1 of the battered chicken breasts in the basket and spray the top with oil spray. Air fry until the top is browned, about 5 minutes. Flip the chicken and spray the second side with oil spray. Air fry until the second side is browned and crispy and the internal temperature reaches 165ºF (74ºC). Remove the first chicken breast from the air fryer and repeat with the second chicken breast. 5. Serve hot with lemon juice.

Chipotle Drumsticks

Prep time: 5 minutes | Cook time: 25 minutes | Serves 4

1 tablespoon tomato paste
½ teaspoon chipotle powder
¼ teaspoon apple cider vinegar
¼ teaspoon garlic powder
8 chicken drumsticks
½ teaspoon salt
⅛ teaspoon ground black pepper

1. In a small bowl, combine tomato paste, chipotle powder, vinegar, and garlic powder. 2. Sprinkle drumsticks with salt and pepper, then place into a large bowl and pour in tomato paste mixture. Toss or stir to evenly coat all drumsticks in mixture. 3. Place drumsticks into ungreased air fryer basket. Adjust the temperature to 400ºF (204ºC) and air fry for 25 minutes, turning drumsticks halfway through cooking. Drumsticks will be dark red with an internal temperature of at least 165ºF (74ºC) when done. Serve warm.

Hoisin Turkey Burgers

Prep time: 30 minutes | Cook time: 20 minutes | Serves 4

Olive oil
1 pound (454 g) lean ground turkey
¼ cup whole-wheat bread crumbs
¼ cup hoisin sauce
2 tablespoons soy sauce
4 whole-wheat buns

1. Spray the air fryer basket lightly with olive oil. 2. In a large bowl, mix together the turkey, bread crumbs, hoisin sauce, and soy sauce. 3. Form the mixture into 4 equal patties. Cover with plastic wrap and refrigerate the patties for 30 minutes. 4. Place the patties in the air fryer basket in a single layer. Spray the patties lightly with olive oil. 5. Air fry at 370ºF (188ºC) for 10 minutes. Flip the patties over, lightly spray with olive oil, and cook until golden brown, an additional 5 to 10 minutes. 6. Place the patties on buns and top with your choice of low-calorie burger toppings like sliced tomatoes, onions, and cabbage slaw.

Potato-Crusted Chicken

Prep time: 15 minutes | Cook time: 22 to 25 minutes | Serves 4

¼ cup buttermilk
1 large egg, beaten
1 cup instant potato flakes
¼ cup grated Parmesan cheese
1 teaspoon salt
½ teaspoon freshly ground black pepper
2 whole boneless, skinless chicken breasts (about 1 pound / 454 g each), halved
1 to 2 tablespoons oil

1. In a shallow bowl, whisk the buttermilk and egg until blended. In another shallow bowl, stir together the potato flakes, cheese, salt, and pepper. 2. One at a time, dip the chicken pieces in the buttermilk mixture and the potato flake mixture, coating thoroughly. 3. Preheat the air fryer to 400ºF (204ºC). Line the air fryer basket with parchment paper. 4. Place the coated chicken on the parchment and spritz with oil. 5. Cook for 15 minutes. Flip the chicken, spritz it with oil, and cook for 7 to 10 minutes more until the outside is crispy and the inside is no longer pink.

Chicken Schnitzel

Prep time: 15 minutes | Cook time: 5 minutes | Serves 4

½ cup all-purpose flour
1 teaspoon marjoram
½ teaspoon thyme
1 teaspoon dried parsley flakes
½ teaspoon salt
1 egg
Cooking spray
1 teaspoon lemon juice
1 teaspoon water
1 cup breadcrumbs
4 chicken tenders, pounded thin, cut in half lengthwise

1. Preheat the air fryer to 390ºF (199ºC) and spritz with cooking spray. 2. Combine the flour, marjoram, thyme, parsley, and salt in a shallow dish. Stir to mix well. 3. Whisk the egg with lemon juice and water in a large bowl. Pour the breadcrumbs in a separate shallow dish. 4. Roll the chicken halves in the flour mixture first, then in the egg mixture, and then roll over the breadcrumbs to coat well. Shake the excess off. 5. Arrange the chicken halves in the preheated air fryer and spritz with cooking spray on both sides. 6. Air fry for 5 minutes or until the chicken halves are golden brown and crispy. Flip the halves halfway through. 7. Serve immediately.

South Indian Pepper Chicken

Prep time: 30 minutes | Cook time: 15 minutes | Serves 4

Spice Mix:
1 dried red chile, or ½ teaspoon dried red pepper flakes
1-inch piece cinnamon or cassia bark
1½ teaspoons coriander seeds
1 teaspoon fennel seeds
1 teaspoon cumin seeds
1 teaspoon black peppercorns
½ teaspoon cardamom seeds
¼ teaspoon ground turmeric
1 teaspoon kosher salt
Chicken:
1 pound (454 g) boneless, skinless chicken thighs, cut crosswise into thirds
2 medium onions, cut into ½-inch-thick slices
¼ cup olive oil
Cauliflower rice, steamed rice, or naan bread, for serving

1. For the spice mix: Combine the dried chile, cinnamon, coriander, fennel, cumin, peppercorns, and cardamom in a clean coffee or spice grinder. Grind, shaking the grinder lightly so all the seeds and bits get into the blades, until the mixture is broken down to a fine powder. Stir in the turmeric and salt. 2. For the chicken: Place the chicken and onions in resealable plastic bag. Add the oil and 1½ tablespoons of the spice mix. Seal the bag and massage until the chicken is well coated. Marinate at room temperature for 30 minutes or in the refrigerator for up to 24 hours. 3. Place the chicken and onions in the air fryer basket. Set the air fryer to 350ºF (177ºC) for 10 minutes, stirring once halfway through the cooking time. Increase the temperature to 400ºF (204ºC) for 5 minutes. Use a meat thermometer to ensure the chicken has reached an internal temperature of 165ºF (74ºC). 4. Serve with steamed rice, cauliflower rice, or naan.

Pork Rind Fried Chicken

Prep time: 30 minutes | Cook time: 20 minutes | Serves 4

¼ cup buffalo sauce
4 (4-ounce / 113-g) boneless, skinless chicken breasts
½ teaspoon paprika
½ teaspoon garlic powder
¼ teaspoon ground black pepper
2 ounces (57 g) plain pork rinds, finely crushed

1. Pour buffalo sauce into a large sealable bowl or bag. Add chicken and toss to coat. Place sealed bowl or bag into refrigerator and let marinate at least 30 minutes up to overnight. 2. Remove chicken from marinade but do not shake excess sauce off chicken. Sprinkle both sides of thighs with paprika, garlic powder, and pepper. 3. Place pork rinds into a large bowl and press each chicken breast into pork rinds to coat evenly on both sides. 4. Place chicken into ungreased air fryer basket. Adjust the temperature to 400ºF (204ºC) and roast for 20 minutes, turning chicken halfway through cooking. Chicken will be golden and have an internal temperature of at least 165ºF (74ºC) when done. Serve warm.

Juicy Paprika Chicken Breast

Prep time: 5 minutes | Cook time: 30 minutes | Serves 4

Oil, for spraying
4 (6-ounce / 170-g) boneless, skinless chicken breasts
1 tablespoon olive oil
1 tablespoon paprika
1 tablespoon packed light brown sugar
½ teaspoon cayenne pepper
½ teaspoon onion powder
½ teaspoon granulated garlic

1. Line the air fryer basket with parchment and spray lightly with oil. 2. Brush the chicken with the olive oil. 3. In a small bowl, mix together the paprika, brown sugar, cayenne pepper, onion powder, and garlic and sprinkle it over the chicken. 4. Place the chicken in the prepared basket. You may need to work in batches, depending on the size of your air fryer. 5. Air fry at 360°F (182°C) for 15 minutes, flip, and cook for another 15 minutes, or until the internal temperature reaches 165°F (74°C). Serve immediately.

Honey-Glazed Chicken Thighs

Prep time: 5 minutes | Cook time: 14 minutes | Serves 4

Oil, for spraying
4 boneless, skinless chicken thighs, fat trimmed
3 tablespoons soy sauce
1 tablespoon balsamic vinegar
2 teaspoons honey
2 teaspoons minced garlic
1 teaspoon ground ginger

1. Preheat the air fryer to 400°F (204°C). Line the air fryer basket with parchment and spray lightly with oil. 2. Place the chicken in the prepared basket. 3. Cook for 7 minutes, flip, and cook for another 7 minutes, or until the internal temperature reaches 165°F (74°C) and the juices run clear. 4. In a small saucepan, combine the soy sauce, balsamic vinegar, honey, garlic, and ginger and cook over low heat for 1 to 2 minutes, until warmed through. 5. Transfer the chicken to a serving plate and drizzle with the sauce just before serving.

Chapter 5 Beef, Pork, and Lamb

Chapter 5 Beef, Pork, and Lamb

Beef Flank Steak with Sage

Prep time: 13 minutes | Cook time: 7 minutes | Serves 2

⅓ cup sour cream
½ cup green onion, chopped
1 tablespoon mayonnaise
3 cloves garlic, smashed
1 pound (454 g) beef flank steak, trimmed and cubed
2 tablespoons fresh sage, minced
½ teaspoon salt
⅓ teaspoon black pepper, or to taste

1. Season your meat with salt and pepper; arrange beef cubes on the bottom of a baking dish that fits in your air fryer. 2. Stir in green onions and garlic; air fry for about 7 minutes at 385ºF (196ºC). 3. Once your beef starts to tender, add the cream, mayonnaise, and sage; air fry an additional 8 minutes. Bon appétit!

Southern Chili

Prep time: 20 minutes | Cook time: 25 minutes | Serves 4

1 pound (454 g) ground beef (85% lean)
1 cup minced onion
1 (28-ounce / 794-g) can tomato purée
1 (15-ounce / 425-g) can diced tomatoes with green chilies
1 (15-ounce / 425-g) can light red kidney beans, rinsed and drained
¼ cup Chili seasoning

1. Preheat the air fryer to 400ºF (204ºC). 2. In a baking pan, mix the ground beef and onion. Place the pan in the air fryer. 3. Cook for 4 minutes. Stir and cook for 4 minutes more until browned. Remove the pan from the fryer. Drain the meat and transfer to a large bowl. 4. Reduce the air fryer temperature to 350ºF (177ºC). 5. To the bowl with the meat, add in the tomato purée, diced tomatoes and green chilies, kidney beans, and Chili seasoning. Mix well. Pour the mixture into the baking pan. 6. Cook for 25 minutes, stirring every 10 minutes, until thickened.

Herb-Roasted Beef Tips with Onions

Prep time: 5 minutes | Cook time: 10 minutes | Serves 4

1 pound (454 g) rib eye steak, cubed
2 garlic cloves, minced
2 tablespoons olive oil
1 tablespoon fresh oregano
1 teaspoon salt
½ teaspoon black pepper
1 yellow onion, thinly sliced

1. Preheat the air fryer to 380°F (193ºC). 2. In a medium bowl, combine the steak, garlic, olive oil, oregano, salt, pepper, and onion. Mix until all of the beef and onion are well coated. 3. Put the seasoned steak mixture into the air fryer basket. Roast for 5 minutes. Stir and roast for 5 minutes more. 4. Let rest for 5 minutes before serving with some favorite sides.

Carne Asada

Prep time: 5 minutes | Cook time: 15 minutes | Serves 4

3 chipotle peppers in adobo, chopped
⅓ cup chopped fresh oregano
⅓ cup chopped fresh parsley
4 cloves garlic, minced
Juice of 2 limes
1 teaspoon ground cumin seeds
⅓ cup olive oil
1 to 1½ pounds (454 g to 680 g) flank steak
Salt, to taste

1. Combine the chipotle, oregano, parsley, garlic, lime juice, cumin, and olive oil in a large bowl. Stir to mix well. 2. Dunk the flank steak in the mixture and press to coat well. Wrap the bowl in plastic and marinate under room temperature for at least 30 minutes. 3. Preheat the air fryer to 390ºF (199ºC). 4. Discard the marinade and place the steak in the preheated air fryer. Sprinkle with salt. 5. Air fry for 15 minutes or until the steak is medium-rare or it reaches your desired doneness. Flip the steak halfway through the cooking time. 6. Remove the steak from the air fryer and slice to serve.

Cantonese BBQ Pork

Prep time: 30 minutes | Cook time: 15 minutes | Serves 4

¼ cup honey
2 tablespoons dark soy sauce
1 tablespoon sugar
1 tablespoon Shaoxing wine (rice cooking wine)
1 tablespoon hoisin sauce
2 teaspoons minced garlic
2 teaspoons minced fresh ginger
1 teaspoon Chinese five-spice powder
1 pound (454 g) fatty pork shoulder, cut into long, 1-inch-thick pieces

1. In a small microwave-safe bowl, combine the honey, soy sauce, sugar, wine, hoisin, garlic, ginger, and five-spice powder. Microwave in 10-second intervals, stirring in between, until the honey has dissolved. 2. Use a fork to pierce the pork slices to allow the marinade to penetrate better. Place the pork in a large bowl or resealable plastic bag and pour in half the marinade; set aside the remaining marinade to use for the sauce. Toss to coat. Marinate the pork at room temperature for 30 minutes, or cover and refrigerate for up 24 hours. 3. Place the pork in a single layer in the air fryer basket. Set the air fryer to 400ºF (204ºC) for 15 minutes, turning and basting the pork halfway through the cooking time. 4. While the pork is cooking, microwave the reserved marinade on high for 45 to 60 seconds, stirring every 15 seconds, to thicken it slightly to the consistency of a sauce. 5. Transfer the pork to a cutting board and let rest for 10 minutes. Brush with the sauce and serve.

Smoky Pork Tenderloin

Prep time: 5 minutes | Cook time: 19 to 22 minutes | Serves 6

1½ pounds (680 g) pork tenderloin
1 tablespoon avocado oil
1 teaspoon chili powder
1 teaspoon smoked paprika
1 teaspoon garlic powder
1 teaspoon sea salt
1 teaspoon freshly ground black pepper

1. Pierce the tenderloin all over with a fork and rub the oil all over the meat. 2. In a small dish, stir together the chili powder, smoked paprika, garlic powder, salt, and pepper. 3. Rub the spice mixture all over the tenderloin. 4. Set the air fryer to 400°F (204°C). Place the pork in the air fryer basket and air fry for 10 minutes. Flip the tenderloin and cook for 9 to 12 minutes more, until an instant-read thermometer reads at least 145°F (63°C). 5. Allow the tenderloin to rest for 5 minutes, then slice and serve.

Beef Empanadas

Prep time: 15 minutes | Cook time: 25 minutes | Serves 5

2 garlic cloves, chopped
⅓ cup chopped green bell pepper
⅓ medium onion, chopped
8 ounces (227 g) 93% lean ground beef
1 teaspoon hamburger seasoning
Salt and freshly ground black pepper, to taste
15 empanada wrappers
1 cup shredded Mozzarella cheese
1 cup shredded pepper Jack cheese
1 tablespoon butter
Cooking oil spray

1. Spray a skillet with the cooking oil and place it over medium-high heat. Add the garlic, green bell pepper, and onion. Cook until fragrant, about 2 minutes. 2. Add the ground beef to the skillet. Season it with the hamburger seasoning, salt, and pepper. Using a spatula or spoon, break up the beef into small pieces. Cook the beef for about 5 minutes until browned. Drain any excess fat. 3. Lay the empanada wrappers on a work surface. 4. Dip a basting brush in water. Glaze each wrapper along the edges with the wet brush. This will soften the crust and make it easier to roll. You can also dip your fingers in water to moisten the edges. 5. Scoop 2 to 3 tablespoons of the ground beef mixture onto each empanada wrapper. Sprinkle the Mozzarella and pepper Jack cheeses over the beef. 6. Close the empanadas by folding the empanada wrapper in half over the filling. Using the back of a fork, press along the edges to seal. 7. Insert the crisper plate into the basket and the basket into the unit. Preheat the unit by selecting AIR FRY, setting the temperature to 400°F (204°C), and setting the time to 3 minutes. Select START/PAUSE to begin. 8. Once the unit is preheated, spray the crisper plate with cooking oil. Working in batches, place 7 or 8 empanadas into the basket. Spray each with cooking oil. 9. Select AIR FRY, set the temperature to 400°F (204°C), and set the time to 12 minutes. Select START/PAUSE to begin. 10. After 8 minutes, flip the empanadas and spray them with more cooking oil. Resume cooking. 11. When the cooking is complete, transfer the empanadas to a plate. For added flavor, top each hot empanada with a bit of butter and let melt. Repeat steps 8, 9, and 10 for the remaining empanadas. 12. Cool for 5 minutes before serving.

Honey-Baked Pork Loin

Prep time: 30 minutes | Cook time: 22 to 25 minutes | Serves 6

¼ cup honey
¼ cup freshly squeezed lemon juice
2 tablespoons soy sauce
1 teaspoon garlic powder
1 (2-pound / 907-g) pork loin
2 tablespoons vegetable oil

1. In a medium bowl, whisk together the honey, lemon juice, soy sauce, and garlic powder. Reserve half of the mixture for basting during cooking. 2. Cut 5 slits in the pork loin and transfer it to a resealable bag. Add the remaining honey mixture. Seal the bag and refrigerate to marinate for at least 2 hours. 3. Preheat the air fryer to 400°F (204°C). Line the air fryer basket with parchment paper. 4. Remove the pork from the marinade, and place it on the parchment. Spritz with oil, then baste with the reserved marinade. 5. Cook for 15 minutes. Flip the pork, baste with more marinade and spritz with oil again. Cook for 7 to 10 minutes more until the internal temperature reaches 145°F (63°C). Let rest for 5 minutes before serving.

Swedish Meatloaf

Prep time: 10 minutes | Cook time: 35 minutes | Serves 8

1½ pounds (680 g) ground beef (85% lean)
¼ pound (113 g) ground pork
1 large egg (omit for egg-free)
½ cup minced onions
¼ cup tomato sauce
2 tablespoons dry mustard
2 cloves garlic, minced
2 teaspoons fine sea salt
1 teaspoon ground black pepper, plus more for garnish

Sauce:
½ cup (1 stick) unsalted butter
½ cup shredded Swiss or mild Cheddar cheese (about 2 ounces / 57 g)
2 ounces (57 g) cream cheese (¼ cup), softened
⅓ cup beef broth
⅛ teaspoon ground nutmeg
Halved cherry tomatoes, for serving (optional)

1. Preheat the air fryer to 390°F (199°C). 2. In a large bowl, combine the ground beef, ground pork, egg, onions, tomato sauce, dry mustard, garlic, salt, and pepper. Using your hands, mix until well combined. 3. Place the meatloaf mixture in a loaf pan and place it in the air fryer. Cook for 35 minutes, or until cooked through and the internal temperature reaches 145°F (63°C). Check the meatloaf after 25 minutes; if it's getting too brown on the top, cover it loosely with foil to prevent burning. 4. While the meatloaf cooks, make the sauce: Heat the butter in a saucepan over medium-high heat until it sizzles and brown flecks appear, stirring constantly to keep the butter from burning. Turn the heat down to low and whisk in the Swiss cheese, cream cheese, broth, and nutmeg. Simmer for at least 10 minutes. The longer it simmers, the more the flavors open up. 5. When the meatloaf is done, transfer it to a serving tray and pour the sauce over it. Garnish with ground black pepper and serve with cherry tomatoes, if desired. Allow the meatloaf to rest for 10 minutes before slicing so it doesn't crumble apart. 6. Store leftovers in an airtight container in the fridge for 3 days or in the freezer for up to a month. Reheat in a preheated 350°F (177°C) air fryer for 4 minutes, or until heated through.

Spice-Rubbed Pork Loin

Prep time: 5 minutes | Cook time: 20 minutes | Serves 6

1 teaspoon paprika
½ teaspoon ground cumin
½ teaspoon chili powder
½ teaspoon garlic powder
2 tablespoons coconut oil
1 (1½-pound / 680-g) boneless pork loin
½ teaspoon salt
¼ teaspoon ground black pepper

1. In a small bowl, mix paprika, cumin, chili powder, and garlic powder. 2. Drizzle coconut oil over pork. Sprinkle pork loin with salt and pepper, then rub spice mixture evenly on all sides. 3. Place pork loin into ungreased air fryer basket. Adjust the temperature to 400ºF (204ºC) and air fry for 20 minutes, turning pork halfway through cooking. Pork loin will be browned and have an internal temperature of at least 145ºF (63ºC) when done. Serve warm.

Meat and Rice Stuffed Bell Peppers

Prep time: 20 minutes | Cook time: 18 minutes | Serves 4

¾ pound (340 g) lean ground beef
4 ounces (113 g) lean ground pork
¼ cup onion, minced
1 (15-ounce / 425-g) can crushed tomatoes
1 teaspoon Worcestershire sauce
1 teaspoon barbecue seasoning
1 teaspoon honey
½ teaspoon dried basil
½ cup cooked brown rice
½ teaspoon garlic powder
½ teaspoon oregano
½ teaspoon salt
2 small bell peppers, cut in half, stems removed, deseeded
Cooking spray

1. Preheat the air fryer to 360ºF (182ºC) and spritz a baking pan with cooking spray. 2. Arrange the beef, pork, and onion in the baking pan and cook in the preheated air fryer for 8 minutes. Break the ground meat into chunks halfway through the cooking. 3. Meanwhile, combine the tomatoes, Worcestershire sauce, barbecue seasoning, honey, and basil in a saucepan. Stir to mix well. 4. Transfer the cooked meat mixture to a large bowl and add the cooked rice, garlic powder, oregano, salt, and ¼ cup of the tomato mixture. Stir to mix well. 5. Stuff the pepper halves with the mixture, then arrange the pepper halves in the air fryer and air fry for 10 minutes or until the peppers are lightly charred. 6. Serve the stuffed peppers with the remaining tomato sauce on top.

Stuffed Beef Tenderloin with Feta Cheese

Prep time: 10 minutes | Cook time: 10 minutes | Serves 4

1½ pounds (680 g) beef tenderloin, pounded to ¼ inch thick
3 teaspoons sea salt
1 teaspoon ground black pepper
2 ounces (57 g) creamy goat cheese
½ cup crumbled feta cheese
¼ cup finely chopped onions
2 cloves garlic, minced
Cooking spray

1. Preheat the air fryer to 400ºF (204ºC). Spritz the air fryer basket with cooking spray. 2. Unfold the beef tenderloin on a clean work surface. Rub the salt and pepper all over the beef tenderloin to season. 3. Make the filling for the stuffed beef tenderloins: Combine the goat cheese, feta, onions, and garlic in a medium bowl. Stir until well blended. 4. Spoon the mixture in the center of the tenderloin. Roll the tenderloin up tightly like rolling a burrito and use some kitchen twine to tie the tenderloin. 5. Arrange the tenderloin in the air fryer basket and air fry for 10 minutes, flipping the tenderloin halfway through to ensure even cooking, or until an instant-read thermometer inserted in the center of the tenderloin registers 135ºF (57ºC) for medium-rare. 6. Transfer to a platter and serve immediately.

Spicy Lamb Sirloin Chops

Prep time: 30 minutes | Cook time: 15 minutes | Serves 4

½ yellow onion, coarsely chopped
4 coin-size slices peeled fresh ginger
5 garlic cloves
1 teaspoon garam masala
1 teaspoon ground fennel
1 teaspoon ground cinnamon
1 teaspoon ground turmeric
½ to 1 teaspoon cayenne pepper
½ teaspoon ground cardamom
1 teaspoon kosher salt
1 pound (454 g) lamb sirloin chops

1. In a blender, combine the onion, ginger, garlic, garam masala, fennel, cinnamon, turmeric, cayenne, cardamom, and salt. Pulse until the onion is finely minced and the mixture forms a thick paste, 3 to 4 minutes. 2. Place the lamb chops in a large bowl. Slash the meat and fat with a sharp knife several times to allow the marinade to penetrate better. Add the spice paste to the bowl and toss the lamb to coat. Marinate at room temperature for 30 minutes or cover and refrigerate for up to 24 hours. 3. Place the lamb chops in a single layer in the air fryer basket. Set the air fryer to 325ºF (163ºC) for 15 minutes, turning the chops halfway through the cooking time. Use a meat thermometer to ensure the lamb has reached an internal temperature of 145ºF (63ºC) (medium-rare).

Macadamia Nuts Crusted Pork Rack

Prep time: 5 minutes | Cook time: 35 minutes | Serves 2

1 clove garlic, minced
2 tablespoons olive oil
1 pound (454 g) rack of pork
1 cup chopped macadamia nuts
1 tablespoon breadcrumbs
1 tablespoon rosemary, chopped
1 egg
Salt and ground black pepper, to taste

1. Preheat the air fryer to 350ºF (177ºC). 2. Combine the garlic and olive oil in a small bowl. Stir to mix well. 3. On a clean work surface, rub the pork rack with the garlic oil and sprinkle with salt and black pepper on both sides. 4. Combine the macadamia nuts, breadcrumbs, and rosemary in a shallow dish. Whisk the egg in a large bowl. 5. Dredge the pork in the egg, then roll the pork over the macadamia nut mixture to coat well. Shake the excess off. 6. Arrange the pork in the preheated air fryer and air fry for 30 minutes on both sides. Increase to 390ºF (199ºC) and fry for 5 more minutes or until the pork is well browned. 7. Serve immediately.

German Rouladen-Style Steak

Prep time: 20 minutes | Cook time: 15 minutes | Serves 4

Onion Sauce:
2 medium onions, cut into ½-inch-thick slices
Kosher salt and black pepper, to taste
½ cup sour cream
1 tablespoon tomato paste
2 teaspoons chopped fresh parsley
Rouladen:
¼ cup Dijon mustard
1 pound (454 g) flank or skirt steak, ¼ to ½ inch thick
1 teaspoon black pepper
4 slices bacon
¼ cup chopped fresh parsley

1. For the sauce: In a small bowl, mix together the onions with salt and pepper to taste. Place the onions in the air fryer basket. Set the air fryer to 400ºF (204ºC) for 6 minutes, or until the onions are softened and golden brown. 2. Set aside half of the onions to use in the rouladen. Place the rest in a small bowl and add the sour cream, tomato paste, parsley, ½ teaspoon salt, and ½ teaspoon pepper. Stir until well combined, adding 1 to 2 tablespoons of water, if necessary, to thin the sauce slightly. Set the sauce aside. 3. For the rouladen: Evenly spread the mustard over the meat. Sprinkle with the pepper. Top with the bacon slices, reserved onions, and parsley. Starting at the long end, roll up the steak as tightly as possible, ending seam side down. Use 2 or 3 wooden toothpicks to hold the roll together. Using a sharp knife, cut the roll in half so that it better fits in the air fryer basket. 4. Place the steak, seam side down, in the air fryer basket. Set the air fryer to 400ºF (204ºC) for 9 minutes. Use a meat thermometer to ensure the steak has reached an internal temperature of 145ºF (63ºC). (It is critical to not overcook flank steak, so as to not toughen the meat.) 5. Let the steak rest for 10 minutes before cutting into slices. Serve with the sauce.

Fajita Meatball Lettuce Wraps

Prep time: 10 minutes | Cook time: 10 minutes | Serves 4

1 pound (454 g) ground beef (85% lean)
½ cup salsa, plus more for serving if desired
¼ cup chopped onions
¼ cup diced green or red bell peppers
1 large egg, beaten
1 teaspoon fine sea salt
½ teaspoon chili powder
½ teaspoon ground cumin
1 clove garlic, minced
For Serving (Optional):
8 leaves Boston lettuce
Pico de gallo or salsa
Lime slices

1. Spray the air fryer basket with avocado oil. Preheat the air fryer to 350ºF (177ºC). 2. In a large bowl, mix together all the ingredients until well combined. 3. Shape the meat mixture into eight 1-inch balls. Place the meatballs in the air fryer basket, leaving a little space between them. Air fry for 10 minutes, or until cooked through and no longer pink inside and the internal temperature reaches 145ºF (63ºC). 4. Serve each meatball on a lettuce leaf, topped with pico de gallo or salsa, if desired. Serve with lime slices if desired. 5. Store leftovers in an airtight container in the fridge for 3 days or in the freezer for up to a month. Reheat in a preheated 350ºF (177ºC) air fryer for 4 minutes, or until heated through.

Hoisin BBQ Pork Chops

Prep time: 5 minutes | Cook time: 22 minutes | Serves 2 to 3

3 tablespoons hoisin sauce
¼ cup honey
1 tablespoon soy sauce
3 tablespoons rice vinegar
2 tablespoons brown sugar
1½ teaspoons grated fresh ginger
1 to 2 teaspoons Sriracha sauce, to taste
2 to 3 bone-in center cut pork chops, 1-inch thick (about 1¼ pounds / 567 g)
Chopped scallions, for garnish

1. Combine the hoisin sauce, honey, soy sauce, rice vinegar, brown sugar, ginger, and Sriracha sauce in a small saucepan. Whisk the ingredients together and bring the mixture to a boil over medium-high heat on the stovetop. Reduce the heat and simmer the sauce until it has reduced in volume and thickened slightly, about 10 minutes. 2. Preheat the air fryer to 400ºF (204ºC). 3. Place the pork chops into the air fryer basket and pour half the hoisin BBQ sauce over the top. Air fry for 6 minutes. Then, flip the chops over, pour the remaining hoisin BBQ sauce on top and air fry for 5 to 6 more minutes, depending on the thickness of the pork chops. The internal temperature of the pork chops should be 155ºF (68ºC) when tested with an instant read thermometer. 4. Let the pork chops rest for 5 minutes before serving. You can spoon a little of the sauce from the bottom drawer of the air fryer over the top if desired. Sprinkle with chopped scallions and serve.

Bulgogi Burgers

Prep time: 30 minutes | Cook time: 10 minutes | Serves 4

Burgers:
1 pound (454 g) 85% lean ground beef
¼ cup chopped scallions
2 tablespoons gochujang (Korean red chile paste)
1 tablespoon dark soy sauce
2 teaspoons minced garlic
2 teaspoons minced fresh ginger
2 teaspoons sugar
1 tablespoon toasted sesame oil
½ teaspoon kosher salt
Gochujang Mayonnaise:
¼ cup mayonnaise
¼ cup chopped scallions
1 tablespoon gochujang (Korean red chile paste)
1 tablespoon toasted sesame oil
2 teaspoons sesame seeds
4 hamburger buns

1. For the burgers: In a large bowl, mix the ground beef, scallions, gochujang, soy sauce, garlic, ginger, sugar, sesame oil, and salt. Marinate at room temperature for 30 minutes, or cover and refrigerate for up to 24 hours. 2. Divide the meat into four portions and form them into round patties. Make a slight depression in the middle of each patty with your thumb to prevent them from puffing up into a dome shape while cooking. 3. Place the patties in a single layer in the air fryer basket. Set the air fryer to 350ºF (177ºC) for 10 minutes. 4. Meanwhile, for the gochujang mayonnaise: Stir together the mayonnaise, scallions, gochujang, sesame oil, and sesame seeds. 5. At the end of the cooking time, use a meat thermometer to ensure the burgers have reached an internal temperature of 160ºF / 71ºC (medium). 6. To serve, place the burgers on the buns and top with the mayonnaise.

Pork Loin Roast

Prep time: 30 minutes | Cook time: 55 minutes | Serves 6

1½ pounds (680 g) boneless pork loin roast, washed
1 teaspoon mustard seeds
1 teaspoon garlic powder
1 teaspoon porcini powder
1 teaspoon shallot powder
¾ teaspoon sea salt flakes
1 teaspoon red pepper flakes, crushed
2 dried sprigs thyme, crushed
2 tablespoons lime juice

1. Firstly, score the meat using a small knife; make sure to not cut too deep. 2. In a small-sized mixing dish, combine all seasonings in the order listed above; mix to combine well. 3. Massage the spice mix into the pork meat to evenly distribute. Drizzle with lemon juice. 4. Set the air fryer to 360°F (182°C). Place the pork in the air fryer basket; roast for 25 to 30 minutes. Pause the machine, check for doneness and cook for 25 minutes more.

Garlic Butter Steak Bites

Prep time: 5 minutes | Cook time: 16 minutes | Serves 3

Oil, for spraying
1 pound (454 g) boneless steak, cut into 1-inch pieces
2 tablespoons olive oil
1 teaspoon Worcestershire sauce
½ teaspoon granulated garlic
½ teaspoon salt
¼ teaspoon freshly ground black pepper

1. Preheat the air fryer to 400°F (204°C). Line the air fryer basket with parchment and spray lightly with oil. 2. In a medium bowl, combine the steak, olive oil, Worcestershire sauce, garlic, salt, and black pepper and toss until evenly coated. 3. Place the steak in a single layer in the prepared basket. You may have to work in batches, depending on the size of your air fryer. 4. Cook for 10 to 16 minutes, flipping every 3 to 4 minutes. The total cooking time will depend on the thickness of the meat and your preferred doneness. If you want it well done, it may take up to 5 additional minutes.

Sausage and Pork Meatballs

Prep time: 15 minutes | Cook time: 8 to 12 minutes | Serves 8

1 large egg
1 teaspoon gelatin
1 pound (454 g) ground pork
½ pound (227 g) Italian sausage, casings removed, crumbled
⅓ cup Parmesan cheese
¼ cup finely diced onion
1 tablespoon tomato paste
1 teaspoon minced garlic
1 teaspoon dried oregano
¼ teaspoon red pepper flakes
Sea salt and freshly ground black pepper, to taste
Keto-friendly marinara sauce, for serving

1. Beat the egg in a small bowl and sprinkle with the gelatin. Allow to sit for 5 minutes. 2. In a large bowl, combine the ground pork, sausage, Parmesan, onion, tomato paste, garlic, oregano, and red pepper flakes. Season with salt and black pepper. 3. Stir the gelatin mixture, then add it to the other ingredients and, using clean hands, mix to ensure that everything is well combined. Form into 1½-inch round meatballs. 4. Set the air fryer to 400°F (204°C). Place the meatballs in the air fryer basket in a single layer, cooking in batches as needed. Air fry for 5 minutes. Flip and cook for 3 to 7 minutes more, or until an instant-read thermometer reads 160°F (71°C).

Greek Pork with Tzatziki Sauce

Prep time: 30 minutes | Cook time: 50 minutes | Serves 4

Greek Pork:
2 pounds (907 g) pork sirloin roast
Salt and black pepper, to taste
1 teaspoon smoked paprika
½ teaspoon mustard seeds
½ teaspoon celery seeds
1 teaspoon fennel seeds
1 teaspoon Ancho chili powder
1 teaspoon turmeric powder
½ teaspoon ground ginger
2 tablespoons olive oil
2 cloves garlic, finely chopped
Tzatziki:
½ cucumber, finely chopped and squeezed
1 cup full-fat Greek yogurt
1 garlic clove, minced
1 tablespoon extra-virgin olive oil
1 teaspoon balsamic vinegar
1 teaspoon minced fresh dill
A pinch of salt

1. Toss all ingredients for Greek pork in a large mixing bowl. Toss until the meat is well coated. 2. Cook in the preheated air fryer at 360°F (182°C) for 30 minutes; turn over and cook another 20 minutes. 3. Meanwhile, prepare the tzatziki by mixing all the tzatziki ingredients. Place in your refrigerator until ready to use. 4. Serve the pork sirloin roast with the chilled tzatziki on the side. Enjoy!

Greek Lamb Pita Pockets

Prep time: 15 minutes | Cook time: 6 minutes | Serves 4

Dressing:
1 cup plain yogurt
1 tablespoon lemon juice
1 teaspoon dried dill weed, crushed
1 teaspoon ground oregano
½ teaspoon salt
Meatballs:
½ pound (227 g) ground lamb
1 tablespoon diced onion
1 teaspoon dried parsley
1 teaspoon dried dill weed, crushed
¼ teaspoon oregano
¼ teaspoon coriander
¼ teaspoon ground cumin
¼ teaspoon salt
4 pita halves
Suggested Toppings:
1 red onion, slivered
1 medium cucumber, deseeded, thinly sliced
Crumbled feta cheese
Sliced black olives
Chopped fresh peppers

1. Preheat the air fryer to 390°F (199°C). 2. Stir the dressing ingredients together in a small bowl and refrigerate while preparing lamb. 3. Combine all meatball ingredients in a large bowl and stir to distribute seasonings. 4. Shape meat mixture into 12 small meatballs, rounded or slightly flattened if you prefer. 5. Transfer the meatballs in the preheated air fryer and air fry for 6 minutes, until well done. Remove and drain on paper towels. 6. To serve, pile meatballs and the choice of toppings in pita pockets and drizzle with dressing.

Greek-Style Meatloaf

Prep time: 5 minutes | Cook time: 25 minutes | Serves 6

1 pound (454 g) lean ground beef
2 eggs
2 Roma tomatoes, diced
½ white onion, diced
½ cup whole wheat bread crumbs
1 teaspoon garlic powder
1 teaspoon dried oregano
1 teaspoon dried thyme
1 teaspoon salt
1 teaspoon black pepper
2 ounces (57 g) mozzarella cheese, shredded
1 tablespoon olive oil
Fresh chopped parsley, for garnish

1. Preheat the oven to 380°F(193°C). 2. In a large bowl, mix together the ground beef, eggs, tomatoes, onion, bread crumbs, garlic powder, oregano, thyme, salt, pepper, and cheese. 3. Form into a loaf, flattening to 1-inch thick. 4. Brush the top with olive oil, then place the meatloaf into the air fryer basket and cook for 25 minutes. 5. Remove from the air fryer and allow to rest for 5 minutes, before slicing and serving with a sprinkle of parsley.

Chinese-Style Baby Back Ribs

Prep time: 30 minutes | Cook time: 30 minutes | Serves 4

1 tablespoon toasted sesame oil
1 tablespoon fermented black bean paste
1 tablespoon Shaoxing wine (rice cooking wine)
1 tablespoon dark soy sauce
1 tablespoon agave nectar or honey
1 teaspoon minced garlic
1 teaspoon minced fresh ginger
1 (1½-pound / 680-g) slab baby back ribs, cut into individual ribs

1. In a large bowl, stir together the sesame oil, black bean paste, wine, soy sauce, agave, garlic, and ginger. Add the ribs and toss well to coat. Marinate at room temperature for 30 minutes, or cover and refrigerate for up to 24 hours. 2. Place the ribs in the air fryer basket; discard the marinade. Set the air fryer to 350°F (177°C) for 30 minutes.

Roast Beef with Horseradish Cream

Prep time: 5 minutes | Cook time: 35 to 45 minutes | Serves 6

2 pounds (907 g) beef roast top round or eye of round
1 tablespoon salt
2 teaspoons garlic powder
1 teaspoon freshly ground black pepper
1 teaspoon dried thyme
Horseradish Cream:
⅓ cup heavy cream
⅓ cup sour cream
⅓ cup prepared horseradish
2 teaspoons fresh lemon juice
Salt and freshly ground black pepper, to taste

1. Preheat the air fryer to 400°F (204°C). 2. Season the beef with the salt, garlic powder, black pepper, and thyme. Place the beef fat-side down in the basket of the air fryer and lightly coat with olive oil. Pausing halfway through the cooking time to turn the meat, air fry for 35 to 45 minutes, until a thermometer inserted into the thickest part indicates the desired doneness, 125°F (52°C) (rare) to 150°F (66°C) (medium). Let the beef rest for 10 minutes before slicing. 3. To make the horseradish cream: In a small bowl, combine the heavy cream, sour cream, horseradish, and lemon juice. Whisk until thoroughly combined. Season to taste with salt and freshly ground black pepper. Serve alongside the beef.

Sausage and Peppers

Prep time: 7 minutes | Cook time: 35 minutes | Serves 4

Oil, for spraying
2 pounds (907 g) hot or sweet Italian sausage links, cut into thick slices
4 large bell peppers of any color, seeded and cut into slices
1 onion, thinly sliced
1 tablespoon olive oil
1 tablespoon chopped fresh parsley
1 teaspoon dried oregano
1 teaspoon dried basil
1 teaspoon balsamic vinegar

1. Line the air fryer basket with parchment and spray lightly with oil. 2. In a large bowl, combine the sausage, bell peppers, and onion. 3. In a small bowl, whisk together the olive oil, parsley, oregano, basil, and balsamic vinegar. Pour the mixture over the sausage and peppers and toss until evenly coated. 4. Using a slotted spoon, transfer the mixture to the prepared basket, taking care to drain out as much excess liquid as possible. 5. Air fry at 350°F (177°C) for 20 minutes, stir, and cook for another 15 minutes, or until the sausage is browned and the juices run clear.

Lebanese Malfouf (Stuffed Cabbage Rolls)

Prep time: 15 minutes | Cook time: 33 minutes | Serves 4

1 head green cabbage
1 pound (454 g) lean ground beef
½ cup long-grain brown rice
4 garlic cloves, minced
1 teaspoon salt
½ teaspoon black pepper
1 teaspoon ground cinnamon
2 tablespoons chopped fresh mint
Juice of 1 lemon
Olive oil cooking spray
½ cup beef broth
1 tablespoon olive oil

1. Cut the cabbage in half and remove the core. Remove 12 of the larger leaves to use for the cabbage rolls. 2. Bring a large pot of salted water to a boil, then drop the cabbage leaves into the water, boiling them for 3 minutes. Remove from the water and set aside. 3. In a large bowl, combine the ground beef, rice, garlic, salt, pepper, cinnamon, mint, and lemon juice, and mix together until combined. Divide this mixture into 12 equal portions. 4. Preheat the air fryer to 360°F(182°C). Lightly coat a small casserole dish with olive oil cooking spray. 5. Place a cabbage leaf on a clean work surface. Place a spoonful of the beef mixture on one side of the leaf, leaving space on all other sides. Fold the two perpendicular sides inward and then roll forward, tucking tightly as rolled (similar to a burrito roll). Place the finished rolls into the baking dish, stacking them on top of each other if needed. 6. Pour the beef broth over the top of the cabbage rolls so that it soaks down between them, and then brush the tops with the olive oil. 7. Place the casserole dish into the air fryer basket and cook for 30 minutes.

Beef and Goat Cheese Stuffed Peppers

Prep time: 10 minutes | Cook time: 30 minutes | Serves 4

1 pound (454 g) lean ground beef
½ cup cooked brown rice
2 Roma tomatoes, diced
3 garlic cloves, minced
½ yellow onion, diced
2 tablespoons fresh oregano, chopped
1 teaspoon salt
½ teaspoon black pepper
¼ teaspoon ground allspice
2 bell peppers, halved and seeded
4 ounces (113 g) goat cheese
¼ cup fresh parsley, chopped

1. Preheat the air fryer to 360°F(182°C). 2. In a large bowl, combine the ground beef, rice, tomatoes, garlic, onion, oregano, salt, pepper, and allspice. Mix well. 3. Divide the beef mixture equally into the halved bell peppers and top each with about 1 ounce (28 g a quarter of the total) of the goat cheese. 4. Place the peppers into the air fryer basket in a single layer, making sure that they don't touch each other. Cook for 30 minutes. 5. Remove the peppers from the air fryer and top with fresh parsley before serving.

Beef and Broccoli Stir-Fry

Prep time: 30 minutes | Cook time: 20 minutes | Serves 2

½ pound (227 g) sirloin steak, thinly sliced
2 tablespoons coconut aminos
¼ teaspoon grated ginger
¼ teaspoon finely minced garlic
1 tablespoon coconut oil
2 cups broccoli florets
¼ teaspoon crushed red pepper
⅛ teaspoon xanthan gum
½ teaspoon sesame seeds

1. To marinate beef, place it into a large bowl or storage bag and add coconut aminos, ginger, garlic, and coconut oil. Allow to marinate for 1 hour in refrigerator. 2. Remove beef from marinade, reserving marinade, and place beef into the air fryer basket. 3. Adjust the temperature to 320°F (160°C) and air fry for 20 minutes. 4. After 10 minutes, add broccoli and sprinkle red pepper into the basket and shake. 5. Pour the marinade into a skillet over medium heat and bring to a boil, then reduce to simmer. Stir in xanthan gum and allow to thicken. 6. When done, quickly empty fryer basket into skillet and toss. Sprinkle with sesame seeds. Serve immediately.

Air Fried Beef Satay with Peanut Dipping Sauce

Prep time: 30 minutes | Cook time: 5 to 7 minutes | Serves 4

8 ounces (227 g) London broil, sliced into 8 strips
2 teaspoons curry powder
½ teaspoon kosher salt
Cooking spray
Peanut Dipping sauce:
2 tablespoons creamy peanut butter
1 tablespoon reduced-sodium soy sauce
2 teaspoons rice vinegar
1 teaspoon honey
1 teaspoon grated ginger
Special Equipment:
4 bamboo skewers, cut into halves and soaked in water for 20 minutes to keep them from burning while cooking

1. Preheat the air fryer to 360°F (182°C). Spritz the air fryer basket with cooking spray. 2. In a bowl, place the London broil strips and sprinkle with the curry powder and kosher salt to season. Thread the strips onto the soaked skewers. 3. Arrange the skewers in the prepared air fryer basket and spritz with cooking spray. Air fry for 5 to 7 minutes, or until the beef is well browned, turning halfway through. 4. In the meantime, stir together the peanut butter, soy sauce, rice vinegar, honey, and ginger in a bowl to make the dipping sauce. 5. Transfer the beef to the serving dishes and let rest for 5 minutes. Serve with the peanut dipping sauce on the side.

Beefy Poppers

Prep time: 15 minutes | Cook time: 15 minutes | Makes 8 poppers

8 medium jalapeño peppers, stemmed, halved, and seeded
1 (8-ounce / 227-g) package cream cheese (or Kite Hill brand cream cheese style spread for dairy-free), softened
2 pounds (907 g) ground beef
(85% lean)
1 teaspoon fine sea salt
½ teaspoon ground black pepper
8 slices thin-cut bacon
Fresh cilantro leaves, for garnish

1. Spray the air fryer basket with avocado oil. Preheat the air fryer to 400°F (204°C). 2. Stuff each jalapeño half with a few tablespoons of cream cheese. Place the halves back together again to form 8 jalapeños. 3. Season the ground beef with the salt and pepper and mix with your hands to incorporate. Flatten about ¼ pound (113 g) of ground beef in the palm of your hand and place a stuffed jalapeño in the center. Fold the beef around the jalapeño, forming an egg shape. Wrap the beef-covered jalapeño with a slice of bacon and secure it with a toothpick. 4. Place the jalapeños in the air fryer basket, leaving space between them (if you're using a smaller air fryer, work in batches if necessary), and air fry for 15 minutes, or until the beef is cooked through and the bacon is crispy. Garnish with cilantro before serving. 5. Store leftovers in an airtight container in the fridge for 3 days or in the freezer for up to a month. Reheat in a preheated 350°F (177°C) air fryer for 4 minutes, or until heated through and the bacon is crispy.

Rosemary Ribeye Steaks

Prep time: 10 minutes | Cook time: 15 minutes | Serves 2

¼ cup butter
1 clove garlic, minced
Salt and ground black pepper, to taste
1½ tablespoons balsamic vinegar
¼ cup rosemary, chopped
2 ribeye steaks

1. Melt the butter in a skillet over medium heat. Add the garlic and fry until fragrant. 2. Remove the skillet from the heat and add the salt, pepper, and vinegar. Allow it to cool. 3. Add the rosemary, then pour the mixture into a Ziploc bag. 4. Put the ribeye steaks in the bag and shake well, coating the meat well. Refrigerate for an hour, then allow to sit for a further twenty minutes. 5. Preheat the air fryer to 400°F (204°C). 6. Air fry the ribeye steaks for 15 minutes. 7. Take care when removing the steaks from the air fryer and plate up. 8. Serve immediately.

Kheema Burgers

Prep time: 15 minutes | Cook time: 12 minutes | Serves 4

Burgers:
1 pound (454 g) 85% lean ground beef or ground lamb
2 large eggs, lightly beaten
1 medium yellow onion, diced
¼ cup chopped fresh cilantro
1 tablespoon minced fresh ginger
3 cloves garlic, minced
2 teaspoons garam masala
1 teaspoon ground turmeric
½ teaspoon ground cinnamon
⅛ teaspoon ground cardamom
1 teaspoon kosher salt
1 teaspoon cayenne pepper
Raita Sauce:
1 cup grated cucumber
½ cup sour cream
¼ teaspoon kosher salt
¼ teaspoon black pepper
For Serving:
4 lettuce leaves, hamburger buns, or naan breads

1. For the burgers: In a large bowl, combine the ground beef, eggs, onion, cilantro, ginger, garlic, garam masala, turmeric, cinnamon, cardamom, salt, and cayenne. Gently mix until ingredients are thoroughly combined. 2. Divide the meat into four portions and form into round patties. Make a slight depression in the middle of each patty with your thumb to prevent them from puffing up into a dome shape while cooking. 3. Place the patties in the air fryer basket. Set the air fryer to 350ºF (177ºC) for 12 minutes. Use a meat thermometer to ensure the burgers have reached an internal temperature of 160ºF / 71ºC (for medium). 4. Meanwhile, for the sauce: In a small bowl, combine the cucumber, sour cream, salt, and pepper. 5. To serve: Place the burgers on the lettuce, buns, or naan and top with the sauce.

Asian Glazed Meatballs

Prep time: 15 minutes | Cook time: 10 minutes per batch | Serves 4 to 6

1 large shallot, finely chopped
2 cloves garlic, minced
1 tablespoon grated fresh ginger
2 teaspoons fresh thyme, finely chopped
1½ cups brown mushrooms, very finely chopped (a food processor works well here)
2 tablespoons soy sauce
Freshly ground black pepper, to taste
1 pound (454 g) ground beef
½ pound (227 g) ground pork
3 egg yolks
1 cup Thai sweet chili sauce (spring roll sauce)
¼ cup toasted sesame seeds
2 scallions, sliced

1. Combine the shallot, garlic, ginger, thyme, mushrooms, soy sauce, freshly ground black pepper, ground beef and pork, and egg yolks in a bowl and mix the ingredients together. Gently shape the mixture into 24 balls, about the size of a golf ball. 2. Preheat the air fryer to 380ºF (193ºC). 3. Working in batches, air fry the meatballs for 8 minutes, turning the meatballs over halfway through the cooking time. Drizzle some of the Thai sweet chili sauce on top of each meatball and return the basket to the air fryer, air frying for another 2 minutes. Reserve the remaining Thai sweet chili sauce for serving. 4. As soon as the meatballs are done, sprinkle with toasted sesame seeds and transfer them to a serving platter. Scatter the scallions around and serve warm.

London Broil with Herb Butter

Prep time: 30 minutes | Cook time: 20 to 25 minutes | Serves 4

1½ pounds (680 g) London broil top round steak
¼ cup olive oil
2 tablespoons balsamic vinegar
1 tablespoon Worcestershire sauce
4 cloves garlic, minced
Herb Butter:
6 tablespoons unsalted butter, softened
1 tablespoon chopped fresh parsley
¼ teaspoon salt
¼ teaspoon dried ground rosemary or thyme
¼ teaspoon garlic powder
Pinch of red pepper flakes

1. Place the beef in a gallon-size resealable bag. In a small bowl, whisk together the olive oil, balsamic vinegar, Worcestershire sauce, and garlic. Pour the marinade over the beef, massaging gently to coat, and seal the bag. Let sit at room temperature for an hour or refrigerate overnight. 2. To make the herb butter: In a small bowl, mix the butter with the parsley, salt, rosemary, garlic powder, and red pepper flakes until smooth. Cover and refrigerate until ready to use. 3. Preheat the air fryer to 400ºF (204ºC). 4. Remove the beef from the marinade (discard the marinade) and place the beef in the air fryer basket. Pausing halfway through the cooking time to turn the meat, air fry for 20 to 25 minutes, until a thermometer inserted into the thickest part indicates the desired doneness, 125ºF / 52ºC (rare) to 150ºF / 66ºC (medium). Let the beef rest for 10 minutes before slicing. Serve topped with the herb butter.

Lamb Chops with Horseradish Sauce

Prep time: 30 minutes | Cook time: 13 minutes | Serves 4

Lamb:
4 lamb loin chops
2 tablespoons vegetable oil
1 clove garlic, minced
½ teaspoon kosher salt
½ teaspoon black pepper
Horseradish Cream Sauce:
½ cup mayonnaise
1 tablespoon Dijon mustard
1 to 1½ tablespoons prepared horseradish
2 teaspoons sugar
Vegetable oil spray

1. For the lamb: Brush the lamb chops with the oil, rub with the garlic, and sprinkle with the salt and pepper. Marinate at room temperature for 30 minutes. 2. Meanwhile, for the sauce: In a medium bowl, combine the mayonnaise, mustard, horseradish, and sugar. Stir until well combined. Set aside half of the sauce for serving. 3. Spray the air fryer basket with vegetable oil spray and place the chops in the basket. Set the air fryer to 325ºF (163ºC) for 10 minutes, turning the chops halfway through the cooking time. 4. Remove the chops from the air fryer and add to the bowl with the horseradish sauce, turning to coat with the sauce. Place the chops back in the air fryer basket. Set the air fryer to 400ºF (204ºC) for 3 minutes. Use a meat thermometer to ensure the meat has reached an internal temperature of 145ºF (63ºC) (for medium-rare). 5. Serve the chops with the reserved horseradish sauce.

Tomato and Bacon Zoodles

Prep time: 10 minutes | Cook time: 15 to 22 minutes | Serves 2

8 ounces (227 g) sliced bacon
½ cup grape tomatoes
1 large zucchini, spiralized
½ cup ricotta cheese
¼ cup heavy (whipping) cream
⅓ cup finely grated Parmesan cheese, plus more for serving
Sea salt and freshly ground black pepper, to taste

1. Set the air fryer to 400ºF (204ºC). Arrange the bacon strips in a single layer in the air fryer basket—some overlapping is okay because the bacon will shrink, but cook in batches if needed. Air fry for 8 minutes. Flip the bacon strips and air fry for 2 to 5 minutes more, until the bacon is crisp. Remove the bacon from the air fryer. 2. Put the tomatoes in the air fryer basket and air fry for 3 to 5 minutes, until they are just starting to burst. Remove the tomatoes from the air fryer. 3. Put the zucchini noodles in the air fryer and air fry for 2 to 4 minutes, to the desired doneness. 4. Meanwhile, combine the ricotta, heavy cream, and Parmesan in a saucepan over medium-low heat. Cook, stirring often, until warm and combined. 5. Crumble the bacon. Place the zucchini, bacon, and tomatoes in a bowl. Toss with the ricotta sauce. Season with salt and pepper, and sprinkle with additional Parmesan.

Sichuan Cumin Lamb

Prep time: 30 minutes | Cook time: 10 minutes | Serves 4

Lamb:
2 tablespoons cumin seeds
1 teaspoon Sichuan peppercorns, or ½ teaspoon cayenne pepper
1 pound (454 g) lamb (preferably shoulder), cut into ½ by 2-inch pieces
2 tablespoons vegetable oil
1 tablespoon light soy sauce
1 tablespoon minced garlic
2 fresh red chiles, chopped
1 teaspoon kosher salt
¼ teaspoon sugar
For Serving:
2 scallions, chopped
Large handful of chopped fresh cilantro

1. For the lamb: In a dry skillet, toast the cumin seeds and Sichuan peppercorns (if using) over medium heat, stirring frequently, until fragrant, 1 to 2 minutes. Remove from the heat and let cool. Use a mortar and pestle to coarsely grind the toasted spices. 2. Use a fork to pierce the lamb pieces to allow the marinade to penetrate better. In a large bowl or resealable plastic bag, combine the toasted spices, vegetable oil, soy sauce, garlic, chiles, salt, and sugar. Add the lamb to the bag. Seal and massage to coat. Marinate at room temperature for 30 minutes. 3. Place the lamb in a single layer in the air fryer basket. Set the air fryer to 350ºF (177ºC) for 10 minutes. Use a meat thermometer to ensure the lamb has reached an internal temperature of 145ºF (63ºC) (medium-rare). 4. Transfer the lamb to a serving bowl. Stir in the scallions and cilantro and serve.

Chapter 6 Snacks and Appetizers

Chapter 6 Snacks and Appetizers

Garlicky and Cheesy French Fries

Prep time: 5 minutes | Cook time: 20 to 25 minutes | Serves 4

3 medium russet potatoes, rinsed, dried, and cut into thin wedges or classic fry shapes
2 tablespoons extra-virgin olive oil
1 tablespoon granulated garlic
⅓ cup grated Parmesan cheese
½ teaspoon salt
¼ teaspoon freshly ground black pepper
Cooking oil spray
2 tablespoons finely chopped fresh parsley (optional)

1. In a large bowl combine the potato wedges or fries and the olive oil. Toss to coat. 2. Sprinkle the potatoes with the granulated garlic, Parmesan cheese, salt, and pepper, and toss again. 3. Insert the crisper plate into the basket and the basket into the unit. Preheat the unit by selecting AIR FRY, setting the temperature to 400°F (204°C), and setting the time to 3 minutes. Select START/PAUSE to begin. 4. Once the unit is preheated, spray the crisper plate with cooking oil. Place the potatoes into the basket. 5. Select AIR FRY, set the temperature to 400°F (204°C), and set the time to 20 to 25 minutes. Select START/PAUSE to begin. 6. After about 10 minutes, remove the basket and shake it so the fries at the bottom come up to the top. Reinsert the basket to resume cooking. 7. When the cooking is complete, top the fries with the parsley (if using) and serve hot.

Golden Onion Rings

Prep time: 15 minutes | Cook time: 14 minutes per batch | Serves 4

1 large white onion, peeled and cut into ½ to ¾-inch-thick slices (about 2 cups)
½ cup 2% milk
1 cup whole-wheat pastry flour, or all-purpose flour
2 tablespoons cornstarch
¾ teaspoon sea salt, divided
½ teaspoon freshly ground black pepper, divided
¾ teaspoon granulated garlic, divided
1½ cups whole-grain bread crumbs, or gluten-free bread crumbs
Cooking oil spray (coconut, sunflower, or safflower)
Ketchup, for serving (optional)

1. Carefully separate the onion slices into rings—a gentle touch is important here. 2. Place the milk in a shallow bowl and set aside. 3. Make the first breading: In a medium bowl, stir together the flour, cornstarch, ¼ teaspoon of salt, ¼ teaspoon of pepper, and ¼ teaspoon of granulated garlic. Set aside. 4. Make the second breading: In a separate medium bowl, stir together the bread crumbs with the remaining ½ teaspoon of salt, the remaining ½ teaspoon of garlic, and the remaining ½ teaspoon of pepper. Set aside. 5. Insert the crisper plate into the basket and the basket into the unit. Preheat the unit by selecting AIR FRY, setting the temperature to 390°F (199°C), and setting the time to 3 minutes. Select START/PAUSE to begin. 6. Once the unit is preheated, spray the crisper plate and the basket with cooking oil. 7. To make the onion rings, dip one ring into the milk and into the first breading mixture. Dip the ring into the milk again and back into the first breading mixture, coating thoroughly. Dip the ring into the milk one last time and then into the second breading mixture, coating thoroughly. Gently lay the onion ring in the basket. Repeat with additional rings and, as you place them into the basket, do not overlap them too much. Once all the onion rings are in the basket, generously spray the tops with cooking oil. 8. Select AIR FRY, set the temperature to 390°F (199°C), and set the time to 14 minutes. Insert the basket into the unit. Select START/PAUSE to begin. 9. After 4 minutes, open the unit and spray the rings generously with cooking oil. Close the unit to resume cooking. After 3 minutes, remove the basket and spray the onion rings again. Remove the rings, turn them over, and place them back into the basket. Generously spray them again with oil. Reinsert the basket to resume cooking. After 4 minutes, generously spray the rings with oil one last time. Resume cooking for the remaining 3 minutes, or until the onion rings are very crunchy and brown. 10. When the cooking is complete, serve the hot rings with ketchup, or other sauce of choice.

Zucchini Fries with Roasted Garlic Aïoli

Prep time: 20 minutes | Cook time: 12 minutes | Serves 4

1 tablespoon vegetable oil
½ head green or savoy cabbage, finely shredded
Roasted Garlic Aïoli:
1 teaspoon roasted garlic
½ cup mayonnaise
2 tablespoons olive oil
Juice of ½ lemon
Salt and pepper, to taste
Zucchini Fries:
½ cup flour
2 eggs, beaten
1 cup seasoned bread crumbs
Salt and pepper, to taste
1 large zucchini, cut into ½-inch sticks
Olive oil

1. Make the aïoli: Combine the roasted garlic, mayonnaise, olive oil and lemon juice in a bowl and whisk well. Season the aïoli with salt and pepper to taste. 2. Prepare the zucchini fries. Create a dredging station with three shallow dishes. Place the flour in the first shallow dish and season well with salt and freshly ground black pepper. Put the beaten eggs in the second shallow dish. In the third shallow dish, combine the bread crumbs, salt and pepper. Dredge the zucchini sticks, coating with flour first, then dipping them into the eggs to coat, and finally tossing in bread crumbs. Shake the dish with the bread crumbs and pat the crumbs onto the zucchini sticks gently with your hands so they stick evenly. 3. Place the zucchini fries on a flat surface and let them sit at least 10 minutes before air frying to let them dry out a little. Preheat the air fryer to 400°F (204°C). 4. Spray the zucchini sticks with olive oil, and place them into the air fryer basket. You can air fry the zucchini in two layers, placing the second layer in the opposite direction to the first. Air fry for 12 minutes turning and rotating the fries halfway through the cooking time. Spray with additional oil when you turn them over. 5. Serve zucchini fries warm with the roasted garlic aïoli.

Taco-Spiced Chickpeas

Prep time: 5 minutes | Cook time: 17 minutes | Serves 3

Oil, for spraying
1 (15½-ounce / 439-g) can chickpeas, drained
1 teaspoon chili powder
½ teaspoon ground cumin
½ teaspoon salt
½ teaspoon granulated garlic
2 teaspoons lime juice

1. Line the air fryer basket with parchment and spray lightly with oil. Place the chickpeas in the prepared basket. 2. Air fry at 390°F (199°C) for 17 minutes, shaking or stirring the chickpeas and spraying lightly with oil every 5 to 7 minutes. 3. In a small bowl, mix together the chili powder, cumin, salt, and garlic. 4. When 2 to 3 minutes of cooking time remain, sprinkle half of the seasoning mix over the chickpeas. Finish cooking. 5. Transfer the chickpeas to a medium bowl and toss with the remaining seasoning mix and the lime juice. Serve immediately.

Peppery Chicken Meatballs

Prep time: 5 minutes | Cook time: 13 to 20 minutes | Makes 16 meatballs

2 teaspoons olive oil
¼ cup minced onion
¼ cup minced red bell pepper
2 vanilla wafers, crushed
1 egg white
½ teaspoon dried thyme
½ pound (227 g) ground chicken breast

1. Preheat the air fryer to 370°F (188°C). 2. In a baking pan, mix the olive oil, onion, and red bell pepper. Put the pan in the air fryer. Air fry for 3 to 5 minutes, or until the vegetables are tender. 3. In a medium bowl, mix the cooked vegetables, crushed wafers, egg white, and thyme until well combined 4. Mix in the chicken, gently but thoroughly, until everything is combined. 5. Form the mixture into 16 meatballs and place them in the air fryer basket. Air fry for 10 to 15 minutes, or until the meatballs reach an internal temperature of 165°F (74°C) on a meat thermometer. 6. Serve immediately.

Classic Spring Rolls

Prep time: 10 minutes | Cook time: 9 minutes | Makes 16 spring rolls

4 teaspoons toasted sesame oil
6 medium garlic cloves, minced or pressed
1 tablespoon grated peeled fresh ginger
2 cups thinly sliced shiitake mushrooms
4 cups chopped green cabbage
1 cup grated carrot
½ teaspoon sea salt
16 rice paper wrappers
Cooking oil spray (sunflower, safflower, or refined coconut)
Gluten-free sweet and sour sauce or Thai sweet chili sauce, for serving (optional)

1. Place a wok or sauté pan over medium heat until hot. 2. Add the sesame oil, garlic, ginger, mushrooms, cabbage, carrot, and salt. Cook for 3 to 4 minutes, stirring often, until the cabbage is lightly wilted. Remove the pan from the heat. 3. Gently run a rice paper under water. Lay it on a flat nonabsorbent surface. Place about ¼ cup of the cabbage filling in the middle. Once the wrapper is soft enough to roll, fold the bottom up over the filling, fold in the sides, and roll the wrapper all the way up. (Basically, make a tiny burrito.) 4. Repeat step 3 to make the remaining spring rolls until you have the number of spring rolls you want to cook right now (and the amount that will fit in the air fryer basket in a single layer without them touching each other). Refrigerate any leftover filling in an airtight container for about 1 week. 5. Insert the crisper plate into the basket and the basket into the unit. Preheat the unit by selecting AIR FRY, setting the temperature to 390°F (199°C), and setting the time to 3 minutes. Select START/PAUSE to begin. 6. Once the unit is preheated, spray the crisper plate and the basket with cooking oil. Place the spring rolls into the basket, leaving a little room between them so they don't stick to each other. Spray the top of each spring roll with cooking oil. 7. Select AIR FRY, set the temperature to 390°F (199°C), and set the time to 9 minutes. Select START/PAUSE to begin. 8. When the cooking is complete, the egg rolls should be crisp-ish and lightly browned. Serve immediately, plain or with a sauce of choice.

Crispy Cajun Dill Pickle Chips

Prep time: 5 minutes | Cook time: 10 minutes | Makes 16 slices

¼ cup all-purpose flour
½ cup panko bread crumbs
1 large egg, beaten
2 teaspoons Cajun seasoning
2 large dill pickles, sliced into 8 rounds each
Cooking spray

1. Preheat the air fryer to 390°F (199°C). 2. Place the all-purpose flour, panko bread crumbs, and egg into 3 separate shallow bowls, then stir the Cajun seasoning into the flour. 3. Dredge each pickle chip in the flour mixture, then the egg, and finally the bread crumbs. Shake off any excess, then place each coated pickle chip on a plate. 4. Spritz the air fryer basket with cooking spray, then place 8 pickle chips in the basket and air fry for 5 minutes, or until crispy and golden brown. Repeat this process with the remaining pickle chips. 5. Remove the chips and allow to slightly cool on a wire rack before serving.

Spicy Tortilla Chips

Prep time: 5 minutes | Cook time: 8 to 12 minutes | Serves 4

½ teaspoon ground cumin
½ teaspoon paprika
½ teaspoon chili powder
½ teaspoon salt
Pinch cayenne pepper
8 (6-inch) corn tortillas, each cut into 6 wedges
Cooking spray

1. Preheat the air fryer to 375°F (191°C). Lightly spritz the air fryer basket with cooking spray. 2. Stir together the cumin, paprika, chili powder, salt, and pepper in a small bowl. 3. Working in batches, arrange the tortilla wedges in the air fryer basket in a single layer. Lightly mist them with cooking spray. Sprinkle some seasoning mixture on top of the tortilla wedges. 4. Air fry for 4 to 6 minutes, shaking the basket halfway through, or until the chips are lightly browned and crunchy. 5. Repeat with the remaining tortilla wedges and seasoning mixture. 6. Let the tortilla chips cool for 5 minutes and serve.

Egg Roll Pizza Sticks

Prep time: 10 minutes | Cook time: 5 minutes | Serves 4

Olive oil
8 pieces reduced-fat string cheese
8 egg roll wrappers
24 slices turkey pepperoni
Marinara sauce, for dipping (optional)

1. Spray the air fryer basket lightly with olive oil. Fill a small bowl with water. 2. Place each egg roll wrapper diagonally on a work surface. It should look like a diamond. 3. Place 3 slices of turkey pepperoni in a vertical line down the center of the wrapper. 4. Place 1 Mozzarella cheese stick on top of the turkey pepperoni. 5. Fold the top and bottom corners of the egg roll wrapper over the cheese stick. 6. Fold the left corner over the cheese stick and roll the cheese stick up to resemble a spring roll. Dip a finger in the water and seal the edge of the roll 7. Repeat with the rest of the pizza sticks. 8. Place them in the air fryer basket in a single layer, making sure to leave a little space between each one. Lightly spray the pizza sticks with oil. You may need to cook these in batches. 9. Air fry at 375°F (191°C) until the pizza sticks are lightly browned and crispy, about 5 minutes. 10. These are best served hot while the cheese is melted. Accompany with a small bowl of marinara sauce, if desired.

Roasted Grape Dip

Prep time: 10 minutes | Cook time: 8 to 12 minutes | Serves 6

2 cups seedless red grapes, rinsed and patted dry
1 tablespoon apple cider vinegar
1 tablespoon honey
1 cup low-fat Greek yogurt
2 tablespoons 2% milk
2 tablespoons minced fresh basil

1. In the air fryer basket, sprinkle the grapes with the cider vinegar and drizzle with the honey. Toss to coat. Roast the grapes at 380°F (193°C) for 8 to 12 minutes, or until shriveled but still soft. Remove from the air fryer. 2. In a medium bowl, stir together the yogurt and milk. 3. Gently blend in the grapes and basil. Serve immediately, or cover and chill for 1 to 2 hours.

Greek Potato Skins with Olives and Feta

Prep time: 5 minutes | Cook time: 45 minutes | Serves 4

2 russet potatoes
3 tablespoons olive oil, divided, plus more for drizzling (optional)
1 teaspoon kosher salt, divided
¼ teaspoon black pepper
2 tablespoons fresh cilantro, chopped, plus more for serving
¼ cup Kalamata olives, diced
¼ cup crumbled feta
Chopped fresh parsley, for garnish (optional)

1. Preheat the air fryer to 380°F(193°C). 2. Using a fork, poke 2 to 3 holes in the potatoes, then coat each with about ½ tablespoon olive oil and ½ teaspoon salt. 3. Place the potatoes into the air fryer basket and cook for 30 minutes. 4. Remove the potatoes from the air fryer, and slice in half. Using a spoon, scoop out the flesh of the potatoes, leaving a ½-inch layer of potato inside the skins, and set the skins aside. 5. In a medium bowl, combine the scooped potato middles with the remaining 2 tablespoons of olive oil, ½ teaspoon of salt, black pepper, and cilantro. Mix until well combined. 6. Divide the potato filling into the now-empty potato skins, spreading it evenly over them. Top each potato with a tablespoon each of the olives and feta. 7. Place the loaded potato skins back into the air fryer and cook for 15 minutes. 8. Serve with additional chopped cilantro or parsley and a drizzle of olive oil, if desired.

Skinny Fries

Prep time: 10 minutes | Cook time: 15 minutes per batch | Serves 2

2 to 3 russet potatoes, peeled and cut into ¼-inch sticks
2 to 3 teaspoons olive or vegetable oil
Salt, to taste

1. Cut the potatoes into ¼-inch strips. (A mandolin with a julienne blade is really helpful here.) Rinse the potatoes with cold water several times and let them soak in cold water for at least 10 minutes or as long as overnight. 2. Preheat the air fryer to 380°F (193°C). 3. Drain and dry the potato sticks really well, using a clean kitchen towel. Toss the fries with the oil in a bowl and then air fry the fries in two batches at 380°F (193°C) for 15 minutes, shaking the basket a couple of times while they cook. 4. Add the first batch of French fries back into the air fryer basket with the finishing batch and let everything warm through for a few minutes. As soon as the fries are done, season them with salt and transfer to a plate or basket. Serve them warm with ketchup or your favorite dip.

Mozzarella Arancini

Prep time: 5 minutes | Cook time: 8 to 11 minutes | Makes 16 arancini

2 cups cooked rice, cooled
2 eggs, beaten
1½ cups panko bread crumbs, divided
½ cup grated Parmesan cheese
2 tablespoons minced fresh basil
16 ¾-inch cubes Mozzarella cheese
2 tablespoons olive oil

1. Preheat the air fryer to 400°F (204°C). 2. In a medium bowl, combine the rice, eggs, ½ cup of the bread crumbs, Parmesan cheese, and basil. Form this mixture into 16 1½-inch balls. 3. Poke a hole in each of the balls with your finger and insert a Mozzarella cube. Form the rice mixture firmly around the cheese. 4. On a shallow plate, combine the remaining 1 cup of the bread crumbs with the olive oil and mix well. Roll the rice balls in the bread crumbs to coat. 5. Air fry the arancini in batches for 8 to 11 minutes or until golden brown. 6. Serve hot.

Garlic-Roasted Tomatoes and Olives

Prep time: 5 minutes | Cook time: 20 minutes | Serves 6

2 cups cherry tomatoes
4 garlic cloves, roughly chopped
½ red onion, roughly chopped
1 cup black olives
1 cup green olives
1 tablespoon fresh basil, minced
1 tablespoon fresh oregano, minced
2 tablespoons olive oil
¼ to ½ teaspoon salt

1. Preheat the air fryer to 380°F(193°C). 2. In a large bowl, combine all of the ingredients and toss together so that the tomatoes and olives are coated well with the olive oil and herbs. 3. Pour the mixture into the air fryer basket, and roast for 10 minutes. Stir the mixture well, then continue roasting for an additional 10 minutes. 4. Remove from the air fryer, transfer to a serving bowl, and enjoy.

Stuffed Figs with Goat Cheese and Honey

Prep time: 5 minutes | Cook time: 10 minutes | Serves 4

8 fresh figs
2 ounces (57 g) goat cheese
¼ teaspoon ground cinnamon
1 tablespoon honey, plus more for serving
1 tablespoon olive oil

1. Preheat the air fryer to 360°F(182°C). 2. Cut the stem off of each fig. 3. Cut an X into the top of each fig, cutting halfway down the fig. Leave the base intact. 4. In a small bowl, mix together the goat cheese, cinnamon, and honey. 5. Spoon the goat cheese mixture into the cavity of each fig. 6. Place the figs in a single layer in the air fryer basket. Drizzle the olive oil over top of the figs and roast for 10 minutes. 7. Serve with an additional drizzle of honey.

Caramelized Onion Dip

Prep time: 5 minutes | Cook time: 30 minutes | Serves 8 to 10

1 tablespoon butter
1 medium yellow onion, halved and thinly sliced
¼ teaspoon kosher salt, plus additional for seasoning
4 ounces (113 g) cream cheese, softened
½ cup sour cream
¼ teaspoon onion powder
1 tablespoon chopped fresh chives
Black pepper, to taste
Thick-cut potato chips or vegetable chips

1. Place the butter in a baking pan. Place the pan in the air fryer basket. Set the air fryer to 200°F (93°C) for 1 minute, or until the butter is melted. Add the onions and salt to the pan. 2. Set the air fryer to 200°F (93°C) for 15 minutes, or until onions are softened. Set the air fryer to 375°F (191°C) for 15 minutes, until onions are a deep golden brown, stirring two or three times during the cooking time. Let cool completely. 3. In a medium bowl, stir together the cooked onions, cream cheese, sour cream, onion powder, and chives. Season with salt and pepper. Cover and refrigerate for 2 hours to allow the flavors to blend. 4. Serve the dip with potato chips or vegetable chips.

Kale Chips with Tex-Mex Dip

Prep time: 10 minutes | Cook time: 5 to 6 minutes | Serves 8

1 cup Greek yogurt
1 tablespoon chili powder
⅓ cup low-sodium salsa, well drained
1 bunch curly kale
1 teaspoon olive oil
¼ teaspoon coarse sea salt

1. In a small bowl, combine the yogurt, chili powder, and drained salsa; refrigerate. 2. Rinse the kale thoroughly, and pat dry. Remove the stems and ribs from the kale, using a sharp knife. Cut or tear the leaves into 3-inch pieces. 3. Toss the kale with the olive oil in a large bowl. 4. Air fry the kale in small batches at 390°F (199°C) until the leaves are crisp. This should take 5 to 6 minutes. Shake the basket once during cooking time. 5. As you remove the kale chips, sprinkle them with a bit of the sea salt. 6. When all of the kale chips are done, serve with the dip.

Jalapeño Poppers

Prep time: 10 minutes | Cook time: 20 minutes | Serves 4

Oil, for spraying
8 ounces (227 g) cream cheese
¾ cup gluten-free bread crumbs, divided
2 tablespoons chopped fresh parsley
½ teaspoon granulated garlic
½ teaspoon salt
10 jalapeño peppers, halved and seeded

1. Line the air fryer basket with parchment and spray lightly with oil. 2. In a medium bowl, mix together the cream cheese, half of the bread crumbs, the parsley, garlic, and salt. 3. Spoon the mixture into the jalapeño halves. Gently press the stuffed jalapeños in the remaining bread crumbs. 4. Place the stuffed jalapeños in the prepared basket. 5. Air fry at 370°F (188°C) for 20 minutes, or until the cheese is melted and the bread crumbs are crisp and golden brown.

Asian Five-Spice Wings

Prep time: 30 minutes | Cook time: 13 to 15 minutes | Serves 4

2 pounds (907 g) chicken wings
½ cup Asian-style salad dressing
2 tablespoons Chinese five-spice powder

1. Cut off wing tips and discard or freeze for stock. Cut remaining wing pieces in two at the joint. 2. Place wing pieces in a large sealable plastic bag. Pour in the Asian dressing, seal bag, and massage the marinade into the wings until well coated. Refrigerate for at least an hour. 3. Remove wings from bag, drain off excess marinade, and place wings in air fryer basket. 4. Air fry at 360°F (182°C) for 13 to 15 minutes or until juices run clear. About halfway through cooking time, shake the basket or stir wings for more even cooking. 5. Transfer cooked wings to plate in a single layer. Sprinkle half of the Chinese five-spice powder on the wings, turn, and sprinkle other side with remaining seasoning.

Onion Pakoras

Prep time: 30 minutes | Cook time: 10 minutes per batch | Serves 2

2 medium yellow or white onions, sliced (2 cups)
½ cup chopped fresh cilantro
2 tablespoons vegetable oil
1 tablespoon chickpea flour
1 tablespoon rice flour, or 2 tablespoons chickpea flour
1 teaspoon ground turmeric
1 teaspoon cumin seeds
1 teaspoon kosher salt
½ teaspoon cayenne pepper
Vegetable oil spray

1. In a large bowl, combine the onions, cilantro, oil, chickpea flour, rice flour, turmeric, cumin seeds, salt, and cayenne. Stir to combine. Cover and let stand for 30 minutes or up to overnight. (This allows the onions to release moisture, creating a batter.) Mix well before using. 2. Spray the air fryer basket generously with vegetable oil spray. Drop half of the batter in 6 heaping tablespoons into the basket. Set the air fryer to 350°F (177°C) for 8 minutes. Carefully turn the pakoras over and spray with oil spray. Set the air fryer for 2 minutes, or until the batter is cooked through and crisp. 3. Repeat with remaining batter to make 6 more pakoras, checking at 6 minutes for doneness. Serve hot.

Lemon-Pepper Chicken Drumsticks

Prep time: 30 minutes | Cook time: 30 minutes | Serves 2

2 teaspoons freshly ground coarse black pepper
1 teaspoon baking powder
½ teaspoon garlic powder
4 chicken drumsticks (4 ounces / 113 g each)
Kosher salt, to taste
1 lemon

1. In a small bowl, stir together the pepper, baking powder, and garlic powder. Place the drumsticks on a plate and sprinkle evenly with the baking powder mixture, turning the drumsticks so they're well coated. Let the drumsticks stand in the refrigerator for at least 1 hour or up to overnight. 2. Sprinkle the drumsticks with salt, then transfer them to the air fryer, standing them bone-end up and leaning against the wall of the air fryer basket. Air fry at 375°F (191°C) until cooked through and crisp on the outside, about 30 minutes. 3. Transfer the drumsticks to a serving platter and finely grate the zest of the lemon over them while they're hot. Cut the lemon into wedges and serve with the warm drumsticks.

Grilled Ham and Cheese on Raisin Bread

Prep time: 5 minutes | Cook time: 10 minutes | Serves 1

2 slices raisin bread
2 tablespoons butter, softened
2 teaspoons honey mustard
3 slices thinly sliced honey ham (about 3 ounces / 85 g)
4 slices Muenster cheese (about 3 ounces / 85 g)
2 toothpicks

1. Preheat the air fryer to 370°F (188°C). 2. Spread the softened butter on one side of both slices of raisin bread and place the bread, buttered side down on the counter. Spread the honey mustard on the other side of each slice of bread. Layer 2 slices of cheese, the ham and the remaining 2 slices of cheese on one slice of bread and top with the other slice of bread. Remember to leave the buttered side of the bread on the outside. 3. Transfer the sandwich to the air fryer basket and secure the sandwich with toothpicks. 4. Air fry for 5 minutes. Flip the sandwich over, remove the toothpicks and air fry for another 5 minutes. Cut the sandwich in half and enjoy!

Lemon Shrimp with Garlic Olive Oil

Prep time: 5 minutes | Cook time: 6 minutes | Serves 4

1 pound (454 g) medium shrimp, cleaned and deveined
¼ cup plus 2 tablespoons olive oil, divided
Juice of ½ lemon
3 garlic cloves, minced and divided
½ teaspoon salt
¼ teaspoon red pepper flakes
Lemon wedges, for serving (optional)
Marinara sauce, for dipping (optional)

1. Preheat the air fryer to 380°F (193°C). 2. In a large bowl, combine the shrimp with 2 tablespoons of the olive oil, as well as the lemon juice, ⅓ of the minced garlic, salt, and red pepper flakes. Toss to coat the shrimp well. 3. In a small ramekin, combine the remaining ¼ cup of olive oil and the remaining minced garlic. 4. Tear off a 12-by-12-inch sheet of aluminum foil. Pour the shrimp into the center of the foil, then fold the sides up and crimp the edges so that it forms an aluminum foil bowl that is open on top. Place this packet into the air fryer basket. 5. Roast the shrimp for 4 minutes, then open the air fryer and place the ramekin with oil and garlic in the basket beside the shrimp packet. Cook for 2 more minutes. 6. Transfer the shrimp on a serving plate or platter with the ramekin of garlic olive oil on the side for dipping. You may also serve with lemon wedges and marinara sauce, if desired.

Cheesy Hash Brown Bruschetta

Prep time: 5 minutes | Cook time: 6 to 8 minutes | Serves 4

4 frozen hash brown patties
1 tablespoon olive oil
⅓ cup chopped cherry tomatoes
3 tablespoons diced fresh Mozzarella
2 tablespoons grated Parmesan cheese
1 tablespoon balsamic vinegar
1 tablespoon minced fresh basil

1. Preheat the air fryer to 400°F (204°C). 2. Place the hash brown patties in the air fryer in a single layer. Air fry for 6 to 8 minutes, or until the potatoes are crisp, hot, and golden brown. 3. Meanwhile, combine the olive oil, tomatoes, Mozzarella, Parmesan, vinegar, and basil in a small bowl. 4. When the potatoes are done, carefully remove from the basket and arrange on a serving plate. Top with the tomato mixture and serve.

Pickle Chips

Prep time: 30 minutes | Cook time: 12 minutes | Serves 4

Oil, for spraying
2 cups sliced dill or sweet pickles, drained
1 cup buttermilk
2 cups all-purpose flour
2 large eggs, beaten
2 cups panko bread crumbs
¼ teaspoon salt

1. Line the air fryer basket with parchment and spray lightly with oil. 2. In a shallow bowl, combine the pickles and buttermilk and let soak for at least 1 hour, then drain. 3. Place the flour, beaten eggs, and bread crumbs in separate bowls. 4. Coat each pickle chip lightly in the flour, dip in the eggs, and dredge in the bread crumbs. Be sure each one is evenly coated. 5. Place the pickle chips in the prepared basket, sprinkle with the salt, and spray lightly with oil. You may need to work in batches, depending on the size of your air fryer. 6. Air fry at 390°F (199°C) for 5 minutes, flip, and cook for another 5 to 7 minutes, or until crispy. Serve hot.

Chapter 7 Vegetables and Sides

Chapter 7 Vegetables and Sides

Spiced Butternut Squash

Prep time: 10 minutes | Cook time: 15 minutes | Serves 4

4 cups 1-inch-cubed butternut squash
2 tablespoons vegetable oil
1 to 2 tablespoons brown sugar
1 teaspoon Chinese five-spice powder

1. In a medium bowl, combine the squash, oil, sugar, and five-spice powder. Toss to coat. 2. Place the squash in the air fryer basket. Set the air fryer to 400°F (204°C) for 15 minutes or until tender.

Baked Jalapeño and Cheese Cauliflower Mash

Prep time: 10 minutes | Cook time: 15 minutes | Serves 6

1 (12-ounce / 340-g) steamer bag cauliflower florets, cooked according to package instructions
2 tablespoons salted butter, softened
2 ounces (57 g) cream cheese, softened
½ cup shredded sharp Cheddar cheese
¼ cup pickled jalapeños
½ teaspoon salt
¼ teaspoon ground black pepper

1. Place cooked cauliflower into a food processor with remaining ingredients. Pulse twenty times until cauliflower is smooth and all ingredients are combined. 2. Spoon mash into an ungreased round nonstick baking dish. Place dish into air fryer basket. Adjust the temperature to 380°F (193°C) and cook for 15 minutes. The top will be golden brown when done. Serve warm.

Garlic and Thyme Tomatoes

Prep time: 10 minutes | Cook time: 15 minutes | Serves 2 to 4

4 Roma tomatoes
1 tablespoon olive oil
Salt and freshly ground black pepper, to taste
1 clove garlic, minced
½ teaspoon dried thyme

1. Preheat the air fryer to 390°F (199°C). 2. Cut the tomatoes in half and scoop out the seeds and any pithy parts with your fingers. Place the tomatoes in a bowl and toss with the olive oil, salt, pepper, garlic and thyme. 3. Transfer the tomatoes to the air fryer, cut side up. Air fry for 15 minutes. The edges should just start to brown. Let the tomatoes cool to an edible temperature for a few minutes and then use in pastas, on top of crostini, or as an accompaniment to any poultry, meat or fish.

Green Bean Casserole

Prep time: 10 minutes | Cook time: 20 minutes | Serves 4

1 pound (454 g) fresh green beans, ends trimmed, strings removed, and chopped into 2-inch pieces
1 (8-ounce / 227-g) package sliced brown mushrooms
½ onion, sliced
1 clove garlic, minced
1 tablespoon olive oil
½ teaspoon salt
¼ teaspoon freshly ground black pepper
4 ounces (113 g) cream cheese
½ cup chicken stock
¼ teaspoon ground nutmeg
½ cup grated Cheddar cheese

1. Preheat the air fryer to 400°F (204°C). Coat a casserole dish with olive oil and set aside. 2. In a large bowl, combine the green beans, mushrooms, onion, garlic, olive oil, salt, and pepper. Toss until the vegetables are thoroughly coated with the oil and seasonings. 3. Transfer the mixture to the air fryer basket. Pausing halfway through the cooking time to shake the basket, air fry for 10 minutes until tender. 4. While the vegetables are cooking, in a 2-cup glass measuring cup, warm the cream cheese and chicken stock in the microwave on high for 1 to 2 minutes until the cream cheese is melted. Add the nutmeg and whisk until smooth. 5. Transfer the vegetables to the prepared casserole dish and pour the cream cheese mixture over the top. Top with the Cheddar cheese. Air fry for another 10 minutes until the cheese is melted and beginning to brown.

Sausage-Stuffed Mushroom Caps

Prep time: 10 minutes | Cook time: 8 minutes | Serves 2

6 large portobello mushroom caps
½ pound (227 g) Italian sausage
¼ cup chopped onion
2 tablespoons blanched finely ground almond flour
¼ cup grated Parmesan cheese
1 teaspoon minced fresh garlic

1. Use a spoon to hollow out each mushroom cap, reserving scrapings. 2. In a medium skillet over medium heat, brown the sausage about 10 minutes or until fully cooked and no pink remains. Drain and then add reserved mushroom scrapings, onion, almond flour, Parmesan, and garlic. Gently fold ingredients together and continue cooking an additional minute, then remove from heat. 3. Evenly spoon the mixture into mushroom caps and place the caps into a 6-inch round pan. Place pan into the air fryer basket. 4. Adjust the temperature to 375°F (191°C) and set the timer for 8 minutes. 5. When finished cooking, the tops will be browned and bubbling. Serve warm.

Garlic Herb Radishes

Prep time: 10 minutes | Cook time: 10 minutes | Serves 4

1 pound (454 g) radishes
2 tablespoons unsalted butter, melted
½ teaspoon garlic powder
½ teaspoon dried parsley
¼ teaspoon dried oregano
¼ teaspoon ground black pepper

1. Remove roots from radishes and cut into quarters. 2. In a small bowl, add butter and seasonings. Toss the radishes in the herb butter and place into the air fryer basket. 3. Adjust the temperature to 350°F (177°C) and set the timer for 10 minutes. 4. Halfway through the cooking time, toss the radishes in the air fryer basket. Continue cooking until edges begin to turn brown. 5. Serve warm.

Butternut Squash Croquettes

Prep time: 5 minutes | Cook time: 17 minutes | Serves 4

⅓ butternut squash, peeled and grated
⅓ cup all-purpose flour
2 eggs, whisked
4 cloves garlic, minced
1½ tablespoons olive oil
1 teaspoon fine sea salt
⅓ teaspoon freshly ground black pepper, or more to taste
⅓ teaspoon dried sage
A pinch of ground allspice

1. Preheat the air fryer to 345°F (174°C). Line the air fryer basket with parchment paper. 2. In a mixing bowl, stir together all the ingredients until well combined. 3. Make the squash croquettes: Use a small cookie scoop to drop tablespoonfuls of the squash mixture onto a lightly floured surface and shape into balls with your hands. Transfer them to the air fryer basket. 4. Air fry for 17 minutes until the squash croquettes are golden brown. 5. Remove from the basket to a plate and serve warm.

Air-Fried Okra

Prep time: 10 minutes | Cook time: 10 minutes | Serves 4

1 egg
½ cup almond milk
½ cup crushed pork rinds
¼ cup grated Parmesan cheese
¼ cup almond flour
1 teaspoon garlic powder
¼ teaspoon freshly ground black pepper
½ pound (227 g) fresh okra, stems removed and chopped into 1-inch slices

1. Preheat the air fryer to 400°F (204°C). 2. In a shallow bowl, whisk together the egg and milk. 3. In a second shallow bowl, combine the pork rinds, Parmesan, almond flour, garlic powder, and black pepper. 4. Working with a few slices at a time, dip the okra into the egg mixture followed by the crumb mixture. Press lightly to ensure an even coating. 5. Working in batches if necessary, arrange the okra in a single layer in the air fryer basket and spray lightly with olive oil. Pausing halfway through the cooking time to turn the okra, air fry for 10 minutes until tender and golden brown. Serve warm.

Glazed Sweet Potato Bites

Prep time: 10 minutes | Cook time: 25 minutes | Serves 4

Oil, for spraying
3 medium sweet potatoes, peeled and cut into 1-inch pieces
2 tablespoons honey
1 tablespoon olive oil
2 teaspoons ground cinnamon

1. Line the air fryer basket with parchment and spray lightly with oil. 2. In a large bowl, toss together the sweet potatoes, honey, olive oil, and cinnamon until evenly coated. 3. Place the potatoes in the prepared basket. 4. Air fry at 400°F (204°C) for 20 to 25 minutes, or until crispy and easily pierced with a fork.

Cheesy Cauliflower Tots

Prep time: 15 minutes | Cook time: 12 minutes | Makes 16 tots

1 large head cauliflower
1 cup shredded Mozzarella cheese
½ cup grated Parmesan cheese
1 large egg
¼ teaspoon garlic powder
¼ teaspoon dried parsley
⅛ teaspoon onion powder

1. On the stovetop, fill a large pot with 2 cups water and place a steamer in the pan. Bring water to a boil. Cut the cauliflower into florets and place on steamer basket. Cover pot with lid. 2. Allow cauliflower to steam 7 minutes until fork tender. Remove from steamer basket and place into cheesecloth or clean kitchen towel and let cool. Squeeze over sink to remove as much excess moisture as possible. The mixture will be too soft to form into tots if not all the moisture is removed. Mash with a fork to a smooth consistency. 3. Put the cauliflower into a large mixing bowl and add Mozzarella, Parmesan, egg, garlic powder, parsley, and onion powder. Stir until fully combined. The mixture should be wet but easy to mold. 4. Take 2 tablespoons of the mixture and roll into tot shape. Repeat with remaining mixture. Place into the air fryer basket. 5. Adjust the temperature to 320°F (160°C) and set the timer for 12 minutes. 6. Turn tots halfway through the cooking time. Cauliflower tots should be golden when fully cooked. Serve warm.

Sweet and Crispy Roasted Pearl Onions

Prep time: 5 minutes | Cook time: 18 minutes | Serves 3

1 (14½-ounce / 411-g) package frozen pearl onions (do not thaw)
2 tablespoons extra-virgin olive oil
2 tablespoons balsamic vinegar
2 teaspoons finely chopped fresh rosemary
½ teaspoon kosher salt
¼ teaspoon black pepper

1. In a medium bowl, combine the onions, olive oil, vinegar, rosemary, salt, and pepper until well coated. 2. Transfer the onions to the air fryer basket. Set the air fryer to 400°F (204°C) for 18 minutes, or until the onions are tender and lightly charred, stirring once or twice during the cooking time.

Garlic-Parmesan Jícama Fries

Prep time: 10 minutes | Cook time: 25 to 35 minutes | Serves 4

1 medium jícama, peeled
1 tablespoon avocado oil
¼ cup (4 tablespoons) unsalted butter
1 tablespoon minced garlic
¾ teaspoon chopped dried rosemary
¾ teaspoon sea salt
½ teaspoon freshly ground black pepper
⅓ cup grated Parmesan cheese
Chopped fresh parsley, for garnish
Maldon sea salt, for garnish

1. Using a spiralizer or julienne peeler, cut the jícama into shoestrings, then cut them into 3-inch-long sticks. 2. Bring a large pot of water to boil. Add the jícama and cook for about 10 minutes. Drain and dry on paper towels. Transfer to a medium bowl and toss with the oil. 3. Set the air fryer to 400°F (204°C). Arrange the jícama in a single layer in the basket, working in batches if necessary. Air fry for 15 to 25 minutes, checking at intervals, until tender and golden brown. 4. While the fries cook, melt the butter over medium-high heat. Add the garlic, rosemary, salt, and pepper. Cook for about 1 minute. 5. Toss the fries with the garlic butter. Top with the Parmesan cheese, and sprinkle with parsley and Maldon sea salt.

Roasted Potatoes and Asparagus

Prep time: 5 minutes | Cook time: 23 minutes | Serves 4

4 medium potatoes
1 bunch asparagus
⅓ cup cottage cheese
⅓ cup low-fat crème fraiche
1 tablespoon wholegrain mustard
Salt and pepper, to taste
Cooking spray

1. Preheat the air fryer to 390°F (199°C). Spritz the air fryer basket with cooking spray. 2. Place the potatoes in the basket. Air fry the potatoes for 20 minutes. 3. Boil the asparagus in salted water for 3 minutes. 4. Remove the potatoes and mash them with rest of ingredients. Sprinkle with salt and pepper. 5. Serve immediately.

Breaded Green Tomatoes

Prep time: 15 minutes | Cook time: 30 minutes | Serves 4

½ cup all-purpose flour
2 eggs
½ cup yellow cornmeal
½ cup panko bread crumbs
1 teaspoon garlic powder
Salt and freshly ground black pepper, to taste
2 green tomatoes, cut into ½-inch-thick rounds
Cooking oil spray

1. Place the flour in a small bowl. 2. In another small bowl, beat the eggs. 3. In a third small bowl, stir together the cornmeal, panko, and garlic powder. Season with salt and pepper. 4. Dip each tomato slice into the flour, the egg, and finally the cornmeal mixture to coat. 5. Insert the crisper plate into the basket and the basket into the unit. Preheat the unit by selecting AIR FRY, setting the temperature to 400°F (204°C), and setting the time to 3 minutes. Select START/PAUSE to begin. 6. Once the unit is preheated, spray the crisper plate and the basket with cooking oil. Working in batches, place the tomato slices in the air fryer in a single layer. Do not stack them. Spray the tomato slices with the cooking oil. 7. Select AIR FRY, set the temperature to 400°F (204°C), and set the time to 10 minutes. Select START/PAUSE to begin. 8. After 5 minutes, use tongs to flip the tomatoes. Resume cooking for 4 to 5 minutes, or until crisp. 9. When the cooking is complete, transfer the fried green tomatoes to a plate. Repeat steps 6, 7, and 8 for the remaining tomatoes.

Chermoula-Roasted Beets

Prep time: 15 minutes | Cook time: 25 minutes | Serves 4

Chermoula:
1 cup packed fresh cilantro leaves
½ cup packed fresh parsley leaves
6 cloves garlic, peeled
2 teaspoons smoked paprika
2 teaspoons ground cumin
1 teaspoon ground coriander
½ to 1 teaspoon cayenne pepper
Pinch crushed saffron (optional)
½ cup extra-virgin olive oil
Kosher salt, to taste
Beets:
3 medium beets, trimmed, peeled, and cut into 1-inch chunks
2 tablespoons chopped fresh cilantro
2 tablespoons chopped fresh parsley

1. For the chermoula: In a food processor, combine the cilantro, parsley, garlic, paprika, cumin, coriander, and cayenne. Pulse until coarsely chopped. Add the saffron, if using, and process until combined. With the food processor running, slowly add the olive oil in a steady stream; process until the sauce is uniform. Season to taste with salt. 2. For the beets: In a large bowl, drizzle the beets with ½ cup of the chermoula, or enough to coat. Arrange the beets in the air fryer basket. Set the air fryer to 375°F (191°C) for 25 to minutes, or until the beets are tender. 3. Transfer the beets to a serving platter. Sprinkle with chopped cilantro and parsley and serve.

Asparagus Fries

Prep time: 15 minutes | Cook time: 5 to 7 minutes per batch | Serves 4

12 ounces (340 g) fresh asparagus spears with tough ends trimmed off
2 egg whites
¼ cup water
¾ cup panko bread crumbs
¼ cup grated Parmesan cheese, plus 2 tablespoons
¼ teaspoon salt
Oil for misting or cooking spray

1. Preheat the air fryer to 390°F (199°C). 2. In a shallow dish, beat egg whites and water until slightly foamy. 3. In another shallow dish, combine panko, Parmesan, and salt. 4. Dip asparagus spears in egg, then roll in crumbs. Spray with oil or cooking spray. 5. Place a layer of asparagus in air fryer basket, leaving just a little space in between each spear. Stack another layer on top, crosswise. Air fry at 390°F (199°C) for 5 to 7 minutes, until crispy and golden brown. 6. Repeat to cook remaining asparagus.

Sesame-Ginger Broccoli

Prep time: 10 minutes | Cook time: 15 minutes | Serves 4

3 tablespoons toasted sesame oil
2 teaspoons sesame seeds
1 tablespoon chili-garlic sauce
2 teaspoons minced fresh ginger
½ teaspoon kosher salt
½ teaspoon black pepper
1 (16-ounce / 454-g) package frozen broccoli florets (do not thaw)

1. In a large bowl, combine the sesame oil, sesame seeds, chili-garlic sauce, ginger, salt, and pepper. Stir until well combined. Add the broccoli and toss until well coated. 2. Arrange the broccoli in the air fryer basket. Set the air fryer to 325ºF (163ºC) for 15 minutes, or until the broccoli is crisp, tender, and the edges are lightly browned, gently tossing halfway through the cooking time.

Broccoli Tots

Prep time: 15 minutes | Cook time: 10 minutes | Makes 24 tots

2 cups broccoli florets (about ½ pound / 227 g broccoli crowns)
1 egg, beaten
⅛ teaspoon onion powder
¼ teaspoon salt
⅛ teaspoon pepper
2 tablespoons grated Parmesan cheese
¼ cup panko bread crumbs
Oil for misting

1. Steam broccoli for 2 minutes. Rinse in cold water, drain well, and chop finely. 2. In a large bowl, mix broccoli with all other ingredients except the oil. 3. Scoop out small portions of mixture and shape into 24 tots. Lay them on a cookie sheet or wax paper as you work. 4. Spray tots with oil and place in air fryer basket in single layer. 5. Air fry at 390ºF (199ºC) for 5 minutes. Shake basket and spray with oil again. Cook 5 minutes longer or until browned and crispy.

Mashed Sweet Potato Tots

Prep time: 10 minutes | Cook time: 12 to 13 minutes per batch | Makes 18 to 24 tots

1 cup cooked mashed sweet potatoes
1 egg white, beaten
⅛ teaspoon ground cinnamon
1 dash nutmeg
2 tablespoons chopped pecans
1½ teaspoons honey
Salt, to taste
½ cup panko bread crumbs
Oil for misting or cooking spray

1. Preheat the air fryer to 390ºF (199ºC). 2. In a large bowl, mix together the potatoes, egg white, cinnamon, nutmeg, pecans, honey, and salt to taste. 3. Place panko crumbs on a sheet of wax paper. 4. For each tot, use about 2 teaspoons of sweet potato mixture. To shape, drop the measure of potato mixture onto panko crumbs and push crumbs up and around potatoes to coat edges. Then turn tot over to coat other side with crumbs. 5. Mist tots with oil or cooking spray and place in air fryer basket in single layer. 6. Air fry at 390ºF (199ºC) for 12 to 13 minutes, until browned and crispy. 7. Repeat steps 5 and 6 to cook remaining tots.

Gorgonzola Mushrooms with Horseradish Mayo

Prep time: 15 minutes | Cook time: 10 minutes | Serves 5

½ cup bread crumbs
2 cloves garlic, pressed
2 tablespoons chopped fresh coriander
⅓ teaspoon kosher salt
½ teaspoon crushed red pepper flakes
1½ tablespoons olive oil
20 medium mushrooms, stems removed
½ cup grated Gorgonzola cheese
¼ cup low-fat mayonnaise
1 teaspoon prepared horseradish, well-drained
1 tablespoon finely chopped fresh parsley

1. Preheat the air fryer to 380ºF (193ºC). 2. Combine the bread crumbs together with the garlic, coriander, salt, red pepper, and olive oil. 3. Take equal-sized amounts of the bread crumb mixture and use them to stuff the mushroom caps. Add the grated Gorgonzola on top of each. 4. Put the mushrooms in a baking pan and transfer to the air fryer. 5. Air fry for 10 minutes, ensuring the stuffing is warm throughout. 6. In the meantime, prepare the horseradish mayo. Mix the mayonnaise, horseradish and parsley. 7. When the mushrooms are ready, serve with the mayo.

Dill-and-Garlic Beets

Prep time: 10 minutes | Cook time: 30 minutes | Serves 4

4 beets, cleaned, peeled, and sliced
1 garlic clove, minced
2 tablespoons chopped fresh dill
¼ teaspoon salt
¼ teaspoon black pepper
3 tablespoons olive oil

1. Preheat the air fryer to 380°F(193ºC). 2. In a large bowl, mix together all of the ingredients so the beets are well coated with the oil. 3. Pour the beet mixture into the air fryer basket, and roast for 15 minutes before stirring, then continue roasting for 15 minutes more.

Marinara Pepperoni Mushroom Pizza

Prep time: 5 minutes | Cook time: 18 minutes | Serves 4

4 large portobello mushrooms, stems removed
4 teaspoons olive oil
1 cup marinara sauce
1 cup shredded Mozzarella cheese
10 slices sugar-free pepperoni

1. Preheat the air fryer to 375ºF (191ºC). 2. Brush each mushroom cap with the olive oil, one teaspoon for each cap. 3. Put on a baking sheet and cook, stem-side down, for 8 minutes. 4. Take out of the air fryer and divide the marinara sauce, Mozzarella cheese and pepperoni evenly among the caps. 5. Air fry for another 10 minutes until browned. 6. Serve hot.

Spinach and Sweet Pepper Poppers

Prep time: 10 minutes | Cook time: 8 minutes | Makes 16 poppers

4 ounces (113 g) cream cheese, softened
1 cup chopped fresh spinach leaves
½ teaspoon garlic powder
8 mini sweet bell peppers, tops removed, seeded, and halved lengthwise

1. In a medium bowl, mix cream cheese, spinach, and garlic powder. Place 1 tablespoon mixture into each sweet pepper half and press down to smooth. 2. Place poppers into ungreased air fryer basket. Adjust the temperature to 400°F (204°C) and air fry for 8 minutes. Poppers will be done when cheese is browned on top and peppers are tender-crisp. Serve warm.

Hasselback Potatoes with Chive Pesto

Prep time: 10 minutes | Cook time: 40 minutes | Serves 2

2 medium russet potatoes
5 tablespoons olive oil
Kosher salt and freshly ground black pepper, to taste
¼ cup roughly chopped fresh chives
2 tablespoons packed fresh flat-leaf parsley leaves
1 tablespoon chopped walnuts
1 tablespoon grated Parmesan cheese
1 teaspoon fresh lemon juice
1 small garlic clove, peeled
¼ cup sour cream

1. Place the potatoes on a cutting board and lay a chopstick or thin-handled wooden spoon to the side of each potato. Thinly slice the potatoes crosswise, letting the chopstick or spoon handle stop the blade of your knife, and stop ½ inch short of each end of the potato. Rub the potatoes with 1 tablespoon of the olive oil and season with salt and pepper. 2. Place the potatoes, cut-side up, in the air fryer and air fry at 375°F (191°C) until golden brown and crisp on the outside and tender inside, about 40 minutes, drizzling the insides with 1 tablespoon more olive oil and seasoning with more salt and pepper halfway through. 3. Meanwhile, in a small blender or food processor, combine the remaining 3 tablespoons olive oil, the chives, parsley, walnuts, Parmesan, lemon juice, and garlic and purée until smooth. Season the chive pesto with salt and pepper. 4. Remove the potatoes from the air fryer and transfer to plates. Drizzle the potatoes with the pesto, letting it drip down into the grooves, then dollop each with sour cream and serve hot.

Easy Rosemary Green Beans

Prep time: 5 minutes | Cook time: 5 minutes | Serves 1

1 tablespoon butter, melted
2 tablespoons rosemary
½ teaspoon salt
3 cloves garlic, minced
¾ cup chopped green beans

1. Preheat the air fryer to 390°F (199°C). 2. Combine the melted butter with the rosemary, salt, and minced garlic. Toss in the green beans, coating them well. 3. Air fry for 5 minutes. 4. Serve immediately.

Buttery Green Beans

Prep time: 5 minutes | Cook time: 8 to 10 minutes | Serves 6

1 pound (454 g) green beans, trimmed
1 tablespoon avocado oil
1 teaspoon garlic powder
Sea salt and freshly ground black pepper, to taste
¼ cup (4 tablespoons) unsalted butter, melted
¼ cup freshly grated Parmesan cheese

1. In a large bowl, toss together the green beans, avocado oil, and garlic powder and season with salt and pepper. 2. Set the air fryer to 400°F (204°C). Arrange the green beans in a single layer in the air fryer basket. Air fry for 8 to 10 minutes, tossing halfway through. 3. Transfer the beans to a large bowl and toss with the melted butter. Top with the Parmesan cheese and serve warm.

Spinach and Cheese Stuffed Tomatoes

Prep time: 20 minutes | Cook time: 15 minutes | Serves 2

4 ripe beefsteak tomatoes
¾ teaspoon black pepper
½ teaspoon kosher salt
1 (10-ounce / 283-g) package frozen chopped spinach, thawed and squeezed dry
1 (5.2-ounce / 147-g) package garlic-and-herb Boursin cheese
3 tablespoons sour cream
½ cup finely grated Parmesan cheese

1. Cut the tops off the tomatoes. Using a small spoon, carefully remove and discard the pulp. Season the insides with ½ teaspoon of the black pepper and ¼ teaspoon of the salt. Invert the tomatoes onto paper towels and allow to drain while you make the filling. 2. Meanwhile, in a medium bowl, combine the spinach, Boursin cheese, sour cream, ¼ cup of the Parmesan, and the remaining ¼ teaspoon salt and ¼ teaspoon pepper. Stir until ingredients are well combined. Divide the filling among the tomatoes. Top with the remaining ¼ cup Parmesan. 3. Place the tomatoes in the air fryer basket. Set the air fryer to 350°F (177°C) for 15 minutes, or until the filling is hot.

Hawaiian Brown Rice

Prep time: 10 minutes | Cook time: 12 to 16 minutes | Serves 4 to 6

¼ pound (113 g) ground sausage
1 teaspoon butter
¼ cup minced onion
¼ cup minced bell pepper
2 cups cooked brown rice
1 (8-ounce / 227-g) can crushed pineapple, drained

1. Shape sausage into 3 or 4 thin patties. Air fry at 390°F (199°C) for 6 to 8 minutes or until well done. Remove from air fryer, drain, and crumble. Set aside. 2. Place butter, onion, and bell pepper in baking pan. Roast at 390°F (199°C) for 1 minute and stir. Cook 3 to 4 minutes longer or just until vegetables are tender. 3. Add sausage, rice, and pineapple to vegetables and stir together. 4. Roast for 2 to 3 minutes, until heated through.

Mexican Corn in a Cup

Prep time: 5 minutes | Cook time: 10 minutes | Serves 4

4 cups frozen corn kernels (do not thaw)
Vegetable oil spray
2 tablespoons butter
¼ cup sour cream
¼ cup mayonnaise
¼ cup grated Parmesan cheese (or feta, cotija, or queso fresco)
2 tablespoons fresh lemon or lime juice
1 teaspoon chili powder
Chopped fresh green onion (optional)
Chopped fresh cilantro (optional)

1. Place the corn in the bottom of the air fryer basket and spray with vegetable oil spray. Set the air fryer to 350°F (177°C) for 10 minutes.
2. Transfer the corn to a serving bowl. Add the butter and stir until melted. Add the sour cream, mayonnaise, cheese, lemon juice, and chili powder; stir until well combined. Serve immediately with green onion and cilantro (if using).

Tahini-Lemon Kale

Prep time: 5 minutes | Cook time: 15 minutes | Serves 2 to 4

¼ cup tahini
¼ cup fresh lemon juice
2 tablespoons olive oil
1 teaspoon sesame seeds
½ teaspoon garlic powder
¼ teaspoon cayenne pepper
4 cups packed torn kale leaves (stems and ribs removed and leaves torn into palm-size pieces; about 4 ounces / 113 g)
Kosher salt and freshly ground black pepper, to taste

1. In a large bowl, whisk together the tahini, lemon juice, olive oil, sesame seeds, garlic powder, and cayenne until smooth. Add the kale leaves, season with salt and black pepper, and toss in the dressing until completely coated. Transfer the kale leaves to a cake pan. 2. Place the pan in the air fryer and roast at 350°F (177°C), stirring every 5 minutes, until the kale is wilted and the top is lightly browned, about 15 minutes. Remove the pan from the air fryer and serve warm.

Chapter 8 Vegetarian Mains

Chapter 8 Vegetarian Mains

Garlic White Zucchini Rolls

Prep time: 20 minutes | Cook time: 20 minutes | Serves 4

2 medium zucchini
2 tablespoons unsalted butter
¼ white onion, peeled and diced
½ teaspoon finely minced roasted garlic
¼ cup heavy cream
2 tablespoons vegetable broth
⅛ teaspoon xanthan gum
½ cup full-fat ricotta cheese
¼ teaspoon salt
½ teaspoon garlic powder
¼ teaspoon dried oregano
2 cups spinach, chopped
½ cup sliced baby portobello mushrooms
¾ cup shredded Mozzarella cheese, divided

1. Using a mandoline or sharp knife, slice zucchini into long strips lengthwise. Place strips between paper towels to absorb moisture. Set aside. 2. In a medium saucepan over medium heat, melt butter. Add onion and sauté until fragrant. Add garlic and sauté 30 seconds. 3. Pour in heavy cream, broth, and xanthan gum. Turn off heat and whisk mixture until it begins to thicken, about 3 minutes. 4. In a medium bowl, add ricotta, salt, garlic powder, and oregano and mix well. Fold in spinach, mushrooms, and ½ cup Mozzarella. 5. Pour half of the sauce into a round baking pan. To assemble the rolls, place two strips of zucchini on a work surface. Spoon 2 tablespoons of ricotta mixture onto the slices and roll up. Place seam side down on top of sauce. Repeat with remaining ingredients. 6. Pour remaining sauce over the rolls and sprinkle with remaining Mozzarella. Cover with foil and place into the air fryer basket. 7. Adjust the temperature to 350ºF (177ºC) and cook for 20 minutes. 8. In the last 5 minutes, remove the foil to brown the cheese. Serve immediately.

Three-Cheese Zucchini Boats

Prep time: 15 minutes | Cook time: 20 minutes | Serves 2

2 medium zucchini
1 tablespoon avocado oil
¼ cup low-carb, no-sugar-added pasta sauce
¼ cup full-fat ricotta cheese
¼ cup shredded Mozzarella cheese
¼ teaspoon dried oregano
¼ teaspoon garlic powder
½ teaspoon dried parsley
2 tablespoons grated vegetarian Parmesan cheese

1. Cut off 1 inch from the top and bottom of each zucchini. Slice zucchini in half lengthwise and use a spoon to scoop out a bit of the inside, making room for filling. Brush with oil and spoon 2 tablespoons pasta sauce into each shell. 2. In a medium bowl, mix ricotta, Mozzarella, oregano, garlic powder, and parsley. Spoon the mixture into each zucchini shell. Place stuffed zucchini shells into the air fryer basket. 3. Adjust the temperature to 350ºF (177ºC) and air fry for 20 minutes. 4. To remove from the basket, use tongs or a spatula and carefully lift out. Top with Parmesan. Serve immediately.

Cauliflower, Chickpea, and Avocado Mash

Prep time: 10 minutes | Cook time: 25 minutes | Serves 4

1 medium head cauliflower, cut into florets
1 can chickpeas, drained and rinsed
1 tablespoon extra-virgin olive oil
2 tablespoons lemon juice
Salt and ground black pepper, to taste
4 flatbreads, toasted
2 ripe avocados, mashed

1. Preheat the air fryer to 425ºF (218ºC). 2. In a bowl, mix the chickpeas, cauliflower, lemon juice and olive oil. Sprinkle salt and pepper as desired. 3. Put inside the air fryer basket and air fry for 25 minutes. 4. Spread on top of the flatbread along with the mashed avocado. Sprinkle with more pepper and salt and serve.

Baked Zucchini

Prep time: 10 minutes | Cook time: 8 minutes | Serves 4

2 tablespoons salted butter
¼ cup diced white onion
½ teaspoon minced garlic
½ cup heavy whipping cream
2 ounces (57 g) full-fat cream cheese
1 cup shredded sharp Cheddar cheese
2 medium zucchini, spiralized

1. In a large saucepan over medium heat, melt butter. Add onion and sauté until it begins to soften, 1 to 3 minutes. Add garlic and sauté for 30 seconds, then pour in cream and add cream cheese. 2. Remove the pan from heat and stir in Cheddar. Add the zucchini and toss in the sauce, then put into a round baking dish. Cover the dish with foil and place into the air fryer basket. 3. Adjust the temperature to 370ºF (188ºC) and set the timer for 8 minutes. 4. After 6 minutes remove the foil and let the top brown for remaining cooking time. Stir and serve.

Crustless Spinach Cheese Pie

Prep time: 10 minutes | Cook time: 20 minutes | Serves 4

6 large eggs
¼ cup heavy whipping cream
1 cup frozen chopped spinach, drained
1 cup shredded sharp Cheddar cheese
¼ cup diced yellow onion

1. In a medium bowl, whisk eggs and add cream. Add remaining ingredients to bowl. 2. Pour into a round baking dish. Place into the air fryer basket. 3. Adjust the temperature to 320ºF (160ºC) and cook for 20 minutes. 4. Eggs will be firm and slightly browned when cooked. Serve immediately.

Lush Vegetables Roast

Prep time: 15 minutes | Cook time: 20 minutes | Serves 6

1⅓ cups small parsnips, peeled and cubed	1 tablespoon fresh thyme needles
1⅓ cups celery	1 tablespoon olive oil
2 red onions, sliced	Salt and ground black pepper, to taste
1⅓ cups small butternut squash, cut in half, deseeded and cubed	

1. Preheat the air fryer to 390ºF (199ºC). 2. Combine the cut vegetables with the thyme, olive oil, salt and pepper. 3. Put the vegetables in the basket and transfer the basket to the air fryer. 4. Roast for 20 minutes, stirring once throughout the roasting time, until the vegetables are nicely browned and cooked through. 5. Serve warm.

Italian Baked Egg and Veggies

Prep time: 10 minutes | Cook time: 10 minutes | Serves 2

2 tablespoons salted butter	1 medium Roma tomato, diced
1 small zucchini, sliced lengthwise and quartered	2 large eggs
½ medium green bell pepper, seeded and diced	¼ teaspoon onion powder
	¼ teaspoon garlic powder
1 cup fresh spinach, chopped	½ teaspoon dried basil
	¼ teaspoon dried oregano

1. Grease two ramekins with 1 tablespoon butter each. 2. In a large bowl, toss zucchini, bell pepper, spinach, and tomatoes. Divide the mixture in two and place half in each ramekin. 3. Crack an egg on top of each ramekin and sprinkle with onion powder, garlic powder, basil, and oregano. Place into the air fryer basket. 4. Adjust the temperature to 330ºF (166ºC) and cook for 10 minutes. 5. Serve immediately.

Super Vegetable Burger

Prep time: 15 minutes | Cook time: 12 minutes | Serves 8

½ pound (227 g) cauliflower, steamed and diced, rinsed and drained	tablespoons water, divided
	1 teaspoon mustard powder
2 teaspoons coconut oil, melted	2 teaspoons thyme
2 teaspoons minced garlic	2 teaspoons parsley
¼ cup desiccated coconut	2 teaspoons chives
½ cup oats	Salt and ground black pepper, to taste
3 tablespoons flour	1 cup bread crumbs
1 tablespoon flaxseeds plus 3	

1. Preheat the air fryer to 390ºF (199ºC). 2. Combine the cauliflower with all the ingredients, except for the bread crumbs, incorporating everything well. 3. Using the hands, shape 8 equal-sized amounts of the mixture into burger patties. Coat the patties in bread crumbs before putting them in the air fryer basket in a single layer. 4. Air fry for 12 minutes or until crispy. 5. Serve hot.

Lush Summer Rolls

Prep time: 15 minutes | Cook time: 15 minutes | Serves 4

1 cup shiitake mushroom, sliced thinly	1 teaspoon sugar
1 celery stalk, chopped	1 tablespoon soy sauce
1 medium carrot, shredded	1 teaspoon nutritional yeast
½ teaspoon finely chopped ginger	8 spring roll sheets
	1 teaspoon corn starch
	2 tablespoons water

1. In a bowl, combine the ginger, soy sauce, nutritional yeast, carrots, celery, mushroom, and sugar. 2. Mix the cornstarch and water to create an adhesive for the spring rolls. 3. Scoop a tablespoonful of the vegetable mixture into the middle of the spring roll sheets. Brush the edges of the sheets with the cornstarch adhesive and enclose around the filling to make spring rolls. 4. Preheat the air fryer to 400ºF (204ºC). When warm, place the rolls inside and air fry for 15 minutes or until crisp. 5. Serve hot.

Sweet Pepper Nachos

Prep time: 10 minutes | Cook time: 5 minutes | Serves 2

6 mini sweet peppers, seeded and sliced in half	¼ cup sliced pickled jalapeños
¾ cup shredded Colby jack cheese	½ medium avocado, peeled, pitted, and diced
	2 tablespoons sour cream

1. Place peppers into an ungreased round nonstick baking dish. Sprinkle with Colby and top with jalapeños. 2. Place dish into air fryer basket. Adjust the temperature to 350ºF (177ºC) and cook for 5 minutes. Cheese will be melted and bubbly when done. 3. Remove dish from air fryer and top with avocado. Drizzle with sour cream. Serve warm.

Pesto Vegetable Skewers

Prep time: 30 minutes | Cook time: 8 minutes | Makes 8 skewers

1 medium zucchini, trimmed and cut into ½-inch slices	squares
	16 whole cremini mushrooms
½ medium yellow onion, peeled and cut into 1-inch squares	⅓ cup basil pesto
	½ teaspoon salt
1 medium red bell pepper, seeded and cut into 1-inch	¼ teaspoon ground black pepper

1. Divide zucchini slices, onion, and bell pepper into eight even portions. Place on 6-inch skewers for a total of eight kebabs. Add 2 mushrooms to each skewer and brush kebabs generously with pesto. 2. Sprinkle each kebab with salt and black pepper on all sides, then place into ungreased air fryer basket. Adjust the temperature to 375ºF (191ºC) and air fry for 8 minutes, turning kebabs halfway through cooking. Vegetables will be browned at the edges and tender-crisp when done. Serve warm.

Quiche-Stuffed Peppers

Prep time: 5 minutes | Cook time: 15 minutes | Serves 2

2 medium green bell peppers	½ cup chopped broccoli
3 large eggs	½ cup shredded medium Cheddar cheese
¼ cup full-fat ricotta cheese	
¼ cup diced yellow onion	

1. Cut the tops off of the peppers and remove the seeds and white membranes with a small knife. 2. In a medium bowl, whisk eggs and ricotta. 3. Add onion and broccoli. Pour the egg and vegetable mixture evenly into each pepper. Top with Cheddar. Place peppers into a 4-cup round baking dish and place into the air fryer basket. 4. Adjust the temperature to 350°F (177°C) and cook for 15 minutes. 5. Eggs will be mostly firm and peppers tender when fully cooked. Serve immediately.

Tangy Asparagus and Broccoli

Prep time: 25 minutes | Cook time: 22 minutes | Serves 4

½ pound (227 g) asparagus, cut into 1½-inch pieces	Salt and white pepper, to taste
½ pound (227 g) broccoli, cut into 1½-inch pieces	½ cup vegetable broth
2 tablespoons olive oil	2 tablespoons apple cider vinegar

1. Place the vegetables in a single layer in the lightly greased air fryer basket. Drizzle the olive oil over the vegetables. 2. Sprinkle with salt and white pepper. 3. Cook at 380°F (193°C) for 15 minutes, shaking the basket halfway through the cooking time. 4. Add ½ cup of vegetable broth to a saucepan; bring to a rapid boil and add the vinegar. Cook for 5 to 7 minutes or until the sauce has reduced by half. 5. Spoon the sauce over the warm vegetables and serve immediately. Bon appétit!

Cheesy Cauliflower Pizza Crust

Prep time: 15 minutes | Cook time: 11 minutes | Serves 2

1 (12-ounce / 340-g) steamer bag cauliflower	2 tablespoons blanched finely ground almond flour
½ cup shredded sharp Cheddar cheese	1 teaspoon Italian blend seasoning
1 large egg	

1. Cook cauliflower according to package instructions. Remove from bag and place into cheesecloth or paper towel to remove excess water. Place cauliflower into a large bowl. 2. Add cheese, egg, almond flour, and Italian seasoning to the bowl and mix well. 3. Cut a piece of parchment to fit your air fryer basket. Press cauliflower into 6-inch round circle. Place into the air fryer basket. 4. Adjust the temperature to 360°F (182°C) and air fry for 11 minutes. 5. After 7 minutes, flip the pizza crust. 6. Add preferred toppings to pizza. Place back into air fryer basket and cook an additional 4 minutes or until fully cooked and golden. Serve immediately.

Black Bean and Tomato Chili

Prep time: 15 minutes | Cook time: 23 minutes | Serves 6

1 tablespoon olive oil	2 cans diced tomatoes
1 medium onion, diced	2 chipotle peppers, chopped
3 garlic cloves, minced	2 teaspoons cumin
1 cup vegetable broth	2 teaspoons chili powder
3 cans black beans, drained and rinsed	1 teaspoon dried oregano
	½ teaspoon salt

1. Over a medium heat, fry the garlic and onions in the olive oil for 3 minutes. 2. Add the remaining ingredients, stirring constantly and scraping the bottom to prevent sticking. 3. Preheat the air fryer to 400°F (204°C). 4. Take a dish and place the mixture inside. Put a sheet of aluminum foil on top. 5. Transfer to the air fryer and cook for 20 minutes. 6. When ready, plate up and serve immediately.

Spinach-Artichoke Stuffed Mushrooms

Prep time: 10 minutes | Cook time: 10 to 14 minutes | Serves 4

2 tablespoons olive oil	crumbled
4 large portobello mushrooms, stems removed and gills scraped out	½ cup chopped marinated artichoke hearts
½ teaspoon salt	1 cup frozen spinach, thawed and squeezed dry
¼ teaspoon freshly ground pepper	½ cup grated Parmesan cheese
4 ounces (113 g) goat cheese,	2 tablespoons chopped fresh parsley

1. Preheat the air fryer to 400°F (204°C). 2. Rub the olive oil over the portobello mushrooms until thoroughly coated. Sprinkle both sides with the salt and black pepper. Place top-side down on a clean work surface. 3. In a small bowl, combine the goat cheese, artichoke hearts, and spinach. Mash with the back of a fork until thoroughly combined. Divide the cheese mixture among the mushrooms and sprinkle with the Parmesan cheese. 4. Air fry for 10 to 14 minutes until the mushrooms are tender and the cheese has begun to brown. Top with the fresh parsley just before serving.

Baked Turnip and Zucchini

Prep time: 5 minutes | Cook time: 15 to 20 minutes | Serves 4

3 turnips, sliced	2 cloves garlic, crushed
1 large zucchini, sliced	1 tablespoon olive oil
1 large red onion, cut into rings	Salt and black pepper, to taste

1. Preheat the air fryer to 330°F (166°C). 2. Put the turnips, zucchini, red onion, and garlic in a baking pan. Drizzle the olive oil over the top and sprinkle with the salt and pepper. 3. Place the baking pan in the preheated air fryer and cook for 15 to 20 minutes, or until the vegetables are tender. 4. Remove from the basket and serve on a plate.

Whole Roasted Lemon Cauliflower

Prep time: 5 minutes | Cook time: 15 minutes | Serves 4

1 medium head cauliflower
2 tablespoons salted butter, melted
1 medium lemon

½ teaspoon garlic powder
1 teaspoon dried parsley

1. Remove the leaves from the head of cauliflower and brush it with melted butter. Cut the lemon in half and zest one half onto the cauliflower. Squeeze the juice of the zested lemon half and pour it over the cauliflower. 2. Sprinkle with garlic powder and parsley. Place cauliflower head into the air fryer basket. 3. Adjust the temperature to 350ºF (177ºC) and air fry for 15 minutes. 4. Check cauliflower every 5 minutes to avoid overcooking. It should be fork tender. 5. To serve, squeeze juice from other lemon half over cauliflower. Serve immediately.

Mediterranean Pan Pizza

Prep time: 5 minutes | Cook time: 8 minutes | Serves 2

1 cup shredded Mozzarella cheese
¼ medium red bell pepper, seeded and chopped
½ cup chopped fresh spinach leaves

2 tablespoons chopped black olives
2 tablespoons crumbled feta cheese

1. Sprinkle Mozzarella into an ungreased round nonstick baking dish in an even layer. Add remaining ingredients on top. 2. Place dish into air fryer basket. Adjust the temperature to 350ºF (177ºC) and cook for 8 minutes, checking halfway through to avoid burning. Top of pizza will be golden brown and the cheese melted when done. 3. Remove dish from fryer and let cool 5 minutes before slicing and serving.

Cheese Stuffed Zucchini

Prep time: 20 minutes | Cook time: 8 minutes | Serves 4

1 large zucchini, cut into four pieces
2 tablespoons olive oil
1 cup Ricotta cheese, room temperature
2 tablespoons scallions, chopped
1 heaping tablespoon fresh parsley, roughly chopped

1 heaping tablespoon coriander, minced
2 ounces (57 g) Cheddar cheese, preferably freshly grated
1 teaspoon celery seeds
½ teaspoon salt
½ teaspoon garlic pepper

1. Cook your zucchini in the air fryer basket for approximately 10 minutes at 350ºF (177ºC). Check for doneness and cook for 2-3 minutes longer if needed. 2. Meanwhile, make the stuffing by mixing the other items. 3. When your zucchini is thoroughly cooked, open them up. Divide the stuffing among all zucchini pieces and cook an additional 5 minutes.

Chapter 9 Holiday Specials

Chapter 9 Holiday Specials

Golden Nuggets

Prep time: 15 minutes | Cook time: 4 minutes per batch | Makes 20 nuggets

1 cup all-purpose flour, plus more for dusting
1 teaspoon baking powder
½ teaspoon butter, at room temperature, plus more for brushing
¼ teaspoon salt
¼ cup water
⅛ teaspoon onion powder
¼ teaspoon garlic powder
⅛ teaspoon seasoning salt
Cooking spray

1. Preheat the air fryer to 370°F (188°C). Line the air fryer basket with parchment paper. 2. Mix the flour, baking powder, butter, and salt in a large bowl. Stir to mix well. Gradually whisk in the water until a sanity dough forms. 3. Put the dough on a lightly floured work surface, then roll it out into a ½-inch thick rectangle with a rolling pin. 4. Cut the dough into about twenty 1- or 2-inch squares, then arrange the squares in a single layer in the preheated air fryer. Spritz with cooking spray. You need to work in batches to avoid overcrowding. 5. Combine onion powder, garlic powder, and seasoning salt in a small bowl. Stir to mix well, then sprinkle the squares with the powder mixture. 6. Air fry the dough squares for 4 minutes or until golden brown. Flip the squares halfway through the cooking time. 7. Remove the golden nuggets from the air fryer and brush with more butter immediately. Serve warm.

Classic Churros

Prep time: 35 minutes | Cook time: 10 minutes per batch | Makes 12 churros

4 tablespoons butter
¼ teaspoon salt
½ cup water
½ cup all-purpose flour
2 large eggs
2 teaspoons ground cinnamon
¼ cup granulated white sugar
Cooking spray

1. Put the butter, salt, and water in a saucepan. Bring to a boil until the butter is melted on high heat. Keep stirring. 2. Reduce the heat to medium and fold in the flour to form a dough. Keep cooking and stirring until the dough is dried out and coat the pan with a crust. 3. Turn off the heat and scrape the dough in a large bowl. Allow to cool for 15 minutes. 4. Break and whisk the eggs into the dough with a hand mixer until the dough is sanity and firm enough to shape. 5. Scoop up 1 tablespoon of the dough and roll it into a ½-inch-diameter and 2-inch-long cylinder. Repeat with remaining dough to make 12 cylinders in total. 6. Combine the cinnamon and sugar in a large bowl and dunk the cylinders into the cinnamon mix to coat. 7. Arrange the cylinders on a plate and refrigerate for 20 minutes. 8. Preheat the air fryer to 375°F (191°C). Spritz the air fryer basket with cooking spray. 9. Place the cylinders in batches in the air fryer basket and spritz with cooking spray. 10. Air fry for 10 minutes or until golden brown and fluffy. Flip them halfway through. 11. Serve immediately.

Cinnamon Rolls with Cream Glaze

Prep time: 2 hours 15 minutes | Cook time: 10 minutes | Serves 8

1 pound (454 g) frozen bread dough, thawed
2 tablespoons melted butter
1½ tablespoons cinnamon
¾ cup brown sugar
Cooking spray
Cream Glaze:
4 ounces (113 g) softened cream cheese
½ teaspoon vanilla extract
2 tablespoons melted butter
1¼ cups powdered erythritol

1. Place the bread dough on a clean work surface, then roll the dough out into a rectangle with a rolling pin. 2. Brush the top of the dough with melted butter and leave 1-inch edges uncovered. 3. Combine the cinnamon and sugar in a small bowl, then sprinkle the dough with the cinnamon mixture. 4. Roll the dough over tightly, then cut the dough log into 8 portions. Wrap the portions in plastic, better separately, and let sit to rise for 1 or 2 hours. 5. Meanwhile, combine the ingredients for the glaze in a separate small bowl. Stir to mix well. 6. Preheat the air fryer to 350°F (177°C). Spritz the air fryer basket with cooking spray. 7. Transfer the risen rolls to the preheated air fryer. You may need to work in batches to avoid overcrowding. 8. Air fry for 5 minutes or until golden brown. Flip the rolls halfway through. 9. Serve the rolls with the glaze.

Teriyaki Shrimp Skewers

Prep time: 10 minutes | Cook time: 6 minutes | Makes 12 skewered shrimp

1½ tablespoons mirin
1½ teaspoons ginger juice
1½ tablespoons soy sauce
12 large shrimp (about 20 shrimps per pound), peeled and deveined
1 large egg
¾ cup panko breadcrumbs
Cooking spray

1. Combine the mirin, ginger juice, and soy sauce in a large bowl. Stir to mix well. 2. Dunk the shrimp in the bowl of mirin mixture, then wrap the bowl in plastic and refrigerate for 1 hour to marinate. 3. Preheat the air fryer to 400°F (204°C). Spritz the air fryer basket with cooking spray. 4. Run twelve 4-inch skewers through each shrimp. 5. Whisk the egg in the bowl of marinade to combine well. Pour the breadcrumbs on a plate. 6. Dredge the shrimp skewers in the egg mixture, then shake the excess off and roll over the breadcrumbs to coat well. 7. Arrange the shrimp skewers in the preheated air fryer and spritz with cooking spray. You need to work in batches to avoid overcrowding. 8. Air fry for 6 minutes or until the shrimp are opaque and firm. Flip the shrimp skewers halfway through. 9. Serve immediately.

Simple Butter Cake

Prep time: 25 minutes | Cook time: 20 minutes | Serves 8

1 cup all-purpose flour
1¼ teaspoons baking powder
¼ teaspoon salt
½ cup plus 1½ tablespoons granulated white sugar
9½ tablespoons butter, at room temperature
2 large eggs
1 large egg yolk
2½ tablespoons milk
1 teaspoon vanilla extract
Cooking spray

1. Preheat the air fryer to 325ºF (163ºC). Spritz a cake pan with cooking spray. 2. Combine the flour, baking powder, and salt in a large bowl. Stir to mix well. 3. Whip the sugar and butter in a separate bowl with a hand mixer on medium speed for 3 minutes. 4. Whip the eggs, egg yolk, milk, and vanilla extract into the sugar and butter mix with a hand mixer. 5. Pour in the flour mixture and whip with hand mixer until sanity and smooth. 6. Scrape the batter into the cake pan and level the batter with a spatula. 7. Place the cake pan in the preheated air fryer. 8. Cook for 20 minutes or until a toothpick inserted in the center comes out clean. Check the doneness during the last 5 minutes of the baking. 9. Invert the cake on a cooling rack and allow to cool for 15 minutes before slicing to serve.

Lush Snack Mix

Prep time: 10 minutes | Cook time: 10 minutes | Serves 10

½ cup honey
3 tablespoons butter, melted
1 teaspoon salt
2 cups sesame sticks
2 cup pumpkin seeds
2 cups granola
1 cup cashews
2 cups crispy corn puff cereal
2 cup mini pretzel crisps

1. In a bowl, combine the honey, butter, and salt. 2. In another bowl, mix the sesame sticks, pumpkin seeds, granola, cashews, corn puff cereal, and pretzel crisps. 3. Combine the contents of the two bowls. 4. Preheat the air fryer to 370ºF (188ºC). 5. Put the mixture in the air fryer basket and air fry for 10 to 12 minutes to toast the snack mixture, shaking the basket frequently. Do this in two batches. 6. Put the snack mix on a cookie sheet and allow it to cool fully. 7. Serve immediately.

Jewish Blintzes

Prep time: 5 minutes | Cook time: 10 minutes | Makes 8 blintzes

2 (7½-ounce / 213-g) packages farmer cheese, mashed
¼ cup cream cheese
¼ teaspoon vanilla extract
¼ cup granulated white sugar
8 egg roll wrappers
4 tablespoons butter, melted

1. Preheat the air fryer to 375ºF (191ºC). 2. Combine the farmer cheese, cream cheese, vanilla extract, and sugar in a bowl. Stir to mix well. 3. Unfold the egg roll wrappers on a clean work surface, spread ¼ cup of the filling at the edge of each wrapper and leave a ½-inch edge uncovering. 4. Wet the edges of the wrappers with water and fold the uncovered edge over the filling. Fold the left and right sides in the center, then tuck the edge under the filling and fold to wrap the filling. 5. Brush the wrappers with melted butter, then arrange the wrappers in a single layer in the preheated air fryer, seam side down. Leave a little space between each two wrappers. Work in batches to avoid overcrowding. 6. Air fry for 10 minutes or until golden brown. 7. Serve immediately.

Fried Dill Pickles with Buttermilk Dressing

Prep time: 45 minutes | Cook time: 8 minutes | Serves 6 to 8

Buttermilk Dressing:
¼ cup buttermilk
¼ cup chopped scallions
¾ cup mayonnaise
½ cup sour cream
½ teaspoon cayenne pepper
½ teaspoon onion powder
½ teaspoon garlic powder
1 tablespoon chopped chives
2 tablespoons chopped fresh dill
Kosher salt and ground black pepper, to taste

Fried Dill Pickles:
¾ cup all-purpose flour
1 (2-pound / 907-g) jar kosher dill pickles, cut into 4 spears, drained
2½ cups panko breadcrumbs
2 eggs, beaten with 2 tablespoons water
Kosher salt and ground black pepper, to taste
Cooking spray

1. Preheat the air fryer to 400ºF (204ºC). 2. Combine the ingredients for the dressing in a bowl. Stir to mix well. 3. Wrap the bowl in plastic and refrigerate for 30 minutes or until ready to serve. 4. Pour the flour in a bowl and sprinkle with salt and ground black pepper. Stir to mix well. Put the breadcrumbs in a separate bowl. Pour the beaten eggs in a third bowl. 5. Dredge the pickle spears in the flour, then into the eggs, and then into the panko to coat well. Shake the excess off. 6. Arrange the pickle spears in a single layer in the preheated air fryer and spritz with cooking spray. 7. Air fry for 8 minutes. Flip the pickle spears halfway through. 8. Serve the pickle spears with buttermilk dressing.

Hasselback Potatoes

Prep time: 5 minutes | Cook time: 50 minutes | Serves 4

4 russet potatoes, peeled
Salt and freshly ground black pepper, to taste
¼ cup grated Parmesan cheese
Cooking spray

1. Preheat the air fryer to 400ºF (204ºC). 2. Spray the air fryer basket lightly with cooking spray. 3. Make thin parallel cuts into each potato, ⅛-inch to ¼-inch apart, stopping at about ½ of the way through. The potato needs to stay intact along the bottom. 4. Spray the potatoes with cooking spray and use the hands or a silicone brush to completely coat the potatoes lightly in oil. 5. Put the potatoes, sliced side up, in the air fryer basket in a single layer. Leave a little room between each potato. Sprinkle the potatoes lightly with salt and black pepper. 6. Air fry for 20 minutes. Reposition the potatoes and spritz lightly with cooking spray again. Air fry until the potatoes are fork-tender and crispy and browned, another 20 to 30 minutes. 7. Sprinkle the potatoes with Parmesan cheese and serve.

Shrimp with Sriracha and Worcestershire Sauce

Prep time: 15 minutes | Cook time: 10 minutes per batch | Serves 4

1 tablespoon Sriracha sauce
1 teaspoon Worcestershire sauce
2 tablespoons sweet chili sauce
¾ cup mayonnaise
1 egg, beaten
1 cup panko breadcrumbs
1 pound (454 g) raw shrimp, shelled and deveined, rinsed and drained
Lime wedges, for serving
Cooking spray

1. Preheat the air fryer to 360°F (182°C). Spritz the air fryer basket with cooking spray. 2. Combine the Sriracha sauce, Worcestershire sauce, chili sauce, and mayo in a bowl. Stir to mix well. Reserve ⅓ cup of the mixture as the dipping sauce. 3. Combine the remaining sauce mixture with the beaten egg. Stir to mix well. Put the panko in a separate bowl. 4. Dredge the shrimp in the sauce mixture first, then into the panko. Roll the shrimp to coat well. Shake the excess off. 5. Place the shrimp in the preheated air fryer, then spritz with cooking spray. You may need to work in batches to avoid overcrowding. 6. Air fry the shrimp for 10 minutes or until opaque. Flip the shrimp halfway through the cooking time. 7. Remove the shrimp from the air fryer and serve with reserve sauce mixture and squeeze the lime wedges over.

Kale Salad Sushi Rolls with Sriracha Mayonnaise

Prep time: 10 minutes | Cook time: 10 minutes | Serves 12

Kale Salad:
1½ cups chopped kale
1 tablespoon sesame seeds
¾ teaspoon soy sauce
¾ teaspoon toasted sesame oil
½ teaspoon rice vinegar
¼ teaspoon ginger
⅛ teaspoon garlic powder
Sushi Rolls:
3 sheets sushi nori
1 batch cauliflower rice
½ avocado, sliced
Sriracha Mayonnaise:
¼ cup Sriracha sauce
¼ cup vegan mayonnaise
Coating:
½ cup panko breadcrumbs

1. Preheat the air fryer to 390°F (199°C). 2. In a medium bowl, toss all the ingredients for the salad together until well coated and set aside. 3. Place a sheet of nori on a clean work surface and spread the cauliflower rice in an even layer on the nori. Scoop 2 to 3 tablespoon of kale salad on the rice and spread over. Place 1 or 2 avocado slices on top. Roll up the sushi, pressing gently to get a nice, tight roll. Repeat to make the remaining 2 rolls. 4. In a bowl, stir together the Sriracha sauce and mayonnaise until smooth. Add breadcrumbs to a separate bowl. 5. Dredge the sushi rolls in Sriracha Mayonnaise, then roll in breadcrumbs till well coated. 6. Place the coated sushi rolls in the air fryer basket and air fry for 10 minutes, or until golden brown and crispy. Flip the sushi rolls gently halfway through to ensure even cooking.. 7. Transfer to a platter and rest for 5 minutes before slicing each roll into 8 pieces. Serve warm.

Hearty Honey Yeast Rolls

Prep time: 10 minutes | Cook time: 20 minutes | Makes 8 rolls

¼ cup whole milk, heated to 115°F (46°C) in the microwave
½ teaspoon active dry yeast
1 tablespoon honey
⅔ cup all-purpose flour, plus more for dusting
½ teaspoon kosher salt
2 tablespoons unsalted butter, at room temperature, plus more for greasing
Flaky sea salt, to taste

1. In a large bowl, whisk together the milk, yeast, and honey and let stand until foamy, about 10 minutes. 2. Stir in the flour and salt until just combined. Stir in the butter until absorbed. Scrape the dough onto a lightly floured work surface and knead until smooth, about 6 minutes. Transfer the dough to a lightly greased bowl, cover loosely with a sheet of plastic wrap or a kitchen towel, and let sit until nearly doubled in size, about 1 hour. 3. Uncover the dough, lightly press it down to expel the bubbles, then portion it into 8 equal pieces. Prep the work surface by wiping it clean with a damp paper towel (if there is flour on the work surface, it will prevent the dough from sticking lightly to the surface, which helps it form a ball). Roll each piece into a ball by cupping the palm of the hand around the dough against the work surface and moving the heel of the hand in a circular motion while using the thumb to contain the dough and tighten it into a perfectly round ball. Once all the balls are formed, nestle them side by side in the air fryer basket. 4. Cover the rolls loosely with a kitchen towel or a sheet of plastic wrap and let sit until lightly risen and puffed, 20 to 30 minutes. 5. Preheat the air fryer to 270°F (132°C). 6. Uncover the rolls and gently brush with more butter, being careful not to press the rolls too hard. Air fry until the rolls are light golden brown and fluffy, about 12 minutes. 7. Remove the rolls from the air fryer and brush liberally with more butter, if you like, and sprinkle each roll with a pinch of sea salt. Serve warm.

Air Fried Spicy Olives

Prep time: 10 minutes | Cook time: 5 minutes | Serves 4

12 ounces (340 g) pitted black extra-large olives
¼ cup all-purpose flour
1 cup panko bread crumbs
2 teaspoons dried thyme
1 teaspoon red pepper flakes
1 teaspoon smoked paprika
1 egg beaten with 1 tablespoon water
Vegetable oil for spraying

1. Preheat the air fryer to 400°F (204°C). 2. Drain the olives and place them on a paper towel–lined plate to dry. 3. Put the flour on a plate. Combine the panko, thyme, red pepper flakes, and paprika on a separate plate. Dip an olive in the flour, shaking off any excess, then coat with egg mixture. Dredge the olive in the panko mixture, pressing to make the crumbs adhere, and place the breaded olive on a platter. Repeat with the remaining olives. 4. Spray the olives with oil and place them in a single layer in the air fryer basket. Work in batches if necessary so as not to overcrowd the basket. Air fry for 5 minutes until the breading is browned and crispy. Serve warm

Mushroom and Green Bean Casserole

Prep time: 10 minutes | Cook time: 15 minutes | Serves 4

4 tablespoons unsalted butter
¼ cup diced yellow onion
½ cup chopped white mushrooms
½ cup heavy whipping cream
1 ounce (28 g) full-fat cream cheese
½ cup chicken broth
¼ teaspoon xanthan gum
1 pound (454 g) fresh green beans, edges trimmed
½ ounce (14 g) pork rinds, finely ground

1. In a medium skillet over medium heat, melt the butter. Sauté the onion and mushrooms until they become soft and fragrant, about 3 to 5 minutes. 2. Add the heavy whipping cream, cream cheese, and broth to the pan. Whisk until smooth. Bring to a boil and then reduce to a simmer. Sprinkle the xanthan gum into the pan and remove from heat. 3. Preheat the air fryer to 320ºF (160ºC). 4. Chop the green beans into 2-inch pieces and place into a baking dish. Pour the sauce mixture over them and stir until coated. Top the dish with ground pork rinds. Put into the air fryer basket and cook for 15 minutes. 5. Top will be golden and green beans fork-tender when fully cooked. Serve warm.

Air Fried Blistered Tomatoes

Prep time: 5 minutes | Cook time: 10 minutes | Serves 4 to 6

2 pounds (907 g) cherry tomatoes
2 tablespoons olive oil
2 teaspoons balsamic vinegar
½ teaspoon salt
½ teaspoon ground black pepper

1. Preheat the air fryer with a cake pan to 400ºF (204ºC). 2. Toss the cherry tomatoes with olive oil in a large bowl to coat well. 3. Pour the tomatoes in the cake pan. Air fry the cherry tomatoes for 10 minutes or until the tomatoes are blistered and lightly wilted. Shake the basket halfway through. 4. Transfer the blistered tomatoes to a large bowl and toss with balsamic vinegar, salt, and black pepper before serving.

Custard Donut Holes with Chocolate Glaze

Prep time: 1 hour 50 minutes | Cook time: 4 minutes per batch | Makes 24 donut holes

Dough:
1½ cups bread flour
2 egg yolks
1 teaspoon active dry yeast
½ cup warm milk
½ teaspoon pure vanilla extract
2 tablespoons butter, melted
1 tablespoon sugar
¼ teaspoon salt
Cooking spray

Custard Filling:
1 (3.4-ounce / 96-g) box French vanilla instant pudding mix
¼ cup heavy cream
¾ cup whole milk

Chocolate Glaze:
⅓ cup heavy cream
1 cup chocolate chips

Special Equipment:
A pastry bag with a long tip

1. Combine the ingredients for the dough in a food processor, then pulse until a satiny dough ball forms. 2. Transfer the dough on a lightly floured work surface, then knead for 2 minutes by hand and shape the dough back to a ball. 3. Spritz a large bowl with cooking spray, then transfer the dough ball into the bowl. Wrap the bowl in plastic and let it rise for 1½ hours or until it doubled in size. 4. Transfer the risen dough on a floured work surface, then shape it into a 24-inch long log. Cut the log into 24 parts and shape each part into a ball. 5. Transfer the balls on two or three baking sheets and let sit to rise for 30 more minutes. 6. Preheat the air fryer to 400ºF (204ºC). Arrange the baking sheets in the air fryer. You need to work in batches to avoid overcrowding. 7. Spritz the balls with cooking spray. Cook for 4 minutes or until golden brown. Flip the balls halfway through. 8. Meanwhile, combine the ingredients for the filling in a large bowl and whisk for 2 minutes with a hand mixer until well combined. 9. Pour the heavy cream in a saucepan, then bring to a boil. Put the chocolate chips in a small bowl and pour in the boiled heavy cream immediately. Mix until the chocolate chips are melted and the mixture is smooth. 10. Transfer the cooked donut holes to a large plate, then pierce a hole into each donut hole and lightly hollow them. 11. Pour the filling in a pastry bag with a long tip and gently squeeze the filling into the donut holes. Then top the donut holes with chocolate glaze. 12. Allow to sit for 10 minutes, then serve.

Whole Chicken Roast

Prep time: 10 minutes | Cook time: 1 hour | Serves 6

1 teaspoon salt
1 teaspoon Italian seasoning
½ teaspoon freshly ground black pepper
½ teaspoon paprika
½ teaspoon garlic powder
½ teaspoon onion powder
2 tablespoons olive oil, plus more as needed
1 (4-pound / 1.8-kg) fryer chicken

1. Preheat the air fryer to 360ºF (182ºC). 2. Grease the air fryer basket lightly with olive oil. 3. In a small bowl, mix the salt, Italian seasoning, pepper, paprika, garlic powder, and onion powder. 4. Remove any giblets from the chicken. Pat the chicken dry thoroughly with paper towels, including the cavity. 5. Brush the chicken all over with the olive oil and rub it with the seasoning mixture. 6. Truss the chicken or tie the legs with butcher's twine. This will make it easier to flip the chicken during cooking. 7. Put the chicken in the air fryer basket, breast-side down. Air fry for 30 minutes. Flip the chicken over and baste it with any drippings collected in the bottom drawer of the air fryer. Lightly brush the chicken with olive oil. 8. Air fry for 20 minutes. Flip the chicken over one last time and air fry until a thermometer inserted into the thickest part of the thigh reaches at least 165ºF (74ºC) and it's crispy and golden, 10 more minutes. Continue to cook, checking every 5 minutes until the chicken reaches the correct internal temperature. 9. Let the chicken rest for 10 minutes before carving and serving.

Garlicky Olive Stromboli

Prep time: 25 minutes | Cook time: 25 minutes | Serves 8

4 large cloves garlic, unpeeled
3 tablespoons grated Parmesan cheese
½ cup packed fresh basil leaves
½ cup marinated, pitted green and black olives
¼ teaspoon crushed red pepper
½ pound (227 g) pizza dough, at room temperature
4 ounces (113 g) sliced provolone cheese (about 8 slices)
Cooking spray

1. Preheat the air fryer to 370°F (188°C). Spritz the air fryer basket with cooking spray. 2. Put the unpeeled garlic in the air fryer basket. 3. Air fry for 10 minutes or until the garlic is softened completely. Remove them from the air fryer and allow to cool until you can handle. 4. Peel the garlic and place into a food processor with 2 tablespoons of Parmesan, basil, olives, and crushed red pepper. Pulse to mix well. Set aside. 5. Arrange the pizza dough on a clean work surface, then roll it out with a rolling pin into a rectangle. Cut the rectangle in half. 6. Sprinkle half of the garlic mixture over each rectangle half, and leave ½-inch edges uncover. Top them with the provolone cheese. 7. Brush one long side of each rectangle half with water, then roll them up. Spritz the air fryer basket with cooking spray. Transfer the rolls in the preheated air fryer. Spritz with cooking spray and scatter with remaining Parmesan. 8. Air fry the rolls for 15 minutes or until golden brown. Flip the rolls halfway through. 9. Remove the rolls from the air fryer and allow to cool for a few minutes before serving.

Arancini

Prep time: 5 minutes | Cook time: 30 minutes | Makes 10 arancini

⅔ cup raw white Arborio rice
2 teaspoons butter
½ teaspoon salt
1⅓ cups water
2 large eggs, well beaten
1¼ cups seasoned Italian-style dried breadcrumbs
10 ¾-inch semi-firm Mozzarella cubes
Cooking spray

1. Pour the rice, butter, salt, and water in a pot. Stir to mix well and bring a boil over medium-high heat. Keep stirring. 2. Reduce the heat to low and cover the pot. Simmer for 20 minutes or until the rice is tender. 3. Turn off the heat and let sit, covered, for 10 minutes, then open the lid and fluffy the rice with a fork. Allow to cool for 10 more minutes. 4. Preheat the air fryer to 375°F (191°C). 5. Pour the beaten eggs in a bowl, then pour the breadcrumbs in a separate bowl. 6. Scoop 2 tablespoons of the cooked rice up and form it into a ball, then press the Mozzarella into the ball and wrap. 7. Dredge the ball in the eggs first, then shake the excess off the dunk the ball in the breadcrumbs. Roll to coat evenly. Repeat to make 10 balls in total with remaining rice. 8. Transfer the balls in the preheated air fryer and spritz with cooking spray. You need to work in batches to avoid overcrowding. 9. Air fry for 10 minutes or until the balls are lightly browned and crispy. 10. Remove the balls from the air fryer and allow to cool before serving.

Chapter 10 Family Favorites

Chapter 10 Family Favorites

Pecan Rolls

Prep time: 20 minutes | Cook time: 20 to 24 minutes | Makes 12 rolls

2 cups all-purpose flour, plus more for dusting
2 tablespoons granulated sugar, plus ¼ cup, divided
1 teaspoon salt
3 tablespoons butter, at room temperature
¾ cup milk, whole or 2%
¼ cup packed light brown sugar
½ cup chopped pecans, toasted
1 to 2 tablespoons oil
¼ cup confectioners' sugar (optional)

1. In a large bowl, whisk the flour, 2 tablespoons granulated sugar, and salt until blended. Stir in the butter and milk briefly until a sticky dough forms. 2. In a small bowl, stir together the brown sugar and remaining ¼ cup of granulated sugar. 3. Place a piece of parchment paper on a work surface and dust it with flour. Roll the dough on the prepared surface to ¼ inch thickness. 4. Spread the sugar mixture over the dough. Sprinkle the pecans on top. Roll up the dough jelly roll-style, pinching the ends to seal. Cut the dough into 12 rolls. 5. Preheat the air fryer to 320°F (160°C). 6. Line the air fryer basket with parchment paper and spritz the parchment with oil. Place 6 rolls on the prepared parchment. 7. Cook for 5 minutes. Flip the rolls and cook for 5 to 7 minutes more until lightly browned. Repeat with the remaining rolls. 8. Sprinkle with confectioners' sugar (if using).

Phyllo Vegetable Triangles

Prep time: 15 minutes | Cook time: 6 to 11 minutes | Serves 6

3 tablespoons minced onion
2 garlic cloves, minced
2 tablespoons grated carrot
1 teaspoon olive oil
3 tablespoons frozen baby peas, thawed
2 tablespoons nonfat cream cheese, at room temperature
6 sheets frozen phyllo dough, thawed
Olive oil spray, for coating the dough

1. In a baking pan, combine the onion, garlic, carrot, and olive oil. Air fry at 390°F (199°C) for 2 to 4 minutes, or until the vegetables are crisp-tender. Transfer to a bowl. 2. Stir in the peas and cream cheese to the vegetable mixture. Let cool while you prepare the dough. 3. Lay one sheet of phyllo on a work surface and lightly spray with olive oil spray. Top with another sheet of phyllo. Repeat with the remaining 4 phyllo sheets; you'll have 3 stacks with 2 layers each. Cut each stack lengthwise into 4 strips (12 strips total). 4. Place a scant 2 teaspoons of the filling near the bottom of each strip. Bring one corner up over the filling to make a triangle; continue folding the triangles over, as you would fold a flag. Seal the edge with a bit of water. Repeat with the remaining strips and filling. 5. Air fry the triangles, in 2 batches, for 4 to 7 minutes, or until golden brown. Serve.

Beignets

Prep time: 30 minutes | Cook time: 6 minutes | Makes 9 beignets

Oil, for greasing and spraying
3 cups all-purpose flour, plus more for dusting
1½ teaspoons salt
1 (2¼-teaspoon) envelope active dry yeast
1 cup milk
2 tablespoons packed light brown sugar
1 tablespoon unsalted butter
1 large egg
1 cup confectioners' sugar

1. Oil a large bowl. 2. In a small bowl, mix together the flour, salt, and yeast. Set aside. 3. Pour the milk into a glass measuring cup and microwave in 1-minute intervals until it boils. 4. In a large bowl, mix together the brown sugar and butter. Pour in the hot milk and whisk until the sugar has dissolved. Let cool to room temperature. 5. Whisk the egg into the cooled milk mixture and fold in the flour mixture until a dough forms. 6. On a lightly floured work surface, knead the dough for 3 to 5 minutes. 7. Place the dough in the oiled bowl and cover with a clean kitchen towel. Let rise in a warm place for about 1 hour, or until doubled in size. 8. Roll the dough out on a lightly floured work surface until it's about ¼ inch thick. Cut the dough into 3-inch squares and place them on a lightly floured baking sheet. Cover loosely with a kitchen towel and let rise again until doubled in size, about 30 minutes. 9. Line the air fryer basket with parchment and spray lightly with oil. 10. Place the dough squares in the prepared basket and spray lightly with oil. You may need to work in batches, depending on the size of your air fryer. 11. Air fry at 390°F (199°C) for 3 minutes, flip, spray with oil, and cook for another 3 minutes, until crispy. 12. Dust with the confectioners' sugar before serving.

Elephant Ears

Prep time: 5 minutes | Cook time: 5 minutes | Serves 8

Oil, for spraying
1 (8-ounce / 227-g) can buttermilk biscuits
3 tablespoons sugar
1 tablespoon ground cinnamon
3 tablespoons unsalted butter, melted
8 scoops vanilla ice cream (optional)

1. Line the air fryer basket with parchment and spray lightly with oil. 2. Separate the dough. Using a rolling pin, roll out the biscuits into 6- to 8-inch circles. 3. Place the dough circles in the prepared basket and spray liberally with oil. You may need to work in batches, depending on the size of your air fryer. 4. Air fry at 350°F (177°C) for 5 minutes, or until lightly browned. 5. In a small bowl, mix together the sugar and cinnamon. 6. Brush the elephant ears with the melted butter and sprinkle with the cinnamon-sugar mixture. 7. Top each serving with a scoop of ice cream (if using).

Beef Jerky

Prep time: 30 minutes | Cook time: 2 hours | Serves 8

Oil, for spraying
1 pound (454 g) round steak, cut into thin, short slices
¼ cup soy sauce
3 tablespoons packed light brown sugar
1 tablespoon minced garlic
1 teaspoon ground ginger
1 tablespoon water

1. Line the air fryer basket with parchment and spray lightly with oil. 2. Place the steak, soy sauce, brown sugar, garlic, ginger, and water in a zip-top plastic bag, seal, and shake well until evenly coated. Refrigerate for 30 minutes. 3. Place the steak in the prepared basket in a single layer. You may need to work in batches, depending on the size of your air fryer. 4. Air fry at 180ºF (82ºC) for at least 2 hours. Add more time if you like your jerky a bit tougher.

Veggie Tuna Melts

Prep time: 15 minutes | Cook time: 7 to 11 minutes | Serves 4

2 low-sodium whole-wheat English muffins, split
1 (6-ounce / 170-g) can chunk light low-sodium tuna, drained
1 cup shredded carrot
⅓ cup chopped mushrooms
2 scallions, white and green parts, sliced
⅓ cup nonfat Greek yogurt
2 tablespoons low-sodium stone-ground mustard
2 slices low-sodium low-fat Swiss cheese, halved

1. Place the English muffin halves in the air fryer basket. Air fry at 340ºF (171ºC) for 3 to 4 minutes, or until crisp. Remove from the basket and set aside. 2. In a medium bowl, thoroughly mix the tuna, carrot, mushrooms, scallions, yogurt, and mustard. Top each half of the muffins with one-fourth of the tuna mixture and a half slice of Swiss cheese. 3. Air fry for 4 to 7 minutes, or until the tuna mixture is hot and the cheese melts and starts to brown. Serve immediately.

Fish and Vegetable Tacos

Prep time: 15 minutes | Cook time: 9 to 12 minutes | Serves 4

1 pound (454 g) white fish fillets, such as sole or cod
2 teaspoons olive oil
3 tablespoons freshly squeezed lemon juice, divided
1½ cups chopped red cabbage
1 large carrot, grated
½ cup low-sodium salsa
⅓ cup low-fat Greek yogurt
4 soft low-sodium whole-wheat tortillas

1. Brush the fish with the olive oil and sprinkle with 1 tablespoon of lemon juice. Air fry in the air fryer basket at 390ºF (199ºC) for 9 to 12 minutes, or until the fish just flakes when tested with a fork. 2. Meanwhile, in a medium bowl, stir together the remaining 2 tablespoons of lemon juice, the red cabbage, carrot, salsa, and yogurt. 3. When the fish is cooked, remove it from the air fryer basket and break it up into large pieces. 4. Offer the fish, tortillas, and the cabbage mixture, and let each person assemble a taco.

Mixed Berry Crumble

Prep time: 10 minutes | Cook time: 11 to 16 minutes | Serves 4

½ cup chopped fresh strawberries
½ cup fresh blueberries
⅓ cup frozen raspberries
1 tablespoon freshly squeezed lemon juice
1 tablespoon honey
⅔ cup whole-wheat pastry flour
3 tablespoons packed brown sugar
2 tablespoons unsalted butter, melted

1. In a baking pan, combine the strawberries, blueberries, and raspberries. Drizzle with the lemon juice and honey. 2. In a small bowl, mix the pastry flour and brown sugar. 3. Stir in the butter and mix until crumbly. Sprinkle this mixture over the fruit. 4. Cook at 380ºF (193ºC) for 11 to 16 minutes, or until the fruit is tender and bubbly and the topping is golden brown. Serve warm.

Buffalo Cauliflower

Prep time: 15 minutes | Cook time: 5 minutes | Serves 6

1 large head cauliflower, separated into small florets
1 tablespoon olive oil
½ teaspoon garlic powder
⅓ cup low-sodium hot wing sauce
⅔ cup nonfat Greek yogurt
½ teaspoons Tabasco sauce
1 celery stalk, chopped
1 tablespoon crumbled blue cheese

1. In a large bowl, toss the cauliflower florets with the olive oil. Sprinkle with the garlic powder and toss again to coat. Put half of the cauliflower in the air fryer basket. Air fry at 380ºF (193ºC) for 5 to 7 minutes, until the cauliflower is browned, shaking the basket once during cooking. 2. Transfer to a serving bowl and toss with half of the wing sauce. Repeat with the remaining cauliflower and wing sauce. 3. In a small bowl, stir together the yogurt, Tabasco sauce, celery, and blue cheese. Serve with the cauliflower for dipping.

Chinese-Inspired Spareribs

Prep time: 30 minutes | Cook time: 8 minutes | Serves 4

Oil, for spraying
12 ounces (340 g) boneless pork spareribs, cut into 3-inch-long pieces
1 cup soy sauce
¾ cup sugar
½ cup beef or chicken stock
¼ cup honey
2 tablespoons minced garlic
1 teaspoon ground ginger
2 drops red food coloring (optional)

1. Line the air fryer basket with parchment and spray lightly with oil. 2. Combine the ribs, soy sauce, sugar, beef stock, honey, garlic, ginger, and food coloring (if using) in a large zip-top plastic bag, seal, and shake well until completely coated. Refrigerate for at least 30 minutes. 3. Place the ribs in the prepared basket. 4. Air fry at 375ºF (191ºC) for 8 minutes, or until the internal temperature reaches 165ºF (74ºC).

Steak Tips and Potatoes

Prep time: 10 minutes | Cook time: 20 minutes | Serves 4

Oil, for spraying
8 ounces (227 g) baby gold potatoes, cut in half
½ teaspoon salt
1 pound (454 g) steak, cut into ½-inch pieces
1 teaspoon Worcestershire sauce
1 teaspoon granulated garlic
½ teaspoon salt
½ teaspoon freshly ground black pepper

1. Line the air fryer basket with parchment and spray lightly with oil. 2. In a microwave-safe bowl, combine the potatoes and salt, then pour in about ½ inch of water. Microwave for 7 minutes, or until the potatoes are nearly tender. Drain. 3. In a large bowl, gently mix together the steak, potatoes, Worcestershire sauce, garlic, salt, and black pepper. Spread the mixture in an even layer in the prepared basket. 4. Air fry at 400ºF (204ºC) for 12 to 17 minutes, stirring after 5 to 6 minutes. The cooking time will depend on the thickness of the meat and preferred doneness.

Pork Stuffing Meatballs

Prep time: 10 minutes | Cook time: 12 minutes | Makes 35 meatballs

Oil, for spraying
1½ pounds (680 g) ground pork
1 cup bread crumbs
½ cup milk
¼ cup minced onion
1 large egg
1 tablespoon dried rosemary
1 tablespoon dried thyme
1 teaspoon salt
1 teaspoon freshly ground black pepper
1 teaspoon finely chopped fresh parsley

1. Line the air fryer basket with parchment and spray lightly with oil. 2. In a large bowl, mix together the ground pork, bread crumbs, milk, onion, egg, rosemary, thyme, salt, black pepper, and parsley. 3. Roll about 2 tablespoons of the mixture into a ball. Repeat with the rest of the mixture. You should have 30 to 35 meatballs. 4. Place the meatballs in the prepared basket in a single layer, leaving space between each one. You may need to work in batches, depending on the size of your air fryer. 5. Air fry at 390ºF (199ºC) for 10 to 12 minutes, flipping after 5 minutes, or until golden brown and the internal temperature reaches 160ºF (71ºC).

Apple Pie Egg Rolls

Prep time: 10 minutes | Cook time: 8 minutes | Makes 6 rolls

Oil, for spraying
1 (21-ounce / 595-g) can apple pie filling
1 tablespoon all-purpose flour
½ teaspoon lemon juice
¼ teaspoon ground nutmeg
¼ teaspoon ground cinnamon
6 egg roll wrappers

1. Preheat the air fryer to 400ºF (204ºC). Line the air fryer basket with parchment and spray lightly with oil. 2. In a medium bowl, mix together the pie filling, flour, lemon juice, nutmeg, and cinnamon. 3. Lay out the egg roll wrappers on a work surface and spoon a dollop of pie filling in the center of each. 4. Fill a small bowl with water. Dip your finger in the water and, working one at a time, moisten the edges of the wrappers. Fold the wrapper like an envelope: First fold one corner into the center. Fold each side corner in, and then fold over the remaining corner, making sure each corner overlaps a bit and the moistened edges stay closed. Use additional water and your fingers to seal any open edges. 5. Place the rolls in the prepared basket and spray liberally with oil. You may need to work in batches, depending on the size of your air fryer. 6. Cook for 4 minutes, flip, spray with oil, and cook for another 4 minutes, or until crispy and golden brown. Serve immediately.

Cajun Shrimp

Prep time: 15 minutes | Cook time: 9 minutes | Serves 4

Oil, for spraying
1 pound (454 g) jumbo raw shrimp, peeled and deveined
1 tablespoon Cajun seasoning
6 ounces (170 g) cooked kielbasa, cut into thick slices
½ medium zucchini, cut into ¼-inch-thick slices
½ medium yellow squash, cut into ¼-inch-thick slices
1 green bell pepper, seeded and cut into 1-inch pieces
2 tablespoons olive oil
½ teaspoon salt

1. Preheat the air fryer to 400ºF (204ºC). Line the air fryer basket with parchment and spray lightly with oil. 2. In a large bowl, toss together the shrimp and Cajun seasoning. Add the kielbasa, zucchini, squash, bell pepper, olive oil, and salt and mix well. 3. Transfer the mixture to the prepared basket, taking care not to overcrowd. You may need to work in batches, depending on the size of your air fryer. 4. Cook for 9 minutes, shaking and stirring every 3 minutes. Serve immediately.

Meringue Cookies

Prep time: 15 minutes | Cook time: 1 hour 30 minutes | Makes 20 cookies

Oil, for spraying
4 large egg whites
1 cup sugar
Pinch cream of tartar

1. Preheat the air fryer to 140ºF (60ºC). Line the air fryer basket with parchment and spray lightly with oil. 2. In a small heatproof bowl, whisk together the egg whites and sugar. Fill a small saucepan halfway with water, place it over medium heat, and bring to a light simmer. Place the bowl with the egg whites on the saucepan, making sure the bottom of the bowl does not touch the water. Whisk the mixture until the sugar is dissolved. 3. Transfer the mixture to a large bowl and add the cream of tartar. Using an electric mixer, beat the mixture on high until it is glossy and stiff peaks form. Transfer the mixture to a piping bag or a zip-top plastic bag with a corner cut off. 4. Pipe rounds into the prepared basket. You may need to work in batches, depending on the size of your air fryer. 5. Cook for 1 hour 30 minutes. 6. Turn off the air fryer and let the meringues cool completely inside. The residual heat will continue to dry them out.

Churro Bites

Prep time: 5 minutes | Cook time: 6 minutes | Makes 36 bites

Oil, for spraying
1 (17¼-ounce / 489-g) package frozen puffed pastry, thawed
1 cup granulated sugar
1 tablespoon ground cinnamon
½ cup confectioners' sugar
1 tablespoon milk

1. Preheat the air fryer to 400°F (204°C). Line the air fryer basket with parchment and spray lightly with oil. 2. Unfold the puff pastry onto a clean work surface. Using a sharp knife, cut the dough into 36 bite-size pieces. 3. Place the dough pieces in one layer in the prepared basket, taking care not to let the pieces touch or overlap. 4. Cook for 3 minutes, flip, and cook for another 3 minutes, or until puffed and golden. 5. In a small bowl, mix together the granulated sugar and cinnamon. 6. In another small bowl, whisk together the confectioners' sugar and milk. 7. Dredge the bites in the cinnamon-sugar mixture until evenly coated. 8. Serve with the icing on the side for dipping.

Puffed Egg Tarts

Prep time: 10 minutes | Cook time: 42 minutes | Makes 4 tarts

Oil, for spraying
All-purpose flour, for dusting
1 (12-ounce / 340-g) sheet frozen puff pastry, thawed
¾ cup shredded Cheddar cheese, divided
4 large eggs
2 teaspoons chopped fresh parsley
Salt and freshly ground black pepper, to taste

1. Preheat the air fryer to 390°F (199°C). Line the air fryer basket with parchment and spray lightly with oil. 2. Lightly dust your work surface with flour. Unfold the puff pastry and cut it into 4 equal squares. Place 2 squares in the prepared basket. 3. Cook for 10 minutes. 4. Remove the basket. Press the center of each tart shell with a spoon to make an indentation. 5. Sprinkle 3 tablespoons of cheese into each indentation and crack 1 egg into the center of each tart shell. 6. Cook for another 7 to 11 minutes, or until the eggs are cooked to your desired doneness. 7. Repeat with the remaining puff pastry squares, cheese, and eggs. 8. Sprinkle evenly with the parsley, and season with salt and black pepper. Serve immediately.

Fried Green Tomatoes

Prep time: 15 minutes | Cook time: 6 to 8 minutes | Serves 4

4 medium green tomatoes
⅓ cup all-purpose flour
2 egg whites
¼ cup almond milk
1 cup ground almonds
½ cup panko bread crumbs
2 teaspoons olive oil
1 teaspoon paprika
1 clove garlic, minced

1. Rinse the tomatoes and pat dry. Cut the tomatoes into ½-inch slices, discarding the thinner ends. 2. Put the flour on a plate. In a shallow bowl, beat the egg whites with the almond milk until frothy. And on another plate, combine the almonds, bread crumbs, olive oil, paprika, and garlic and mix well. 3. Dip the tomato slices into the flour, then into the egg white mixture, then into the almond mixture to coat. 4. Place four of the coated tomato slices in the air fryer basket. Air fry at 400°F (204°C) for 6 to 8 minutes or until the tomato coating is crisp and golden brown. Repeat with remaining tomato slices and serve immediately.

Meatball Subs

Prep time: 15 minutes | Cook time: 19 minutes | Serves 6

Oil, for spraying
1 pound (454 g) 85% lean ground beef
½ cup Italian bread crumbs
1 tablespoon dried minced onion
1 tablespoon minced garlic
1 large egg
1 teaspoon salt
1 teaspoon freshly ground black pepper
6 hoagie rolls
1 (18-ounce / 510-g) jar marinara sauce
1½ cups shredded Mozzarella cheese

1. Line the air fryer basket with parchment and spray lightly with oil. 2. In a large bowl, mix together the ground beef, bread crumbs, onion, garlic, egg, salt, and black pepper. Roll the mixture into 18 meatballs. 3. Place the meatballs in the prepared basket. 4. Air fry at 390°F (199°C) for 15 minutes. 5. Place 3 meatballs in each hoagie roll. Top with marinara and Mozzarella cheese. 6. Place the loaded rolls in the air fryer and cook for 3 to 4 minutes, or until the cheese is melted. You may need to work in batches, depending on the size of your air fryer. Serve immediately.

Old Bay Tilapia

Prep time: 15 minutes | Cook time: 6 minutes | Serves 4

Oil, for spraying
1 cup panko bread crumbs
2 tablespoons Old Bay seasoning
2 teaspoons granulated garlic
1 teaspoon onion powder
½ teaspoon salt
¼ teaspoon freshly ground black pepper
1 large egg
4 tilapia fillets

1. Preheat the air fryer to 400°F (204°C). Line the air fryer basket with parchment and spray lightly with oil. 2. In a shallow bowl, mix together the bread crumbs, Old Bay, garlic, onion powder, salt, and black pepper. 3. In a small bowl, whisk the egg. 4. Coat the tilapia in the egg, then dredge in the bread crumb mixture until completely coated. 5. Place the tilapia in the prepared basket. You may need to work in batches, depending on the size of your air fryer. Spray lightly with oil. 6. Cook for 4 to 6 minutes, depending on the thickness of the fillets, until the internal temperature reaches 145°F (63°C). Serve immediately.

Chapter 11 Desserts

Chapter 11 Desserts

Peaches and Apple Crumble

Prep time: 10 minutes | Cook time: 10 to 12 minutes | Serves 4

2 peaches, peeled, pitted, and chopped
1 apple, peeled and chopped
2 tablespoons honey
½ cup quick-cooking oatmeal
⅓ cup whole-wheat pastry flour
2 tablespoons unsalted butter, at room temperature
3 tablespoons packed brown sugar
½ teaspoon ground cinnamon

1. Preheat the air fryer to 380°F (193°C). 2. Mix together the peaches, apple, and honey in a baking pan until well incorporated. 3. In a bowl, combine the oatmeal, pastry flour, butter, brown sugar, and cinnamon and stir to mix well. Spread this mixture evenly over the fruit. 4. Place the baking pan in the air fryer basket and cook for 10 to 12 minutes, or until the fruit is bubbling around the edges and the topping is golden brown. 5. Remove from the basket and serve warm.

Vanilla Scones

Prep time: 20 minutes | Cook time: 10 minutes | Serves 6

4 ounces (113 g) coconut flour
½ teaspoon baking powder
1 teaspoon apple cider vinegar
2 teaspoons mascarpone
¼ cup heavy cream
1 teaspoon vanilla extract
1 tablespoon erythritol
Cooking spray

1. In the mixing bowl, mix coconut flour with baking powder, apple cider vinegar, mascarpone, heavy cream, vanilla extract, and erythritol. 2. Knead the dough and cut into scones. 3. Then put them in the air fryer basket and sprinkle with cooking spray. 4. Cook the vanilla scones at 365°F (185°C) for 10 minutes.

Pumpkin-Spice Bread Pudding

Prep time: 15 minutes | Cook time: 35 minutes | Serves 6

Bread Pudding:
¾ cup heavy whipping cream
½ cup canned pumpkin
⅓ cup whole milk
⅓ cup sugar
1 large egg plus 1 yolk
½ teaspoon pumpkin pie spice
⅛ teaspoon kosher salt
4 cups 1-inch cubed day-old baguette or crusty country bread
4 tablespoons (½ stick) unsalted butter, melted
Sauce:
⅓ cup pure maple syrup
1 tablespoon unsalted butter
½ cup heavy whipping cream
½ teaspoon pure vanilla extract

1. For the bread pudding: In a medium bowl, combine the cream, pumpkin, milk, sugar, egg and yolk, pumpkin pie spice, and salt. Whisk until well combined. 2. In a large bowl, toss the bread cubes with the melted butter. Add the pumpkin mixture and gently toss until the ingredients are well combined. 3. Transfer the mixture to a baking pan. Place the pan in the air fryer basket. Set the fryer to 350°F (177°C) for 35 minutes, or until custard is set in the middle. 4. Meanwhile, for the sauce: In a small saucepan, combine the syrup and butter. Heat over medium heat, stirring, until the butter melts. Stir in the cream and simmer, stirring often, until the sauce has thickened, about 15 minutes. Stir in the vanilla. Remove the pudding from the air fryer. 5. Let the pudding stand for 10 minutes before serving with the warm sauce.

Double Chocolate Brownies

Prep time: 5 minutes | Cook time: 15 to 20 minutes | Serves 8

1 cup almond flour
½ cup unsweetened cocoa powder
½ teaspoon baking powder
⅓ cup Swerve
¼ teaspoon salt
½ cup unsalted butter, melted and cooled
3 eggs
1 teaspoon vanilla extract
2 tablespoons mini semisweet chocolate chips

1. Preheat the air fryer to 350°F (177°C). Line a cake pan with parchment paper and brush with oil. 2. In a large bowl, combine the almond flour, cocoa powder, baking powder, Swerve, and salt. Add the butter, eggs, and vanilla. Stir until thoroughly combined. (The batter will be thick.) Spread the batter into the prepared pan and scatter the chocolate chips on top. 3. Air fry for 15 to 20 minutes until the edges are set. (The center should still appear slightly undercooked.) Let cool completely before slicing. To store, cover and refrigerate the brownies for up to 3 days.

Crispy Pineapple Rings

Prep time: 5 minutes | Cook time: 6 to 8 minutes | Serves 6

1 cup rice milk
⅔ cup flour
½ cup water
¼ cup unsweetened flaked coconut
4 tablespoons sugar
½ teaspoon baking soda
½ teaspoon baking powder
½ teaspoon vanilla essence
½ teaspoon ground cinnamon
¼ teaspoon ground anise star
Pinch of kosher salt
1 medium pineapple, peeled and sliced

1. Preheat the air fryer to 380°F (193°C). 2. In a large bowl, stir together all the ingredients except the pineapple. 3. Dip each pineapple slice into the batter until evenly coated. 4. Arrange the pineapple slices in the basket and air fry for 6 to 8 minutes until golden brown. 5. Remove from the basket to a plate and cool for 5 minutes before serving.arm.

Dark Chocolate Lava Cake

Prep time: 5 minutes | Cook time: 10 minutes | Serves 4

Olive oil cooking spray
¼ cup whole wheat flour
1 tablespoon unsweetened dark chocolate cocoa powder
⅛ teaspoon salt
½ teaspoon baking powder
¼ cup raw honey
1 egg
2 tablespoons olive oil

1. Preheat the air fryer to 380°F(193°C). Lightly coat the insides of four ramekins with olive oil cooking spray. 2. In a medium bowl, combine the flour, cocoa powder, salt, baking powder, honey, egg, and olive oil. 3. Divide the batter evenly among the ramekins. 4. Place the filled ramekins inside the air fryer and cook for 10 minutes. 5. Remove the lava cakes from the air fryer and slide a knife around the outside edge of each cake. Turn each ramekin upside down on a saucer and serve.

Fried Golden Bananas

Prep time: 5 minutes | Cook time: 7 minutes | Serves 6

1 large egg
¼ cup cornstarch
¼ cup plain bread crumbs
3 bananas, halved crosswise
Cooking oil
Chocolate sauce, for drizzling

1. Preheat the air fryer to 375°F (191°C) 2. Separate the biscuit dough into 8 biscuits and place them on a flat work surface. Use a small circle cookie cutter or a biscuit cutter to cut a hole in the center of each biscuit. You can also cut the holes using a knife. 3. Spray the air fryer basket with cooking oil. 4. Put 4 donuts in the air fryer. Do not stack. Spray with cooking oil. Air fry for 4 minutes. 5. Open the air fryer and flip the donuts. Air fry for an additional 4 minutes. 6. Remove the cooked donuts from the air fryer, then repeat steps 3 and 4 for the remaining 4 donuts. 7. Drizzle chocolate sauce over the donuts and enjoy while warm.

Caramelized Fruit Skewers

Prep time: 10 minutes | Cook time: 3 to 5 minutes | Serves 4

2 peaches, peeled, pitted, and thickly sliced
3 plums, halved and pitted
3 nectarines, halved and pitted
1 tablespoon honey
½ teaspoon ground cinnamon
¼ teaspoon ground allspice
Pinch cayenne pepper
Special Equipment:
8 metal skewers

1. Preheat the air fryer to 400°F (204°C). 2. Thread, alternating peaches, plums, and nectarines, onto the metal skewers that fit into the air fryer. 3. Thoroughly combine the honey, cinnamon, allspice, and cayenne in a small bowl. Brush generously the glaze over the fruit skewers. 4. Transfer the fruit skewers to the air fryer basket. You may need to cook in batches to avoid overcrowding. 5. Air fry for 3 to 5 minutes, or until the fruit is caramelized. 6. Remove from the basket and repeat with the remaining fruit skewers. 7. Let the fruit skewers rest for 5 minutes before serving.

Shortcut Spiced Apple Butter

Prep time: 5 minutes | Cook time: 1 hour | Makes 1¼ cups

Cooking spray
2 cups store-bought unsweetened applesauce
⅔ cup packed light brown sugar
3 tablespoons fresh lemon juice
½ teaspoon kosher salt
¼ teaspoon ground cinnamon
⅛ teaspoon ground allspice

1. Spray a cake pan with cooking spray. Whisk together all the ingredients in a bowl until smooth, then pour into the greased pan. Set the pan in the air fryer and cook at 340°F (171°C) until the apple mixture is caramelized, reduced to a thick purée, and fragrant, about 1 hour. 2. Remove the pan from the air fryer, stir to combine the caramelized bits at the edge with the rest, then let cool completely to thicken. Scrape the apple butter into a jar and store in the refrigerator for up to 2 weeks.

Baked Brazilian Pineapple

Prep time: 10 minutes | Cook time: 10 minutes | Serves 4

½ cup brown sugar
2 teaspoons ground cinnamon
1 small pineapple, peeled,
cored, and cut into spears
3 tablespoons unsalted butter, melted

1. In a small bowl, mix the brown sugar and cinnamon until thoroughly combined. 2. Brush the pineapple spears with the melted butter. Sprinkle the cinnamon-sugar over the spears, pressing lightly to ensure it adheres well. 3. Place the spears in the air fryer basket in a single layer. (Depending on the size of your air fryer, you may have to do this in batches.) Set the air fryer to 400°F (204°C) for 10 minutes for the first batch (6 to 8 minutes for the next batch, as the fryer will be preheated). Halfway through the cooking time, brush the spears with butter. 4. The pineapple spears are done when they are heated through and the sugar is bubbling. Serve hot.

Funnel Cake

Prep time: 10 minutes | Cook time: 5 minutes | Serves 4

Oil, for spraying
1 cup self-rising flour, plus more for dusting
1 cup fat-free vanilla Greek yogurt
½ teaspoon ground cinnamon
¼ cup confectioners' sugar

1. Preheat the air fryer to 375°F (191°C). Line the air fryer basket with parchment and spray lightly with oil. 2. In a large bowl, mix together the flour, yogurt, and cinnamon until the mixture forms a ball. 3. Place the dough on a lightly floured work surface and knead for about 2 minutes. 4. Cut the dough into 4 equal pieces, then cut each of those into 6 pieces. You should have 24 total pieces. 5. Roll the pieces into 8- to 10-inch-long ropes. Loosely mound the ropes into 4 piles of 6 ropes. 6. Place the dough piles in the prepared basket and spray liberally with oil. You may need to work in batches, depending on the size of your air fryer. 7. Cook for 5 minutes, or until lightly browned. 8. Dust with the confectioners' sugar before serving.

Chocolate Cake

Prep time: 10 minutes | Cook time: 20 to 23 minutes | Serves 8

½ cup sugar
¼ cup flour, plus 3 tablespoons
3 tablespoons cocoa
½ teaspoon baking powder
½ teaspoon baking soda
¼ teaspoon salt
1 egg
2 tablespoons oil
½ cup milk
½ teaspoon vanilla extract

1. Preheat the air fryer to 330°F (166°C). 2. Grease and flour a baking pan. 3. In a medium bowl, stir together the sugar, flour, cocoa, baking powder, baking soda, and salt. 4. Add all other ingredients and beat with a wire whisk until smooth. 5. Pour batter into prepared pan and cook at 330°F (166°C) for 20 to 23 minutes, until toothpick inserted in center comes out clean or with crumbs clinging to it.

Apple Hand Pies

Prep time: 15 minutes | Cook time: 25 minutes | Serves 8

2 apples, cored and diced
¼ cup honey
1 teaspoon ground cinnamon
1 teaspoon vanilla extract
⅛ teaspoon ground nutmeg
2 teaspoons cornstarch
1 teaspoon water
4 refrigerated piecrusts
Cooking oil spray

1. Insert the crisper plate into the basket and the basket into the unit. Preheat the unit by selecting AIR FRY, setting the temperature to 400°F (204°C), and setting the time to 3 minutes. Select START/PAUSE to begin. 2. In a metal bowl that fits into the basket, stir together the apples, honey, cinnamon, vanilla, and nutmeg. 3. In a small bowl, whisk the cornstarch and water until the cornstarch dissolves. 4. Once the unit is preheated, place the metal bowl with the apples into the basket. 5. Select AIR FRY, set the temperature to 400°F (204°C), and set the time to 5 minutes. Select START/PAUSE to begin. 6. After 2 minutes, stir the apples. Resume cooking for 2 minutes. 7. Remove the bowl and stir the cornstarch mixture into the apples. Reinsert the metal bowl into the basket and resume cooking for about 30 seconds until the sauce thickens slightly. 8. When the cooking is complete, refrigerate the apples while you prepare the piecrust. 9. Cut each piecrust into 2 (4-inch) circles. You should have 8 circles of crust. 10. Lay the piecrusts on a work surface. Divide the apple filling among the piecrusts, mounding the mixture in the center of each round. 11. Fold each piecrust over so the top layer of crust is about an inch short of the bottom layer. (The edges should not meet.) Use the back of a fork to seal the edges. 12. Insert the crisper plate into the basket and the basket into the unit. Preheat the unit by selecting AIR FRY, setting the temperature to 400°F (204°C), and setting the time to 3 minutes. Select START/PAUSE to begin. 13. Once the unit is preheated, spray the crisper plate with cooking oil, line the basket with parchment paper, and spray it with cooking oil. Working in batches, place the hand pies into the basket in a single layer. 14. Select AIR FRY, set the temperature to 400°F (204°C), and set the time to 10 minutes. Select START/PAUSE to begin. 15. When the cooking is complete, let the hand pies cool for 5 minutes before removing from the basket. 16. Repeat steps 13, 14, and 15 with the remaining pies.

Coconut Mixed Berry Crisp

Prep time: 5 minutes | Cook time: 20 minutes | Serves 6

1 tablespoon butter, melted
12 ounces (340 g) mixed berries
⅓ cup granulated Swerve
1 teaspoon pure vanilla extract
½ teaspoon ground cinnamon
¼ teaspoon ground cloves
¼ teaspoon grated nutmeg
½ cup coconut chips, for garnish

1. Preheat the air fryer to 330°F (166°C). Coat a baking pan with melted butter. 2. Put the remaining ingredients except the coconut chips in the prepared baking pan. 3. Cook in the preheated air fryer for 20 minutes. 4. Serve garnished with the coconut chips.

Bourbon Bread Pudding

Prep time: 10 minutes | Cook time: 20 minutes | Serves 4

3 slices whole grain bread, cubed
1 large egg
1 cup whole milk
2 tablespoons bourbon
½ teaspoons vanilla extract
¼ cup maple syrup, divided
½ teaspoons ground cinnamon
2 teaspoons sparkling sugar

1. Preheat the air fryer to 270°F (132°C). 2. Spray a baking pan with nonstick cooking spray, then place the bread cubes in the pan. 3. In a medium bowl, whisk together the egg, milk, bourbon, vanilla extract, 3 tablespoons of maple syrup, and cinnamon. Pour the egg mixture over the bread and press down with a spatula to coat all the bread, then sprinkle the sparkling sugar on top and cook for 20 minutes. 4. Remove the pudding from the air fryer and allow to cool in the pan on a wire rack for 10 minutes. Drizzle the remaining 1 tablespoon of maple syrup on top. Slice and serve warm.

Berry Crumble

Prep time: 10 minutes | Cook time: 15 minutes | Serves 4

For the Filling:
2 cups mixed berries
2 tablespoons sugar
1 tablespoon cornstarch
1 tablespoon fresh lemon juice
For the Topping:
¼ cup all-purpose flour
¼ cup rolled oats
1 tablespoon sugar
2 tablespoons cold unsalted butter, cut into small cubes
Whipped cream or ice cream (optional)

1. Preheat the air fryer to 400°F (204°C). 2. For the filling: In a round baking pan, gently mix the berries, sugar, cornstarch, and lemon juice until thoroughly combined. 3. For the topping: In a small bowl, combine the flour, oats, and sugar. Stir the butter into the flour mixture until the mixture has the consistency of bread crumbs. 4. Sprinkle the topping over the berries. 5. Put the pan in the air fryer basket and air fry for 15 minutes. Let cool for 5 minutes on a wire rack. 6. Serve topped with whipped cream or ice cream, if desired.

Ricotta Lemon Poppy Seed Cake

Prep time: 10 minutes | Cook time: 55 minutes | Serves 4

Unsalted butter, at room temperature
1 cup almond flour
½ cup sugar
3 large eggs
¼ cup heavy cream
¼ cup full-fat ricotta cheese
¼ cup coconut oil, melted
2 tablespoons poppy seeds
1 teaspoon baking powder
1 teaspoon pure lemon extract
Grated zest and juice of 1 lemon, plus more zest for garnish

1. Generously butter a baking pan. Line the bottom of the pan with parchment paper cut to fit. 2. In a large bowl, combine the almond flour, sugar, eggs, cream, ricotta, coconut oil, poppy seeds, baking powder, lemon extract, lemon zest, and lemon juice. Beat with a hand mixer on medium speed until well blended and fluffy. 3. Pour the batter into the prepared pan. Cover the pan tightly with aluminum foil. Set the pan in the air fryer basket. Set the air fryer to 325°F (163°C) for 45 minutes. Remove the foil and cook for 10 to 15 minutes more, until a knife (do not use a toothpick) inserted into the center of the cake comes out clean. 4. Let the cake cool in the pan on a wire rack for 10 minutes. Remove the cake from pan and let it cool on the rack for 15 minutes before slicing. 5. Top with additional lemon zest, slice and serve.

Strawberry Shortcake

Prep time: 10 minutes | Cook time: 25 minutes | Serves 6

2 tablespoons coconut oil
1 cup blanched finely ground almond flour
2 large eggs, whisked
½ cup granular erythritol
1 teaspoon baking powder
1 teaspoon vanilla extract
2 cups sugar-free whipped cream
6 medium fresh strawberries, hulled and sliced

1. In a large bowl, combine coconut oil, flour, eggs, erythritol, baking powder, and vanilla. Pour batter into an ungreased round nonstick baking dish. 2. Place dish into air fryer basket. Adjust the temperature to 300°F (149°C) and cook for 25 minutes. When done, shortcake should be golden and a toothpick inserted in the middle will come out clean. 3. Remove dish from fryer and let cool 1 hour. 4. Once cooled, top cake with whipped cream and strawberries to serve.

Peanut Butter-Honey-Banana Toast

Prep time: 10 minutes | Cook time: 9 minutes | Serves 4

2 tablespoons butter, softened
4 slices white bread
4 tablespoons peanut butter
2 bananas, peeled and thinly sliced
4 tablespoons honey
1 teaspoon ground cinnamon

1. Spread butter on one side of each slice of bread, then peanut butter on the other side. Arrange the banana slices on top of the peanut butter sides of each slice (about 9 slices per toast). Drizzle honey on top of the banana and sprinkle with cinnamon. 2. Cut each slice in half lengthwise so that it will better fit into the air fryer basket. Arrange two pieces of bread, butter sides down, in the air fryer basket. Set the air fryer to 375°F (191°C) for 5 minutes. Then set the air fryer to 400°F (204°C) for an additional 4 minutes, or until the bananas have started to brown. Repeat with remaining slices. Serve hot.

Zucchini Nut Muffins

Prep time: 15 minutes | Cook time: 15 minutes | Serves 4

¼ cup vegetable oil, plus more for greasing
¾ cup all-purpose flour
¾ teaspoon ground cinnamon
¼ teaspoon kosher salt
¼ teaspoon baking soda
¼ teaspoon baking powder
2 large eggs
½ cup sugar
½ cup grated zucchini
¼ cup chopped walnuts

1. Generously grease four 4-ounce (113-g) ramekins or a baking pan with vegetable oil. 2. In a medium bowl, sift together the flour, cinnamon, salt, baking soda, and baking powder. 3. In a separate medium bowl, beat together the eggs, sugar, and vegetable oil. Add the dry ingredients to the wet ingredients. Add the zucchini and nuts and stir gently until well combined. Transfer the batter to the prepared ramekins or baking pan. 4. Place the ramekins or pan in the air fryer basket. Set the air fryer to 325°F (163°C) for 15 minutes, or until a cake tester or toothpick inserted into the center comes out clean. If it doesn't, cook for 3 to 5 minutes more and test again. 5. Let cool in the ramekins or pan on a wire rack for 10 minutes. Carefully remove from the ramekins or pan and let cool completely on the rack before serving.

Pears with Honey-Lemon Ricotta

Prep time: 10 minutes | Cook time: 8 minutes | Serves 4

2 large Bartlett pears
3 tablespoons butter, melted
3 tablespoons brown sugar
½ teaspoon ground ginger
¼ teaspoon ground cardamom
½ cup whole-milk ricotta cheese
1 tablespoon honey, plus additional for drizzling
1 teaspoon pure almond extract
1 teaspoon pure lemon extract

1. Peel each pear and cut in half lengthwise. Use a melon baller to scoop out the core. Place the pear halves in a medium bowl, add the melted butter, and toss. Add the brown sugar, ginger, and cardamom; toss to coat. 2. Place the pear halves, cut side down, in the air fryer basket. Set the air fryer to 375°F (191°C) for 8 to 10 minutes, or until the pears are lightly browned and tender, but not mushy. 3. Meanwhile, in a medium bowl, combine the ricotta, honey, and almond and lemon extracts. Beat with an electric mixer on medium speed until the mixture is light and fluffy, about 1 minute. 4. To serve, divide the ricotta mixture among four small shallow bowls. Place a pear half, cut side up, on top of the cheese. Drizzle with additional honey and serve.

Chickpea Brownies

Prep time: 10 minutes | Cook time: 20 minutes | Serves 6

Vegetable oil
1 (15-ounce / 425-g) can chickpeas, drained and rinsed
4 large eggs
⅓ cup coconut oil, melted
⅓ cup honey
3 tablespoons unsweetened cocoa powder
1 tablespoon espresso powder (optional)
1 teaspoon baking powder
1 teaspoon baking soda
½ cup chocolate chips

1. Preheat the air fryer to 325°F (163°C). 2. Generously grease a baking pan with vegetable oil. 3. In a blender or food processor, combine the chickpeas, eggs, coconut oil, honey, cocoa powder, espresso powder (if using), baking powder, and baking soda. Blend or process until smooth. Transfer to the prepared pan and stir in the chocolate chips by hand. 4. Set the pan in the air fryer basket and cook for 20 minutes, or until a toothpick inserted into the center comes out clean. 5. Let cool in the pan on a wire rack for 30 minutes before cutting into squares. 6. Serve immediately.

Breaded Bananas with Chocolate Topping

Prep time: 10 minutes | Cook time: 10 minutes | Serves 6

¼ cup cornstarch
¼ cup plain bread crumbs
1 large egg, beaten
3 bananas, halved crosswise
Cooking spray
Chocolate sauce, for serving

1. Preheat the air fryer to 350°F (177°C) 2. Place the cornstarch, bread crumbs, and egg in three separate bowls. 3. Roll the bananas in the cornstarch, then in the beaten egg, and finally in the bread crumbs to coat well. 4. Spritz the air fryer basket with the cooking spray. 5. Arrange the banana halves in the basket and mist them with the cooking spray. Air fry for 5 minutes. Flip the bananas and continue to air fry for another 2 minutes. 6. Remove the bananas from the basket to a serving plate. Serve with the chocolate sauce drizzled over the top.

Brown Sugar Banana Bread

Prep time: 20 minutes | Cook time: 22 to 24 minutes | Serves 4

1 cup packed light brown sugar
1 large egg, beaten
2 tablespoons butter, melted
½ cup milk, whole or 2%
2 cups all-purpose flour
1½ teaspoons baking powder
1 teaspoon ground cinnamon
½ teaspoon salt
1 banana, mashed
1 to 2 tablespoons oil
¼ cup confectioners' sugar (optional)

1. In a large bowl, stir together the brown sugar, egg, melted butter, and milk. 2. In a medium bowl, whisk the flour, baking powder, cinnamon, and salt until blended. Add the flour mixture to the sugar mixture and stir just to blend. 3. Add the mashed banana and stir to combine. 4. Preheat the air fryer to 350°F (177°C). Spritz 2 mini loaf pans with oil. 5. Evenly divide the batter between the prepared pans and place them in the air fryer basket. 6. Cook for 22 to 24 minutes, or until a knife inserted into the middle of the loaves comes out clean. 7. Dust the warm loaves with confectioners' sugar (if using).

Blackberry Cobbler

Prep time: 15 minutes | Cook time: 25 to 30 minutes | Serves 6

3 cups fresh or frozen blackberries
1¾ cups sugar, divided
1 teaspoon vanilla extract
8 tablespoons (1 stick) butter, melted
1 cup self-rising flour
1 to 2 tablespoons oil

1. In a medium bowl, stir together the blackberries, 1 cup of sugar, and vanilla. 2. In another medium bowl, stir together the melted butter, remaining ¾ cup of sugar, and flour until a dough forms. 3. Spritz a baking pan with oil. Add the blackberry mixture. Crumble the flour mixture over the fruit. Cover the pan with aluminum foil. 4. Preheat the air fryer to 350°F (177°C). 5. Place the covered pan in the air fryer basket. Cook for 20 to 25 minutes until the filling is thickened. 6. Uncover the pan and cook for 5 minutes more, depending on how juicy and browned you like your cobbler. Let sit for 5 minutes before serving.

Eggless Farina Cake

Prep time: 30 minutes | Cook time: 25 minutes | Serves 6

Vegetable oil
2 cups hot water
1 cup chopped dried fruit, such as apricots, golden raisins, figs, and/or dates
1 cup farina (or very fine semolina)
1 cup milk
1 cup sugar
¼ cup ghee, butter, or coconut oil, melted
2 tablespoons plain Greek yogurt or sour cream
1 teaspoon ground cardamom
1 teaspoon baking powder
½ teaspoon baking soda
Whipped cream, for serving

1. Grease a baking pan with vegetable oil. 2. In a small bowl, combine the hot water and dried fruit; set aside for 20 minutes to plump the fruit. 3. Meanwhile, in a large bowl, whisk together the farina, milk, sugar, ghee, yogurt, and cardamom. Let stand for 20 minutes to allow the farina to soften and absorb some of the liquid. 4. Drain the dried fruit and gently stir it into the batter. Add the baking powder and baking soda and stir until thoroughly combined. 5. Pour the batter into the prepared pan. Set the pan in the air fryer basket. Set the air fryer to 325°F (163°C) for 25 minutes, or until a toothpick inserted into the center of the cake comes out clean. 6. Let the cake cool in the pan on a wire rack for 10 minutes. Remove the cake from the pan and let cool on the rack for 20 minutes before slicing. 7. Slice and serve topped with whipped cream.

Cream Cheese Shortbread Cookies

Prep time: 30 minutes | Cook time: 20 minutes | Makes 12 cookies

¼ cup coconut oil, melted
2 ounces (57 g) cream cheese, softened
½ cup granular erythritol
1 large egg, whisked
2 cups blanched finely ground almond flour
1 teaspoon almond extract

1. Combine all ingredients in a large bowl to form a firm ball. 2. Place dough on a sheet of plastic wrap and roll into a 12-inch-long log shape. Roll log in plastic wrap and place in refrigerator 30 minutes to chill. 3. Remove log from plastic and slice into twelve equal cookies. Cut two sheets of parchment paper to fit air fryer basket. Place six cookies on each ungreased sheet. Place one sheet with cookies into air fryer basket. Adjust the temperature to 320°F (160°C) and cook for 10 minutes, turning cookies halfway through cooking. They will be lightly golden when done. Repeat with remaining cookies. 4. Let cool 15 minutes before serving to avoid crumbling.

Gluten-Free Spice Cookies

Prep time: 10 minutes | Cook time: 12 minutes | Serves 4

4 tablespoons (½ stick) unsalted butter, at room temperature
2 tablespoons agave nectar
1 large egg
2 tablespoons water
2½ cups almond flour
½ cup sugar
2 teaspoons ground ginger
1 teaspoon ground cinnamon
½ teaspoon freshly grated nutmeg
1 teaspoon baking soda
¼ teaspoon kosher salt

1. Line the bottom of the air fryer basket with parchment paper cut to fit. 2. In a large bowl using a hand mixer, beat together the butter, agave, egg, and water on medium speed until light and fluffy. 3. Add the almond flour, sugar, ginger, cinnamon, nutmeg, baking soda, and salt. Beat on low speed until well combined. 4. Roll the dough into 2-tablespoon balls and arrange them on the parchment paper in the basket. (They don't really spread too much, but try to leave a little room between them.) Set the air fryer to 325°F (163°C) for 12 minutes, or until the tops of cookies are lightly browned. 5. Transfer to a wire rack and let cool completely. Store in an airtight container for up to a week.

Cream-Filled Sandwich Cookies

Prep time: 8 minutes | Cook time: 8 minutes | Makes 8 cookies

Oil, for spraying
1 (8-ounce / 227-g) can refrigerated crescent rolls
¼ cup milk
8 cream-filled sandwich cookies
1 tablespoon confectioners' sugar

1. Line the air fryer basket with parchment and spray lightly with oil. 2. Unroll the crescent dough and separate it into 8 triangles. Lay out the triangles on a work surface. 3. Pour the milk into a shallow bowl. Quickly dip each cookie in the milk, then place in the center of a dough triangle. 4. Wrap the dough around the cookie, cutting off any excess and pinching the ends to seal. You may be able to combine the excess into enough dough to cover additional cookies, if desired. 5. Place the wrapped cookies in the prepared basket, seam-side down, and spray lightly with oil. 6. Cook at 350°F (177°C) for 4 minutes, flip, spray with oil, and cook for another 3 to 4 minutes, or until puffed and golden brown. 7. Dust with the confectioners' sugar and serve.

Pumpkin Cookie with Cream Cheese Frosting

Prep time: 10 minutes | Cook time: 7 minutes | Serves 6

½ cup blanched finely ground almond flour
½ cup powdered erythritol, divided
2 tablespoons butter, softened
1 large egg
½ teaspoon unflavored gelatin
½ teaspoon baking powder
½ teaspoon vanilla extract
½ teaspoon pumpkin pie spice
2 tablespoons pure pumpkin purée
½ teaspoon ground cinnamon, divided
¼ cup low-carb, sugar-free chocolate chips
3 ounces (85 g) full-fat cream cheese, softened

1. In a large bowl, mix almond flour and ¼ cup erythritol. Stir in butter, egg, and gelatin until combined. 2. Stir in baking powder, vanilla, pumpkin pie spice, pumpkin purée, and ¼ teaspoon cinnamon, then fold in chocolate chips. 3. Pour batter into a round baking pan. Place pan into the air fryer basket. 4. Adjust the temperature to 300°F (149°C) and cook for 7 minutes. 5. When fully cooked, the top will be golden brown and a toothpick inserted in center will come out clean. Let cool at least 20 minutes. 6. To make the frosting: mix cream cheese, remaining ¼ teaspoon cinnamon, and remaining ¼ cup erythritol in a large bowl. Using an electric mixer, beat until it becomes fluffy. Spread onto the cooled cookie. Garnish with additional cinnamon if desired.

Easy Chocolate Donuts

Prep time: 5 minutes | Cook time: 8 minutes | Serves 8

1 (8-ounce / 227-g) can jumbo biscuits
Cooking oil
Chocolate sauce, for drizzling

1. Preheat the air fryer to 375°F (191°C) 2. Separate the biscuit dough into 8 biscuits and place them on a flat work surface. Use a small circle cookie cutter or a biscuit cutter to cut a hole in the center of each biscuit. You can also cut the holes using a knife. 3. Spray the air fryer basket with cooking oil. 4. Put 4 donuts in the air fryer. Do not stack. Spray with cooking oil. Air fry for 4 minutes. 5. Open the air fryer and flip the donuts. Air fry for an additional 4 minutes. 6. Remove the cooked donuts from the air fryer, then repeat steps 3 and 4 for the remaining 4 donuts. 7. Drizzle chocolate sauce over the donuts and enjoy while warm.

Cinnamon-Sugar Almonds

Prep time: 5 minutes | Cook time: 8 minutes | Serves 4

1 cup whole almonds
2 tablespoons salted butter, melted

1 tablespoon sugar
½ teaspoon ground cinnamon

1. In a medium bowl, combine the almonds, butter, sugar, and cinnamon. Mix well to ensure all the almonds are coated with the spiced butter. 2. Transfer the almonds to the air fryer basket and shake so they are in a single layer. Set the air fryer to 300°F (149°C) for 8 minutes, stirring the almonds halfway through the cooking time. 3. Let cool completely before serving.

Chapter 12 Staples, Sauces, Dips, and Dressings

Chapter 12 Staples, Sauces, Dips, and Dressings

Traditional Caesar Dressing

Prep time: 10 minutes | Cook time: 5 minutes | Makes 1½ cups

2 teaspoons minced garlic
4 large egg yolks
¼ cup wine vinegar
½ teaspoon dry mustard
Dash Worcestershire sauce
1 cup extra-virgin olive oil
¼ cup freshly squeezed lemon juice
Sea salt and freshly ground black pepper, to taste

1. To a small saucepan, add the garlic, egg yolks, vinegar, mustard, and Worcestershire sauce and place over low heat. 2. Whisking constantly, cook the mixture until it thickens and is a little bubbly, about 5 minutes. 3. Remove from saucepan from the heat and let it stand for about 10 minutes to cool. 4. Transfer the egg mixture to a large stainless steel bowl. Whisking constantly, add the olive oil in a thin stream. 5. Whisk in the lemon juice and season the dressing with salt and pepper. 6. Transfer the dressing to an airtight container and keep in the refrigerator for up to 3 days.

Blue Cheese Dressing

Prep time: 5 minutes | Cook time: 0 minutes | Serves 12

¾ cup sugar-free mayonnaise
¼ cup sour cream
½ cup heavy (whipping) cream
1 teaspoon minced garlic
1 tablespoon freshly squeezed lemon juice
1 tablespoon apple cider vinegar
1 teaspoon hot sauce
½ teaspoon sea salt
4 ounces (113 g) blue cheese, crumbled (about ¾ cup)

1. In a medium bowl, whisk together the mayonnaise, sour cream, and heavy cream. 2. Stir in the garlic, lemon juice, apple cider vinegar, hot sauce, and sea salt. 3. Add the blue cheese crumbles, and stir until well combined. 4. Transfer to an airtight container, and refrigerate for up to 1 week.

Sweet Ginger Teriyaki Sauce

Prep time: 5 minutes | Cook time: 0 minutes | Serves 4

¼ cup pineapple juice
¼ cup low-sodium soy sauce
2 tablespoons packed brown sugar
1 tablespoon arrowroot powder or cornstarch
1 tablespoon grated fresh ginger
1 teaspoon garlic powder

1. Mix together all the ingredients in a small bowl and whisk to incorporate. 2. Serve immediately, or transfer to an airtight container and refrigerate until ready to use.

Vegan Lentil Dip

Prep time: 10 minutes | Cook time: 15 minutes | Makes 3 cups

2½ cups water, divided
1 cup dried green or brown lentils, rinsed
⅓ cup tahini
1 garlic clove
½ teaspoon salt, plus additional as needed

1. Mix 2 cups of water and lentils in a medium pot and bring to a boil over high heat. 2. Once it starts to boil, reduce the heat to low, and bring to a simmer for 15 minutes, or until the lentils are tender. If there is any water remaining in the pot, simply drain it off. 3. Transfer the cooked lentils to a food processor, along with the remaining ingredients. Pulse until a hummus-like consistency is achieved. 4. Taste and add additional salt as needed. 5. It's tasty used as a sandwich spread, and you can also serve it over whole-wheat pita bread or crackers.

Cauliflower Alfredo Sauce

Prep time: 2 minutes | Cook time: 0 minutes | Makes 4 cups

2 tablespoons olive oil
6 garlic cloves, minced
3 cups unsweetened almond milk
1 (1-pound / 454-g) head cauliflower, cut into florets
1 teaspoon salt
¼ teaspoon freshly ground black pepper
Juice of 1 lemon
4 tablespoons nutritional yeast

1. In a medium saucepan, heat the olive oil over medium-high heat. Add the garlic and sauté for 1 minute or until fragrant. Add the almond milk, stir, and bring to a boil. 2. Gently add the cauliflower. Stir in the salt and pepper and return to a boil. Continue cooking over medium-high heat for 5 minutes or until the cauliflower is soft. Stir frequently and reduce heat if needed to prevent the liquid from boiling over. 3. Carefully transfer the cauliflower and cooking liquid to a food processor, using a slotted spoon to scoop out the larger pieces of cauliflower before pouring in the liquid. Add the lemon and nutritional yeast and blend for 1 to 2 minutes until smooth. 4. Serve immediately.

Cashew Mayo

Prep time: 5 minutes | Cook time: 0 minutes | Makes 18 tablespoons

1 cup cashews, soaked in hot water for at least 1 hour
¼ cup plus 3 tablespoons milk
1 tablespoon apple cider vinegar
1 tablespoon freshly squeezed lemon juice
1 tablespoon Dijon mustard
1 tablespoon aquafaba
⅛ teaspoon pink Himalayan salt

1. In a food processor, combine all the ingredients and blend until creamy and smooth.

Gochujang Dip

Prep time: 5 minutes | Cook time: 0 minutes | Serves 4

2 tablespoons gochujang (Korean red pepper paste)
1 tablespoon mayonnaise
1 tablespoon toasted sesame oil
1 tablespoon minced fresh ginger
1 tablespoon minced garlic
1 teaspoon agave nectar

1. In a small bowl, combine the gochujang, mayonnaise, sesame oil, ginger, garlic, and agave. Stir until well combined. 2. Use immediately or store in the refrigerator, covered, for up to 3 days.

Lemon Cashew Dip

Prep time: 10 minutes | Cook time: 0 minutes | Makes 1 cup

¾ cup cashews, soaked in water for at least 4 hours and drained
Juice and zest of 1 lemon
¼ cup water
2 tablespoons chopped fresh dill
¼ teaspoon salt, plus additional as needed

1. Blend the cashew, lemon juice and zest, and water in a blender until smooth and creamy. 2. Fold in the dill and salt and blend again. 3. Taste and add additional salt as needed. 4. Transfer to the refrigerator to chill for at least 1 hour to blend the flavors. 5. This dip perfectly goes with the crackers or tacos. It also can be used as a sauce for roasted vegetables or a sandwich spread.

Tahini Dressing

Prep time: 5 minutes | Cook time: 0 minutes | Serves 8 to 10

½ cup tahini
¼ cup freshly squeezed lemon juice (about 2 to 3 lemons)
¼ cup extra-virgin olive oil
1 garlic clove, finely minced or ½ teaspoon garlic powder
2 teaspoons salt

1. In a glass mason jar with a lid, combine the tahini, lemon juice, olive oil, garlic, and salt. Cover and shake well until combined and creamy. Store in the refrigerator for up to 2 weeks.

Red Buffalo Sauce

Prep time: 5 minutes | Cook time: 20 minutes | Makes 2 cups

¼ cup olive oil
4 garlic cloves, roughly chopped
1 (5-ounce / 142-g) small red onion, roughly chopped
6 red chiles, roughly chopped (about 2 ounces / 56 g in total)
1 cup water
½ cup apple cider vinegar
½ teaspoon salt
½ teaspoon freshly ground black pepper

1. In a large nonstick sauté pan, heat ¼ cup olive oil over medium-high heat. Once it's hot, add the garlic, onion, and chiles. Cook for 5 minutes, stirring occasionally, until onions are golden brown. 2. Add the water and bring to a boil. Cook for about 10 minutes or until the water has nearly evaporated. 3. Transfer the cooked onion and chile mixture to a food processor or blender and blend briefly to combine. Add the apple cider vinegar, salt, and pepper. Blend again for 30 seconds. 4. Using a mesh sieve, strain the sauce into a bowl. Use a spoon or spatula to scrape and press all the liquid from the pulp.

Pepper Sauce

Prep time: 10 minutes | Cook time: 20 minutes | Makes 4 cups

2 red hot fresh chiles, seeded
2 dried chiles
½ small yellow onion, roughly chopped
2 garlic cloves, peeled
2 cups water
2 cups white vinegar

1. In a medium saucepan, combine the fresh and dried chiles, onion, garlic, and water. Bring to a simmer and cook for 20 minutes, or until tender. Transfer to a food processor or blender. 2. Add the vinegar and blend until smooth.

Artichoke Dip

Prep time: 15 minutes | Cook time: 0 minutes | Serves 3

1 (14-ounce / 397-g) can artichoke hearts, drained
1 pound (454 g) goat cheese
2 tablespoons extra-virgin olive oil
2 teaspoons lemon juice
1 garlic clove, minced
1 tablespoon chopped parsley
1 tablespoon chopped chives
½ tablespoon chopped basil
½ teaspoon sea salt
½ teaspoon freshly ground black pepper
Dash of cayenne pepper (optional)
½ cup freshly grated Pecorino Romano

1. In a food processor, combine all the ingredients, except the Pecorino Romano, and process until well incorporated and creamy. 2. Top with the freshly grated Pecorino Romano. Store in an airtight container in the refrigerator for up to 3 days.

Peachy Barbecue Sauce

Prep time: 10 minutes | Cook time: 0 minutes | Makes 2¼ cups

1 cup peach preserves
1 cup ketchup
2 tablespoons apple cider vinegar
2 tablespoons light brown sugar

1 teaspoon chili powder
½ teaspoon freshly ground black pepper
½ teaspoon dry mustard

1. In a medium bowl, stir together the peach preserves, ketchup, and vinegar until blended. 2. In a small bowl, whisk the brown sugar, chili powder, pepper, and dry mustard to combine. Add the brown sugar mixture to the peach preserves mixture. Mix well to combine. 3. Transfer the barbecue sauce to an airtight container. Refrigerate for up to 1 week until ready to use as a sauce or marinade.

Apple Cider Dressing

Prep time: 5 minutes | Cook time: 0 minutes | Serves 2

2 tablespoons apple cider vinegar
⅓ lemon, juiced

⅓ lemon, zested
Salt and freshly ground black pepper, to taste

1. In a jar, combine the vinegar, lemon juice, and zest. Season with salt and pepper, cover, and shake well.

Lemony Tahini

Prep time: 5 minutes | Cook time: 0 minutes | Serves 4

¾ cup water
½ cup tahini
3 garlic cloves, minced

Juice of 3 lemons
½ teaspoon pink Himalayan salt

1. In a bowl, whisk together all the ingredients until mixed well.

Appendix 1 Measurement Conversion Chart

MEASUREMENT CONVERSION CHART

VOLUME EQUIVALENTS(DRY)

US STANDARD	METRIC (APPROXIMATE)
1/8 teaspoon	0.5 mL
1/4 teaspoon	1 mL
1/2 teaspoon	2 mL
3/4 teaspoon	4 mL
1 teaspoon	5 mL
1 tablespoon	15 mL
1/4 cup	59 mL
1/2 cup	118 mL
3/4 cup	177 mL
1 cup	235 mL
2 cups	475 mL
3 cups	700 mL
4 cups	1 L

VOLUME EQUIVALENTS(LIQUID)

US STANDARD	US STANDARD (OUNCES)	METRIC (APPROXIMATE)
2 tablespoons	1 fl.oz.	30 mL
1/4 cup	2 fl.oz.	60 mL
1/2 cup	4 fl.oz.	120 mL
1 cup	8 fl.oz.	240 mL
1 1/2 cup	12 fl.oz.	355 mL
2 cups or 1 pint	16 fl.oz.	475 mL
4 cups or 1 quart	32 fl.oz.	1 L
1 gallon	128 fl.oz.	4 L

TEMPERATURES EQUIVALENTS

FAHRENHEIT(F)	CELSIUS(C) (APPROXIMATE)
225 °F	107 °C
250 °F	120 °C
275 °F	135 °C
300 °F	150 °C
325 °F	160 °C
350 °F	180 °C
375 °F	190 °C
400 °F	205 °C
425 °F	220 °C
450 °F	235 °C
475 °F	245 °C
500 °F	260 °C

WEIGHT EQUIVALENTS

US STANDARD	METRIC (APPROXIMATE)
1 ounce	28 g
2 ounces	57 g
5 ounces	142 g
10 ounces	284 g
15 ounces	425 g
16 ounces (1 pound)	455 g
1.5 pounds	680 g
2 pounds	907 g

Appendix 2 Air Fryer Cooking Chart

Air Fryer Cooking Chart

Beef

Item	Temp (°F)	Time (mins)	Item	Temp (°F)	Time (mins)
Beef Eye Round Roast (4 lbs.)	400 °F	45 to 55	Meatballs (1-inch)	370 °F	7
Burger Patty (4 oz.)	370 °F	16 to 20	Meatballs (3-inch)	380 °F	10
Filet Mignon (8 oz.)	400 °F	18	Ribeye, bone-in (1-inch, 8 oz)	400 °F	10 to 15
Flank Steak (1.5 lbs.)	400 °F	12	Sirloin steaks (1-inch, 12 oz)	400 °F	9 to 14
Flank Steak (2 lbs.)	400 °F	20 to 28			

Chicken

Item	Temp (°F)	Time (mins)	Item	Temp (°F)	Time (mins)
Breasts, bone in (1 ¼ lb.)	370 °F	25	Legs, bone-in (1 ¾ lb.)	380 °F	30
Breasts, boneless (4 oz)	380 °F	12	Thighs, boneless (1 ½ lb.)	380 °F	18 to 20
Drumsticks (2 ½ lb.)	370 °F	20	Wings (2 lb.)	400 °F	12
Game Hen (halved 2 lb.)	390 °F	20	Whole Chicken	360 °F	75
Thighs, bone-in (2 lb.)	380 °F	22	Tenders	360 °F	8 to 10

Pork & Lamb

Item	Temp (°F)	Time (mins)	Item	Temp (°F)	Time (mins)
Bacon (regular)	400 °F	5 to 7	Pork Tenderloin	370 °F	15
Bacon (thick cut)	400 °F	6 to 10	Sausages	380 °F	15
Pork Loin (2 lb.)	360 °F	55	Lamb Loin Chops (1-inch thick)	400 °F	8 to 12
Pork Chops, bone in (1-inch, 6.5 oz)	400 °F	12	Rack of Lamb (1.5 – 2 lb.)	380 °F	22

Fish & Seafood

Item	Temp (°F)	Time (mins)	Item	Temp (°F)	Time (mins)
Calamari (8 oz)	400 °F	4	Tuna Steak	400 °F	7 to 10
Fish Fillet (1-inch, 8 oz)	400 °F	10	Scallops	400 °F	5 to 7
Salmon, fillet (6 oz)	380 °F	12	Shrimp	400 °F	5
Swordfish steak	400 °F	10			

Air Fryer Cooking Chart

Vegetables					
INGREDIENT	AMOUNT	PREPARATION	OIL	TEMP	COOK TIME
Asparagus	2 bunches	Cut in half, trim stems	2 Tbsp	420°F	12-15 mins
Beets	1½ lbs	Peel, cut in ½-inch cubes	1 Tbsp	390°F	28-30 mins
Bell peppers (for roasting)	4 peppers	Cut in quarters, remove seeds	1 Tbsp	400°F	15-20 mins
Broccoli	1 large head	Cut in 1-2-inch florets	1 Tbsp	400°F	15-20 mins
Brussels sprouts	1 lb	Cut in half, remove stems	1 Tbsp	425°F	15-20 mins
Carrots	1 lb	Peel, cut in ¼-inch rounds	1 Tbsp	425°F	10-15 mins
Cauliflower	1 head	Cut in 1-2-inch florets	2 Tbsp	400°F	20-22 mins
Corn on the cob	7 ears	Whole ears, remove husks	1 Tbps	400°F	14-17 mins
Green beans	1 bag (12 oz)	Trim	1 Tbps	420°F	18-20 mins
Kale (for chips)	4 oz	Tear into pieces, remove stems	None	325°F	5-8 mins
Mushrooms	16 oz	Rinse, slice thinly	1 Tbps	390°F	25-30 mins
Potatoes, russet	1½ lbs	Cut in 1-inch wedges	1 Tbps	390°F	25-30 mins
Potatoes, russet	1 lb	Hand-cut fries, soak 30 mins in cold water, then pat dry	½-3 Tbps	400°F	25-28 mins
Potatoes, sweet	1 lb	Hand-cut fries, soak 30 mins in cold water, then pat dry	1 Tbps	400°F	25-28 mins
Zucchini	1 lb	Cut in eighths lengthwise, then cut in half	1 Tbps	400°F	15-20 mins

Printed in Great Britain
by Amazon